The ʿAlids

For Kaspar and Samuel

The ʿAlids

The First Family of Islam, 750–1200

Teresa Bernheimer

EDINBURGH
University Press

Edinburgh University Press Ltd
22 George Square, Edinburgh EH8 9LF
www.euppublishing.com

Typeset in Times Beyrut Roman by
3btype.com, and
printed and bound in Great Britain by
CPI Group (UK) Ltd, Croydon CR0 4YY

A CIP record for this book is available from the British Library

ISBN 978 0 7486 3847 5 (hardback)
ISBN 978 0 7486 3848 2 (webready PDF)
ISBN 978 0 7486 8295 9 (epub)

Contents

Acknowledgements vii

1. Introduction 1
2. Genealogy, Money and the Drawing of Boundaries 13
3. Shifting Hierarchies and Emphasising Kinship: ʿAlid Marriage Patterns 32
4. The *Niqāba*, the Headship of the ʿAlid Family 51
5. The ʿAlids as Local Nobility 71
6. Conclusion 87

Bibliography 91
Index 113

Acknowledgements

This book is a revised version of my DPhil dissertation, submitted to the Oriental Institute in Oxford in October 2006. I reiterate my thanks to all those who supported me then, in particular Chase Robinson, my supervisor throughout my graduate studies.

During my doctoral research and the revisions for this book, I profited much from a number of visits to Princeton University and from the suggestions and comments by Hossein Modarressi, Patricia Crone and Michael Cook. I benefited hugely from the questions and discussions during the intensive course on 'Sayyids and Sharifs: The Kinsfolk of the Prophet in Muslim Societies' taught by Kazuo Morimoto at Princeton in March 2010. To Kazuo Morimoto I express my particular gratitude for so generously sharing his knowledge on all aspects of Ṭālibid genealogy and the kinsfolk of the Prophet, and for giving me the opportunity to present my work in Tokyo in 2008 and 2009.

I am indebted to a number of colleagues for their kind advice and patience with my ʿAlid questions: Asad Ahmed, Michael Bates, Karen Bauer, Tamima Bayhom-Daou, Evrim Binbas, Mark Cohen, Amikam Elad, Arnold Franklin, Geert Jan van Gelder, Robert Gleave, Sebastian Günther, Najam Haider, Gerald Hawting, Hugh Kennedy, Etan Kohlberg, Arzina Lalani, Wilferd Madelung, Raffaele Mauriello, Christopher Melchert, Roy Mottahedeh, Stephennie Mulder, Judith Pfeiffer, Marina Pyrovolaki, Yossi Rapoport, Biancamaria Scaria Amoretti, Petra Sijpesteijn and Luke Treadwell. John Parker commented on final chapters of the book, and Arezou Azad, Marina Pyrovolaki and Bella Tendler-Krieger found references for me when I was not near a good library.

Many thanks also to my colleagues at SOAS, University of London, especially Ben Fortna, Nelida Fuccaro, Konrad Hirschler and George Lane, who have made the entry into a 'real' academic career so enjoyable.

Many thanks to Nicola Ramsey and Eddie Clark at EUP for their support and patience; to Damien Bove for the maps; and to Laura Booth for copy-editing. I am particularly grateful to Hanna Siurua for her help with the index and invaluable suggestions and corrections at the editing stage. Any remaining errors are, of course, my own.

An earlier version of Chapter 5 was published in *Studia Islamica* 2005, and some of the material on marriage patterns appeared in an article entitled 'Genealogy, Marriage, and the Drawing of Boundaries among the ʿAlids (Eighth–twelfth Centuries)', in Kazuo Morimoto (ed.), *Sayyids and Sharifs in Muslim Societies: The Living Link to the Prophet* (London/New York, 2012), pp. 75–91.

I thank my parents and sisters for their support in all matters. Especially and most of all I thank Kaspar for all his help, and his unfailing optimism and encouragement. This book is for you and Samuel.

1

Introduction

The respect and veneration accorded to the family of the Prophet Muḥammad are unparalleled in Islamic society. Political or religious affiliations notwithstanding, the Prophet's family – most importantly his descendants through his daughter Fāṭima and his cousin ʿAlī b. Abī Ṭālib, collectively known as the ʿAlids – were held in high esteem even by those who rejected their claims to the leadership of the Muslim community. Within the hierarchy of Islamic society, the ʿAlids were 'a blood aristocracy without peer'.[1]

Although they clearly occupied a privileged place among Muslims from the earliest period of Islam, the social prominence of the Prophet's kin was by no means a foregone conclusion. In political as well as religious terms, those who became the heirs and successors to the Prophet in the majority of Muslim communities were generally not his descendants: Political authority came to be exercised by the caliphs while religious leadership went to the scholars. Yet, despite their virtual exclusion from the leadership of the Muslim communities, both politically and religiously, the ʿAlids nevertheless became the one indisputable nobility of Islam.

This book provides the first social history of the ʿAlids in the crucial five centuries from the ʿAbbāsid Revolution to the Saljūqs (second/eighth to sixth/twelfth centuries). This period saw the formulation of many aspects still associated with the special position of *sayyid*s and *sharīf*s in Muslim societies, from their exemption from some of the rules that governed ordinary Muslims to the development of 'ʿAlidism'. In contrast to Shiʿism, defined as the political and religious claims made by some members of the Prophet's family or by others on their behalf, ʿAlidism is characterised by a distinctly cross-sectarian reverence and support for the Prophet's family. As even a staunch Sunni like Ibn Taymiyya (d. 728/1328) notes: 'There is no doubt that Muḥammad's family (*āl Muḥammad*) has a right on the Muslim society (*umma*) that no other people share and that they are entitled to an added love and affection to which no other branches of Quraysh are entitled.'[2]

Because of the richness of the source material, this study focuses especially on

1 Richard Bulliet, *The Patricians of Nishapur. A Study in Medieval Islamic Social History* (Cambridge, MA, 1972), p. 234.

2 Ibn Taymiyya, *Minhāj al-sunna al-nabawiyya*, cited in Kazuo Morimoto, 'Introduction', in Kazuo Morimoto (ed.), *Sayyids and Sharifs in Muslim Societies: The Living Links to the Prophet* (London/New York, 2012), p. 2.

the eastern part of the Islamic world,[3] although the Prophet's family certainly attained a position of similar distinction in other places as well.[4] Their role and status varied considerably not only over time but also at any given time and from place to place. They could even seem contradictory: As some ʿAlids came to be revered as Shiʿite imāms, others became scholars in a Sunni school of law. Some supported the ʿAbbāsids while others were persecuted by them. Some were fabulously wealthy; others were very poor. The ʿAlids were therefore by no means a homogeneous group. The one important phenomenon that united them despite their differences was their increasing sense of themselves as a distinct social force – as the First Family of Islam. To trace and explain its development is the aim of this book.

Definitions

The fourth-/tenth-century genealogist Abū Naṣr al-Bukhārī explains the kinship relations between the Prophet's descendants and the Arabs more generally in the following way:

> It should be noted that every Fāṭimī in the world is also an ʿAlawī; but not every ʿAlawī is a Fāṭimī. Every ʿAlawī is a Ṭālibī; but not every Ṭālibī is an ʿAlawī. Every Ṭālibī is a Hāshimī, but not every Hāshimī is a Ṭālibī. Every Hāshimī is a Qurashī, but not every Qurashī is a Hāshimī. Every Qurashī is an Arab, yet not every Arab a Qurashī.[5]

Throughout this book, I use the term 'the ʿAlids' – the English version of the *nisba* 'al-ʿAlawī' – to mean the Prophet's family, and in particular his descendants through Fāṭima, the Ḥasanids and the Ḥusaynids. As al-Bukhārī points out, this is technically imprecise: ʿAlī had sons from wives other than Fāṭima, who are also called ʿAlids. However, to use the term 'Fāṭimī' (or the anglicised 'Fāṭimid') in this book would have been not only inconsistent with the bulk of previous scholarship but also confusing: 'Fāṭimid' commonly refers not to the Prophet's descendants but to the dynasty that ruled in the Maghreb and later in Egypt from 297/909 until 567/1171.

Moreover, it would have excluded many relations of the Prophet who are not strictly speaking his descendants but who are nonetheless included in the phenomenon described in this book. The Ḥasanids and the Ḥusaynids were clearly central to the emergence of the Prophet's family as the First Family of Islam; theirs was the 'most noble lineage', since al-Ḥasan and al-Ḥusayn, as children of ʿAlī and Fāṭima, were related to the Prophet on both their mother's side and their father's – a point repeatedly made in the sources.[6] But other agnates of the Prophet, such as the

3 That is, the areas of today's Iraq, Iran, Afghanistan and Central Asia.

4 For 'sharīfism' as a mark of distinction and as a basis for authority in North African society, especially after the fifth/eleventh century, see David Powers, *Law, Society and Culture in the Maghrib, 1300–1500* (Cambridge, 2002), pp. 13–14 and 167–205.

5 Abū Naṣr al-Bukhārī, *Sirr al-silsila al-ʿAlawiyya*, ed. Muḥammad Ṣādiq Baḥr al-ʿUlūm (Najaf, 1962), p. 1.

6 Al-Thaʿālibī (d. 429/1038), *Laṭāʾif al-maʿārif*, ed. P. de Jong (Leiden, 1867); English translation C. E. Bosworth, *The Book of Curious and Entertaining Information* (Edinburgh, 1968), p. 79.

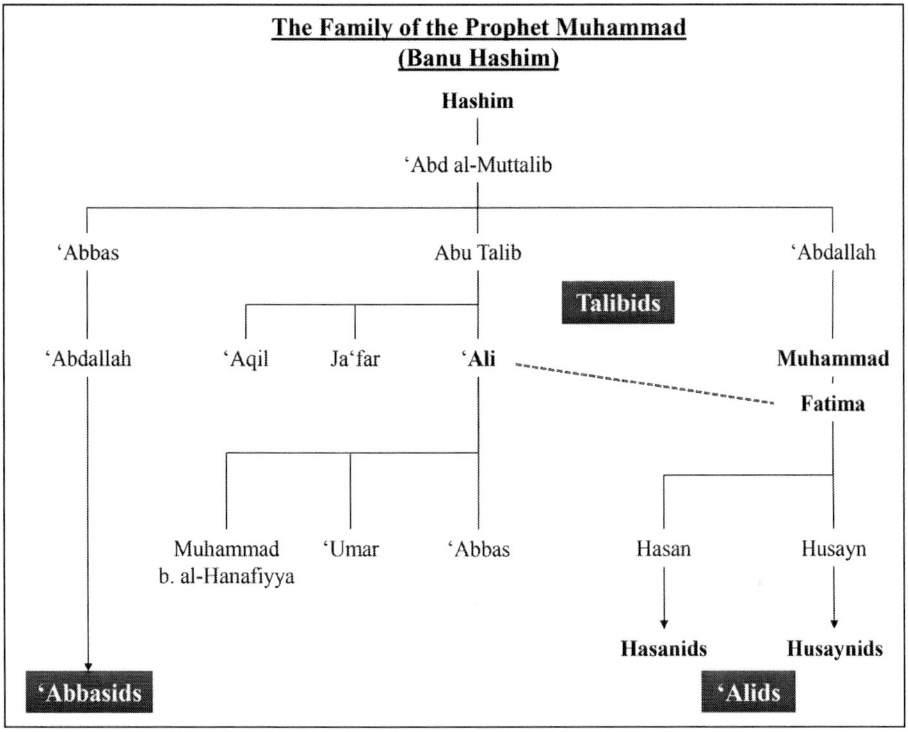

Figure 1.1 Family tree of the Prophet Muḥammad

other ʿAlids (descendants of ʿAlī's other sons Muḥammad b. al-Ḥanafiyya, ʿUmar and ʿAbbās), the Ṭālibids (descendants of ʿAlī's father, Abū Ṭālib, through ʿAlī as well as his other sons Jaʿfar and ʿAqīl) and even the Hāshimites (the clan that included the Ṭālibids and the ʿAbbāsids) were part of the story as well. They came to be addressed as *sayyid*s and *sharīf*s, were recorded in the family registers and were part of the pool of eligible marriage partners for the Prophet's descendants.[7]

Our terminology is also consistent with the sources themselves, which are frequently ambiguous, speaking of ʿAlids when they mean Ḥasanids and Ḥusaynids, or when other Ṭālibids are included. Of course, there were many attempts to define the Prophet's family (*ahl al-bayt*) precisely, to determine exactly which kinship groups could call themselves *sayyid*s and *sharīf*s, and to establish who was entitled to share in the varying privileges of membership. To give just one example: The Egyptian scholar al-Suyūṭī (d. 911/1505) defines the Prophet's family widely as the descendants of Hāshim and al-Muṭṭalib (thus including the ʿAbbāsids) and discusses

7 Roy Mottahedeh has drawn attention to an important family of Jaʿfarid *sharīf*s in fourth-/tenth- and fifth-/eleventh-century Qazwīn; see Roy Mottahedeh, 'Administration in Būyid Qazwīn', in D. S. Richards (ed.), *Islamic Civilisation 950–1150* (Oxford, 1983), pp. 33–45. See also Ibn Funduq al-Bayhaqī, *Tārīkh-i Bayhaq*, ed. Aḥmad Bahmanyār (Tehran, 1938), p. 63 for a discussion of Jaʿfarids as *sayyids* (actually called Zaynabīs because of their descent from Zaynab bt. ʿAlī).

in some detail the status of the Zaynabīs, descendants of Zaynab, a daughter of Fāṭima and ʿAlī. He concludes that even the Zaynabīs, who played a prominent role in Egypt in his time, are indeed *sharīfs*, as members of the wider family of the Prophet, and should be allowed to share in some of the endowments dedicated to its support.[8] Thus, definitions were by no means rigid, but shifting and dependent on the particular context; even matrilineal descent could at times qualify for membership.

The ambiguity extends to the terms '*sayyid*' (pl. *sāda*, *sādāt*) and '*sharīf*' (pl. *ashrāf*, *shurafāʾ*), the honorific titles by which many members of the Prophet's family came to be known. While these honorifics are often said to be specific – someone of Ḥasanid descent is a *sharīf*, and someone claiming a Ḥusaynid lineage is a *sayyid*[9] – for our period and geographical area (the eastern Islamic world) these distinctions do not apply. Although '*sayyid*' is more common than '*sharīf*' for Ḥasanids as well as Ḥusaynids, both terms were used to address members of the Prophet's family, sometimes at the same time.[10]

Historical overview

The ʿAbbāsid Revolution was a watershed in the history of the ʿAlid family. The ʿAbbāsids came to power in 133/750 through a revolution that had called for the return of the caliphate to the family of the Prophet. The revolutionary slogan 'the chosen one from the family of Muḥammad' (*al-riḍā min āl Muḥammad*) had been broadly defined so as to be all of the Banū Hāshim, the wider clan of the Prophet that included both the ʿAbbāsids and the Ṭālibids;[11] once the ʿAbbāsids were chosen, however, many supporters of the revolution claimed to have expected the office of the caliph to be filled by the other branch of the family, and a closer relative of the Prophet – such as an ʿAlid. When it became clear that the ʿAbbāsids had settled into the caliphate, the ʿAlids as well as their various Shiʿite supporters began to sharpen their identities, respectively as the true family and the true heirs of the Prophet.[12]

The first and the perhaps most serious challenge to ʿAbbāsid authority came just a few years after the revolution, early in the reign of the second ʿAbbāsid caliph

8 Jalāl al-Dīn Al-Suyūṭī, 'al-ʿAjāja al-zarnabiyya fī al-sulāla al-Zaynabiyya', in al-Suyūṭī, *al-Ḥāwī li-l-fatāwī*, 2 vols (Cairo, 1352/1933), vol. II, pp. 31–4.

9 For more details, see C. van Arendonk and W. A. Graham, 'Sharīf', in *Encyclopaedia of Islam*, 2nd edn (henceforth *EI2*). How early the title '*sayyid*' came to be used for the Prophet's family and whether it can be linked to the emergence of the ʿAlids as a social force deserves more study; I am grateful to Najam Haider for pointing this out.

10 Thus '*al-sayyid al-sharīf…*' or '*al-sharīf al-sayyid …*'; see, for instance, Abū al-Ḥasan al-ʿUmarī al-Nassāba (d. 450/1058), *al-Majdī fī ansāb al-Ṭālibiyyīn*, ed. Aḥmad al-Mahdāwī al-Dāmghānī (Qum, 1409), p. 207.

11 P. Crone, 'On the Meaning of the ʿAbbāsid call to *al-riḍā*', in C. E. Bosworth (ed.), *The Islamic World: Essays in Honor of Bernard Lewis* (Princeton, 1989), pp. 95–111, and P. Crone, *God's Rule: Government and Islam* (New York, 2004), pp. 72–3; on Hāshimite Shiʿism, see W. Madelung, 'The Hāshimiyyāt of al-Kumayt and Hāshimī Shiʿism', *Studia Islamica* 70 (1989), pp. 5–26.

12 For the development of Shiʿism in this period see now Najam Haider, *The Origins of the Shīʿa: Identity, Ritual, and Sacred Space in Eighth-Century Kūfa* (Cambridge, 2011).

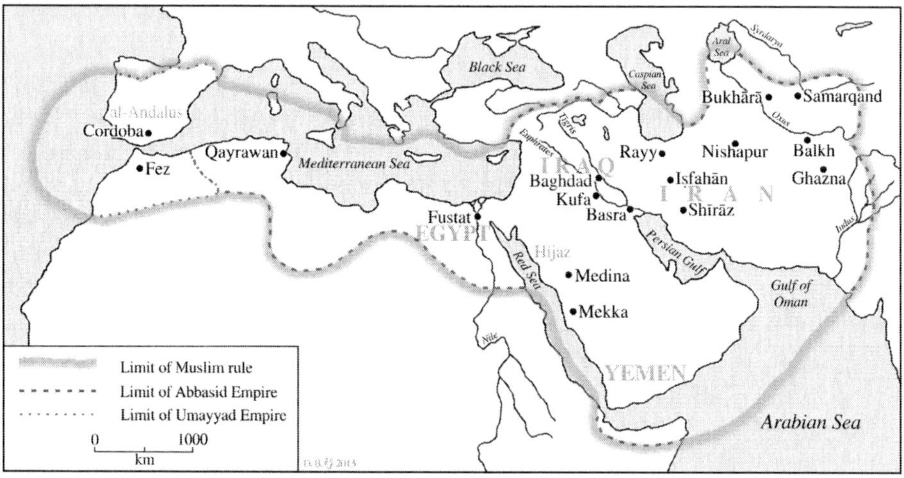

Figure 1.2 The Middle East in the early ʿAbbāsid period

al-Manṣūr (r. 754–75). Muḥammad b. ʿAbdallāh b. al-Ḥasan b. al-Ḥasan b. ʿAlī, known as al-Nafs al-Zakiyya (the Pure Soul), rose up in Medina in 145/762–3, while his brother Ibrāhīm revolted in Basra shortly after.[13] Despite a long period of preparation – according to the sources, the movement had already begun in the late Umayyad period, when Muḥammad's father ʿAbdallāh had played an important role in preparing his son Muḥammad for the caliphate, calling him al-Mahdī and securing the oath of allegiance for him from a group of ʿAlids in Medina – the revolts were quickly crushed. Ibrāhīm was slightly more successful, managing briefly to establish control over Basra, where he minted coins dated 145 AH (762–3 CE).[14]

The brothers' revolt was significant in that it set for the first time one branch of the Prophet's family against another. As the fourth-/tenth-century historian al-Masʿūdī put it: 'It caused a split between the descendants of al-ʿAbbās b. ʿAbd al-Muṭṭalib and the family of Abū Ṭālib; prior to this, their cause was one (*wa-kāna qabla dhālika amruhum wāḥid*)'.[15] In the decades that followed there were still some ʿAlids who supported the ʿAbbāsids, such as al-Ḥasan b. Zayd b. al-Ḥasan b. ʿAlī,

13 For a detailed discussion of the history and historiography of Nafs al-Zakiyya's revolt, see Amikam Elad, *The Rebellion of Muḥammad al-Nafs al-Zakiyya in 145/762: A Study of the Relations Between the Early ʿAbbāsīs and the Ṭālibī Factions* (Leiden, forthcoming).

14 The Qurʾānic verse written on Ibrāhīm's coins is *sūra* XVII:83, 'Truth is come and falsehood is vanished. Verily, falsehood is a vanishing thing'; see Nicholas Lowick, 'Une Monnaie ʿAlide d'al-Baṣrah datée de 145 H. (762–3 après J.-C.)', *Revue Numismatique*, 6th ser., 21 (1979), pp. 218–24; Samīr Shamma, 'Arbaʿa darāhim lihā Taʾrīkh', *Yarmouk Numismatics*, Yarmouk University Publication 4 (1992), pp. 13–25.

15 Al-Masʿūdī, *Murūj al-dhahab*, ed. C. Pellat (Beirut, 1966–79), vol. IV, p. 22. Similarly, the Muʿtazilite ʿAbd al-Jabbār (d. 415/1025): 'At that time [of the Revolution], the Hāshimites were united, without disagreements or splits. The descendants of al-ʿAbbās, ʿAlī, and ʿAqīl and Jaʿfar, and all the other Hāshimites, were in agreement. They only came to disagree when sovereignty passed to the ʿAbbāsids, in the days of Abū Jaʿfar al-Manṣūr, when well known events took place between him and his Ḥasanid kinsmen'; quoted in Crone, *God's Rule*, p. 89.

who was governor of Medina for caliphs al-Manṣūr and al-Mahdī (r. 775–85).[16] Some branches of the two families also continued to inter-marry, perhaps as part of the ʿAbbāsids' conciliatory policies and attempts to draw certain family branches into their power structures. Overall, however, relations between ʿAbbāsids and ʿAlids were clearly altered.

Soon after the accession of the fourth ʿAbbāsid caliph al-Hādī (r. 785–6), another ʿAlid revolt erupted in the Ḥijāz. Al-Hādī, who appears to have adopted a less conciliatory policy towards the ʿAlids than had his predecessor al-Mahdī, appointed one ʿUmar b. ʿAbd al-Azīz b. ʿAbdallāh al-ʿUmarī governor of Medina. The sources unanimously identify the immediate cause of the revolt as the ʿAlids' ill-treatment at the hands of the governor. A number of Ṭālibids joined this uprising, most prominently Yaḥyā (d. 189/805) and Idrīs (d. 175/791), two younger brothers of Muḥammad al-Nafs al-Zakiyya and Ibrāhīm. But the movement could not draw on the support of the Ḥijāzī elites in the way that the Ḥasanid brothers had in 145/762–3.[17] Again, the revolt was quickly defeated. Significantly, however, it triggered the beginning of the dispersal of the Prophet's family from the Ḥijāz. Both Yaḥyā and Idrīs, who fled in the aftermath of the revolt, staged their own challenges to the ʿAbbāsids far away from their ancestral heartlands, in Daylam in the Caspian region and in North Africa respectively.[18] One was successful, the other not; yet both led the ʿAlids to areas that came to be populated with the Prophet's kin in the following centuries.

Except at the fringes of the empire, such as in parts of North Africa, around the Caspian Sea and in Yemen, the ʿAlids never managed to maintain control for very long. The effort of the caliph al-Maʾmūn (r. 198–218/813–33) to bring the ʿAlids back to the centre and to reunite the two branches of the family through his appointment of the Ḥusaynid ʿAlī al-Riḍā (d. 203/818) as his heir apparent in 201/817 was short-lived; animosity continued and the persecution of many members of the ʿAlid family only intensified during the reign of the caliph al-Mutawakkil (r. 232–47/847–61), who also ordered the destruction of the burial places of prominent ʿAlids at Najaf and Karbalāʾ.

From the time of the ʿAbbāsid Revolution to the middle of the third/ninth century, the ʿAlids remained below the historical radar, except when they rebelled against ʿAbbāsid authority. By the late third/ninth century, however, they had emerged as

16 He was 'the first ʿAlid to wear black', black being the colour of the ʿAbbāsids; al-Bukhārī, *Sirr al-silsila,* p. 21. His son al-Qāsim was also part of the ʿAbbāsid army, and he reportedly delivered the news of the ʿAlid defeat to al-Manṣūr; see al-Ṭabarī (d. 310/923), *Taʾrīkh al-rusul wa-l-mulūk*, ed. M. J. de Goeje *et al.* (Leiden, 1879–1901), vol. III, p. 252; English translation *The History of al-Ṭabarī*, ed. E. Yarshater, 39 vols (Albany, NY, 1989–98). Another example is Muḥammad b. Mūsā al-Mubarqaʿa, a descendant of ʿAlī al-Riḍā and boon companion to Caliph al-Mutawakkil; see al-Bukhārī, *Sirr al-silsila,* p. 41.

17 See Asad Ahmed, *The Religious Elite of the Early Islamic Ḥijāz: Five Prosopographical Case Studies* (Oxford, 2011) for the ways in which other important Ḥijāzī families were successfully courted by the ʿAbbāsids in the early decades of their caliphate.

18 See Najam Haider, 'Yaḥyā b. ʿAbdāh b. al-Ḥasan b. al-Ḥasan b. ʿAlī', in M. Haleem and M. A. Shah (eds), *IB Tauris Biographical Dictionary of Islamic Civilisation* (London, forthcoming); and see Daniel Eustache, 'ʿIdrīsids', *EI2*, for references.

part of local elites all over the Islamic world, after many had left the Ḥijāz and settled in cities such as Nishapur, Hamadān, Qum, Rayy and Samarqand. Another century later, ʿAlids were playing leading roles in the politics of a number of cities, especially in the Islamic East. At the centre in Baghdad, too, the Ḥusaynid brothers al-Sharīf al-Raḍī (d. 406/1016) and al-Sharīf al-Murtaḍā (d. 436/1044) dominated Būyid politics for half a century.[19] By the late fifth/eleventh century, the rise of many ʿAlid families to a distinct and often privileged social position, based primarily on their claim to Prophetic descent, was clearly discernable.

Studying the Prophet's family

In the last few years, the role of the Prophet's family in Muslim societies has received increased scholarly attention. A number of international conferences,[20] a graduate workshop[21] and several monographs have examined various aspects of the family's affairs.[22] The publication of early Ṭālibid genealogies by the Marʿashī library in Qum has made important source material on the Prophet's family accessible to a wider audience.[23] The potential of these works to shed light on various aspects of the history of the Prophet's kin has been brought out in the studies by Kazuo Morimoto, who has taken the lead in this intensified effort in 'sayyido–sharifology'.[24]

This book contributes to this endeavour. It focuses on the period and manner in which the ʿAlids came to attain their special position, to which little attention has been paid. The historical chronicles, by authors such as al-Ṭabarī (d. 310/923), al-Yaʿqūbī (d. 292/905) or al-Balādhurī (d. 279/892), mention the ʿAlids mainly when they revolt; some other information can be found there as well, but the main focus is on ʿAlid–ʿAbbāsid relations. Al-Iṣfahānī's (d. 356/967) *Maqātil al-Ṭālibiyyīn*

19 In addition to other positions in the Būyid administration, both served as *naqīb al-Ṭālibiyyīn* in Baghdad, as did their father and al-Raḍī's son; see Moktar Djebli, 'al-Sharīf al-Raḍī, Abū 'l-Ḥasan Muḥammad b. Abī Aḥmad al-Ḥusayn b. Mūsā', *EI2*.

20 In Rome (1998) and Tokyo (2009), with the proceedings published as Biancamaria Scarcia Amoretti and L. Bottini (eds), 'The Role of the *Sādāt/Ashrāf* in Muslim History and Civilisation: Proceedings of the International Conference (Rome, 2–4 March 1998)', *Oriente Moderno*, n.s., 18 (1999), and Morimoto (ed.), *Sayyids and Sharifs in Muslim Societies*. The papers from a 2007 Middle East Studies Association (MESA) panel on 'Sharing Sanctity: Veneration of the Family of the Prophet as Non-Sectarian Social Praxis' will be published as part of a forthcoming special issue of *Studia Islamica*.

21 'Sayyids and Sharifs: The Kinsfolk of the Prophet in Muslim Societies', organised by Michael Cook and taught by Kazuo Morimoto in Princeton, March 2010.

22 Raffaele Mauriello, *Descendants of the Family of the Prophet in Contemporary History: A Case Study, the Shīʿī Religious Establishment of al-Najaf (Iraq)* (Pisa and Rome, 2011); Kazuo Morimoto, *The Guardian of Authenticity: Genealogy of the Prophet's Family in Medieval Islam* (forthcoming); and Stephennie Mulder, *The Shrines of the ʿAlids in Medieval Syria: Sunnis, Shiʿis, and the Architecture of Coexistence* (Edinburgh, forthcoming). Asad Ahmed, *Religious Elite*, chapter 5, contains a thorough examination of the marriage relations of the descendents of ʿAlī b. Abī Ṭālib.

23 For bibliographical references see Chapter 2.

24 For the term, see Kazuo Morimoto, 'Toward the Formation of Sayyido–Sharifology: Questioning Accepted Fact', *Journal of Sophia Asian Studies* 22 (2004), pp. 87–103, and Morimoto, *Sayyids and Sharifs in Muslim Societies*, pp. 1–12.

provides a pro-ʿAlid angle, yet similarly focuses on the interactions of the ʿAlids with the authorities and discusses in chronological order all the Ṭālibids who suffered at the hands of the Umayyads and the ʿAbbāsids.[25] Given this emphasis in the Arabic historical chronicles, usually the main group of sources for historians of early Islam, it is not surprising that the secondary literature has thus far focused on the revolts.

There are some detailed studies on individual uprisings, such as the studies of Amikam Elad and Tilman Nagel on the revolt of Muḥammad al-Nafs al-Zakiyya in 145/762–3 and Laura Veccia Vaglieri's study of this same revolt and the uprising of al-Ḥusayn b. ʿAlī, the Ṣāḥib Fakhkh, in 169/789.[26] Maher Jarrar's recent edition of the *Akhbār Fakhkh* includes a detailed study of this revolt and its actors,[27] and Najam Haider emphasises its importance in the context of his revised narrative of the origins of the Shiʿa.[28] The most comprehensive survey of the rebellions remains Hugh Kennedy's chapter in his *The Early ʿAbbāsid Caliphate*. His discussion covers the period up to Abū al-Sarāyā's revolt in Kufa in 199/815, which he says 'marked a turning point in the history of the ʿAlid movement', as it was the last large-scale popular uprising in the central Islamic lands.[29] There were, however, a number of smaller rebellions in the Ḥijāz and Iraq in the mid-third/ninth century that were important to the history of the ʿAlid family, not least because many ʿAlids left the Ḥijāz in their aftermath. Al-Masʿūdī (d. 345/956 or 346), for instance, remarks of ʿĪsā b. al-Shaykh al-Shaybānī, who was confirmed as governor of Filasṭīn and al-Urdunn in 252/866, that 'he brought with him from Egypt large sums of money and a group of ʿAlids who had fled disturbances in the Ḥijāz'.[30] The uprising of the Zanj in 255–70/868–83 in southern Iraq, moreover, showed what potency an ʿAlid association could still have in rallying anti-ʿAbbāsid factions.[31]

Aside from the ʿAlid rebels, a second major focus of the secondary literature is the

25 As Haider aptly put it, it is 'a text designed to emphasize the oppression of the Ṭālibids'; Najam Haider, 'The Contested Life of Īsā b. Zayd (d. 166/783): Notes on the Construction of Zaydī Historical Narratives' (*Journal of Near Eastern Studies*, forthcoming).

26 Amikam Elad, 'The Rebellion of Muḥammad b. ʿAbd Allāh b. al-Ḥasan (Known as al-Nafs al-Zakīya) in 145/762', in James E. Montgomery (ed.), *ʿAbbasid Studies: Occasional Papers of the School of ʿAbbasid Studies, Cambridge, 6–10 July 2002* (Leuven, 2004), pp. 145–98; Tilman Nagel, 'Ein früher Bericht über den Aufstand von Muḥammad b. ʿAbdallāh im Jahre 145 H.', *Der Islam* 46 (1970), pp. 227–62; Laura Veccia Vaglieri, 'Divagazioni su due Rivolte Alidi', in *A Francesco Gabrieli: Studi orientalistici offerti nel sessantesimo compleanno dai suoi colleghi e discepoli* (Rome, 1964), pp. 315–50; see also Veccia Vaglieri's article 'al-Ḥusayn b. ʿAlī, Ṣāḥib Fakhkh', *EI2*.

27 Maher Jarrar, 'Introduction', in Aḥmad b. Sahl al-Rāzī, *Akhbār Fakhkh*, ed. Maher Jarrar (Tunis, 2011), pp. 9–129.

28 Haider, *Origins of the Shīʿa*, pp. 207–9.

29 Hugh Kennedy, *The Early Abbasid Caliphate* (London, 1981), p. 211.

30 Al-Masʿūdī, *Murūj al-dhahab*, ed. C. Pellat (Beirut, 1966–79), vol. VII, pp. 395–6, quoted in Paul Cobb, *White Banners: Contention in ʿAbbāsid Syria, 750–880* (Albany, NY, 2001), p. 39.

31 See al-Ṭabarī, *Taʾrīkh*, vol. III, pp. 1,742–87. The main discussions in the secondary scholarship are Heinz Halm, *Die Traditionen über den Aufstand ʿAlī b. Muḥammads, des 'Herren der Zanǧ': Eine quellenkritische Untersuchung* (Bonn, 1967); A. Popovic, *La révolte des esclaves en Iraq au III/IX siècle* (Paris, 1976); and David Waines, 'The Third Century Internal Crisis of the Abbasids', *Journal of the Economic and Social History of the Orient* 20 (1977), pp. 301–3.

role of quietist ʿAlids, such as Jaʿfar al-Ṣādiq, in the development of Shiʿism. While some of the studies discuss certain ʿAlid imāms, they do not examine the ʿAlid family as a whole; their attention is on the emergence of Shiʿite doctrine, particularly the development of Imāmism, not on the social history of the ʿAlids.[32] Curiously, despite the important role that certain ʿAlids played in Shiʿite beliefs, relatively few ʿAlids took part in the early formulation of Shiʿism. Hossein Modarressi's study on the early transmitters of Imāmī writings, for instance, lists only one Ḥusaynid.[33] Even in later generations, only a small number of ʿAlids appear in the Imāmī *rijāl* works, the biographical dictionaries of the most important scholars. There were certainly more ʿAlids among the early Zaydī scholars, as Madelung's study on Imām al-Qāsim shows; but even here, most of the ʿAlids included in Ibrāhīm b. al-Qāsim al-Shuhārī's (d. c. 1142/1730) *Ṭabaqāt al-Zaydiyya al-kubrā* lived in the fifth/eleventh century and after.

Studies on the ʿAlid family in the ʿAbbāsid period so far have thus either emphasised the revolts or focused on the role of certain quietist ʿAlids in the development of Shiʿite doctrine. Both the revolts and the development of Shiʿism are important aspects of the history of the ʿAlid family, but not all ʿAlids were rebels, nor were they all Shiʿites. Indeed, many of the prominent ʿAlids who emerged during the period from the second/eighth to the fifth/eleventh century are best described as local notables. One such ʿAlid family in fifth-/eleventh-century Nishapur is discussed by Richard Bulliet in his *Patricians of Nishapur*. These Ḥasanids, from a branch of the Āl Buṭḥānī, who also appear frequently throughout this book, were Sunni, and their sons married the daughters of other prominent Sunnis in the city.[34]

Bulliet's study is based on an analysis of the local histories of Nishapur, and these works, as well as other local histories of Iran, are also important sources here.[35] Biancamaria Scarcia Amoretti, who has examined various aspects of the roles of *sayyids* and *sharīfs* in the medieval period for some decades, recently highlighted how a close reading of the local histories of Iran provides much insight into the history of the ʿAlid family.[36] Indeed, the local histories give some clues to the ʿAlids'

32 See, for instance, M. G. S. Hodgson, 'How Did the Early Shīʿa Become Sectarian?', *Journal of the American Oriental Society* 75 (1955), pp. 1–13; H. M. Jafri, 'The Early Development of Legitimist Shiʿism with Special Reference to the Role of Imām Jaʿfar al-Ṣādiq' (PhD thesis, School of Oriental and African Studies, 1966; published as *Origins and Early Development of Shia Islam* [London, 1979]); and Arzina Lalani, *Early Shī ʿī Thought: The Teachings of Imām Muḥammad al-Bāqir* (London, 2004).

33 Hossein Modarressi, *Tradition and Survival: A Bibliographical Survey of Early Shīʿite Literature* (Oxford, 2003), p. 280. The Ḥusaynid is Abū ʿAbdallāh Ḥusayn b. Zayd b. ʿAlī b. al-Ḥusayn, known as Dhū al-Damʿa. For two other Ṭālibids, see pp. 143–5 and 294.

34 Bulliet, *Patricians*, pp. 234–45. See the discussion of the Buṭḥānīs in Hamadān and the Buṭḥānīs in Nishapur in this volume.

35 The development of a historiographic tradition of local histories from the late third/ninth century onwards has been linked to the decline of ʿAbbāsid authority and the emergence of alternative centres of political power in the Islamic empire. The availability of local patronage and a desire of the rulers to have their rise to power documented may well have contributed to their production. For a discussion of patronage and local history, see Charles Melville, 'The Caspian Provinces: A World Apart. Three Local Histories of Mazandaran', *Iranian Studies* 33 (2000), pp. 49–63.

36 Biancamaria Scarcia Amoretti, 'A Historical Atlas on the ʿAlids: A Proposal and a Few Samples', in Kazuo

prominence in several cities and provinces in the Islamic East. Several works include a separate chapter on *sayyid*s, in addition to discussing them in the biographical sections among the local notables. Information is particularly rich in works such as the *Tārīkh-i Qum* of al-Qummī (d. 406/1015) or the *Tārīkh-i Bayhaq* of Ibn Funduq al-Bayhaqī (d. 565/1169): The latter has a chapter on the *sādāt* of Bayhaq, gives individual entries to many ʿAlids in the long biographical section and also includes a short discussion on the *sayyid*s buried in the region.[37]

Summary and structure

This book does not provide a narrative history of the ʿAlids in the ʿAbbāsid period but rather seeks to trace and explain their emergence as a social force from a variety of angles. While local histories provide important details on the ʿAlids in specific locations, of central importance to a study of the Prophet's family from a more general point of view are the Ṭālibid genealogies. Chapter 2 discusses these works as the historiographic footprint of the emergence of the Prophet's descendants as the First Family of Islam: Written mostly by and for the family of the Prophet, these works reflect not only a 'changing notion of nobility'[38] but also an increasing concern with defining the boundaries of an elite group. In terms of content, the genealogies are certainly selective regarding whom they include, yet in contrast to many other sources that focus on one or another group of ʿAlids – the historical chronicles focusing mainly on the rebels and some government supporters, the *rijāl* works on the scholars and the local histories on the ʿAlids (who are often also scholars) in a particular region – they are inclusive, giving the names, at least, of the Prophet's alleged kin regardless of background. The Ṭālibid genealogies are most comprehensive on the ʿAlids in the eastern part of the Islamic world, because this is where the authors themselves were mostly based.[39]

The Ṭālibid genealogies provide extensive prosopographical data on the Prophet's kin, which I mine and analyse for information on the ʿAlids' financial privileges, false claimants to ʿAlid status and the ʿAlids' marriage patterns, discussed in Chapter 3. The data show that as they rose to the top of the hierarchy of Muslim society, the

Morimoto (ed.), *Sayyids and Sharifs in Muslim Societies: The Living Links to the Prophet* (London and New York, 2012), pp. 92–122.

37 Ibn Funduq, *Tārīkh-i Bayhaq*, pp. 54–65, 254–5 and *passim*. Dorothea Krawulsky notes the abundance of ʿAlids in the region at the time of Ibn Funduq's writing ('. . . *daß es zur Zeit von Ibn Funduq in Bayhaq nichts so im Überfluss gab wie ʿAlīden*'); see Dorothea Krawulsky, 'Untersuchungen zur Shīʿitischen Tradition von Bayhaq: Ein Beitrag zur Frage der Verbreitung der Shīʿa in Persien', in Wadād al-Qāḍī (ed.), *Studia Arabica et Islamica: Festschrift für Iḥsān ʿAbbās* (Beirut, 1981), p. 308.

38 This phrase is taken from Ahmed, *Religious Elite*, n. 12, and it refers to 'the shift of emphasis from belonging to a tribe to closeness to the Prophet', as discussed in Ibn Rasūl's *Turfat al-asḥāb fī maʿrifat al-ansāb*.

39 Morimoto's insights into these works and their authors have provided important reference points for this book; see Kazuo Morimoto, 'The Formation and Development of the Science of Ṭālibid Genealogies in the 10th and 11th Century Middle East', *Oriente Moderno*, n.s., 18 (1999), pp. 541–70.

ʿAlids increasingly married within the family; even though there is little in Shiʿite or Sunni law to explicitly restrict marriage choices, ʿAlid women came to overwhelmingly marry ʿAlid men. Moreover, a close look at the material reveals that the maternal lineage mattered, much more than is usually accounted for. As the genealogical material is arranged vertically – when someone recounts his descent, he mentions his father, grandfather, great-grandfather and so on, not his brothers, cousins and uncles or other relations of marriage – scholars have generally failed to explore these latter connections.[40] However, Asad Ahmed shows in his detailed study of the ʿAlids and other prominent Ḥijāzī families in the first two centuries of Islam that cognate relations formed the basis of social and political alliances and could determine and explain the behaviour of a clan.[41] As dreary as they may at first seem, marriage patterns reveal the internal workings of the ʿAlids more clearly than any other accounts.

Chapter 4 examines the emergence of the ʿAlids as the First Family of Islam through an examination of the *niqāba*, 'the headship' of the ʿAlid family. Morimoto's study of the subject has provided important groundwork, compiling the many references to the *niqāba* in the genealogies to date its diffusion across the Islamic lands.[42] The study confirms that the *niqāba* was not a Būyid innovation, and it challenges the 'division theory', first put forward by Adam Mez, according to which there was one *naqīb* for both Ṭālibids and ʿAbbāsids (*naqīb al-Hāshimiyyīn*) until the end of the fourth/tenth century, when the two clans each got their own.[43] The chapter here focuses on the still little-understood origins and functions of the office, as well as the extent of a *naqīb*'s power, his autonomy from the authorities and his duties towards the ʿAlids. The final chapter then draws together the themes of the previous chapters and gives a case study of two prominent families in the Islamic East, the Āl Zubāra and the Āl Buṯhānī. Both families combined their sacred descent with other sources of elite status, such as wealth and learning, to ensure their place as the *primi inter pares* of the Eastern Islamic elites.

40 Similarly Raffaele Mauriello, 'Genealogical Prestige and Marriage Strategy among the *Ahl al-Bayt*: The Case of the al-Sadr Family in Recent Times', in Sarah Savant and Helena de Felipe (eds), *Genealogy and Knowledge in Muslim Societies: Understanding the Past* (Edinburgh, forthcoming): 'My interviews with members of the al-Sadr family suggest that their memory of genealogy is not only focused vertically, that is to say on the family's distant ancestors, but that it is equally nourished horizontally by bonds established with eminent families with whom they allied.'

41 See Ahmed, *Religious Elite*, especially chapter 5, at pp. 137–8.

42 Kazuo Morimoto, 'A Preliminary Study on the Diffusion of the *Niqāba al-Ṭālibīyīn*: Towards an Understanding of the Early Dispersal of *Sayyids*', in Hidemitsu Kuroki (ed.), *The Influence of Human Mobility in Muslim Societies* (London, 2003), pp. 3–42.

43 The 'Būyid innovation' was suggested by M. Kabir, *The Buwayhid Dynasty, 334/946–447/1055* (Calcutta, 1964), p. 187. For the 'division theory', see Adam Mez, *Die Renaissance des Islāms* (Heidelberg, 1922), p. 145; van Arendonk and Graham, 'Sharīf', *EI2*; Axel Havemann, 'Naḳīb al-ashrāf', *EI2*; and E. Tyan, *Histoire de l'organisation judiciaire en pays d'Islam*, 2nd edn (Leiden, 1960), pp. 550–8. According to Louis Massignon, the *niqāba* of the Ṭālibids was not established until 305/917, with the help of the vizier Ibn Furāt; unfortunately he does not give his source. See Louis Massignon, 'Cadis et *naqībs* baghdadiens', *Wiener Zeitschrift für die Kunde des Morgenlandes* 51 (1948), p. 113.

Finally, a note on authenticity. When presenting my work on the ʿAlids, I have often been asked whether all of these *sayyid*s, now and throughout history, really were descendants of the Prophet. To my mind, this is of little concern: What matters is that, on the whole, the *sayyid*s themselves as well as the rest of society believed that they were the descendants of the Prophet and acted accordingly. As Kazuo Morimoto puts it, 'the *sayyid/sharīf* pedigree is something that could be socially generated at the same time as it was, and was always believed to be, biological'.[44]

44 Morimoto, 'Toward the Formation of Sayyido–Sharifology', p. 90.

2

Genealogy, Money and the Drawing of Boundaries

Central to the ʿAlids' claims to social distinction and entitlement to a variety of privileges was their close genealogical connection to the Prophet. With the dispersal of the family to all parts of the Islamic world, which accelerated after the failed revolt of Ḥusayn b. ʿAlī at Fakhkh in 169/789, the establishment of certain controls over this connection became increasingly important. This concern is reflected in the appearance of Ṭālibid genealogies, genealogical works focusing explicitly on the Ṭālibid branch of the Banū Hāshim, from the mid-third/ninth century onwards. The *ʿUmdat al-ṭālib* of Ibn ʿInaba (d. 828/1424–5), which dates from the early ninth/fifteenth century, is the most famous and widely used of such works, yet it stands at the end of the development of a specific genre or group of works: genealogies of the family of the Prophet, based on family (or local) registers, which were written by genealogists who were themselves predominantly ʿAlids or Ṭālibids.[1]

Genealogy, of course, was by no means a new genre. Arab genealogy was a central form of early Islamic historiography, recording the heritage of the Arab pre-Islamic past in Islamic terms.[2] The major difference between the Ṭālibid works and the earlier Arab genealogies, such as Ibn al-Kalbī's (d. 204/819) *Jamharat al-nasab*, is the former's concern with contemporary lineages. Whereas the general Arab

1 Ibn ʿInaba, *ʿUmdat al-ṭālib fī ansāb āl Abī Ṭālib* (Najaf, 1961), new edn Mahdī al-Rajāʾī (Qum, 1425q/2004); for Ibn ʿInaba see Biancamaria Scarcia Amoretti, 'Ibn ʿInaba', *EI2*; and Biancamaria Scarcia Amoretti, 'Sulla *ʿUmdat al-Ṭālib fī ansāb āl Abī Ṭālib*, e sul suo autore Ǧamāl al-Dīn Aḥmad ibn ʿInaba', *Annali dell'Instituto Orientale di Napoli*, n.s., 13 (1963), pp. 287–94. Many of the earlier Ṭālibid genealogies have only recently become available in printed form. These include Yaḥyā b. al-Ḥasan b. Jaʿfar al-ʿAqīqī (d. 277/891), *Kitāb al-Muʿaqqibān min wuld al-imām amīr al-muʾminīn*, ed. Muḥammad Kāẓim al-Maḥmūdī (Qum, 2001); Abū Naṣr al-Bukhārī (d. mid-fourth/tenth century), *Sirr al-silsila*; Shaykh al-Sharaf al-ʿUbaydalī (d. 435/1043), *Tahdhīb al-ansāb wa-nihāyat al-aʿqāb*, ed. Muḥammad Kāẓim al-Maḥmūdī (Qum, 1413/1992–3); Abū al-Ḥasan al-ʿUmarī al-Nassāba (d. 450/1058), *al-Majdī fī ansāb al-Ṭālibiyyīn*, ed. Aḥmad al-Mahdāwī al-Dāmghānī (Qum, 1409/1988/9); Abū Ismāʿīl Ibrāhīm Ibn Ṭabāṭabā (d. second half of the fifth/eleventh century), *Muntaqilat al-Ṭālibiyya*, ed. Muḥammad Mahdī al-Sayyid Ḥasan al-Kharsān (Najaf, 1388/1968); Ibn Funduq al-Bayhaqī (d. 565/1169), *Lubāb al-ansāb*, ed. Mahdī al-Rajāʾī (Qum, 1410/1989/90); Fakhr al-Dīn al-Rāzī (d. 606/1209), *al-Shajara al-mubāraka fī ansāb al-Ṭālibiyya*, ed. Maḥmūd al-Marʿashī (Qum, 1409/1988/9); Ismaʿīl b. al- Ḥusayn al-Marwazī al-Azwarqānī (d. after 614/1217), *al-Fakhrī fī ansāb al-Ṭālibiyyīn*, ed. Mahdī al-Rajāʾī (Qum, 1409/1988/9); and Muḥammad b. ʿAlī Ibn al-Ṭiqṭaqā (d. 708/1308), *al-Aṣīlī fī ansāb al-Ṭālibiyyīn*, ed. Mahdī al-Rajāʾī (Qum, 1418/1997).

2 See Asad Ahmed, *Religious Elite*, Introduction, and discussion below.

genealogies may be termed a 'backward-looking genre',[3] the Ṭālibid works are by contrast 'forward-looking' and concerned with their current times: Which lineages have survived? Where have they settled? What is their status? Do they belong to the families of *nuqabāʾ*? How can a genealogy be proved or disproved? The frequent references to false claimants in the genealogies suggest that such discussions were not merely of a theoretical nature, but that some very real interests were at stake.

While the genealogies do not always provide rich accounts – they often give little more than a long list of names, with few stories and even fewer dates – they do give a lot of prosopographical information, and this can be analysed for a number of insights into the history and development of the ʿAlids. As is the case with much of the early Islamic source material, few of the Ṭālibid genealogies were written in the period under focus in this study; most date from a slightly later period, mainly from the fifth/eleventh to ninth/fifteenth centuries. Moreover, some of the main works have not survived, at least not in their original multi-volume form. For example, the early fifth-/eleventh-century author Shaykh al-Sharaf al-ʿUbaydalī (d. 435/1043) says that his work *Tahdhīb al-ansāb* is an abridgement of a much larger version of 10,000 pages, which is no longer extant, and the work of the frequently quoted Abū al-Ghanāʾim al-Dimashqī (d. 438/1046) appears to be lost entirely.[4] Some of the extant works, such as al-ʿAqīqī's (d. 277/891) *Kitāb al-Muʿaqqibīn*, also seem to have contained more material than what survives today. In the case of the *Kitāb al-Muʿaqqibīn*, this can be inferred from frequent quotations of al-ʿAqīqī in later works that contain additional or variant details.[5]

In terms of geography, the authors of most of the Ṭālibid genealogies were based in the eastern part of the Islamic world: Accordingly, information is most detailed on ʿAlids in the areas of Iraq, Iran and Central Asia, as well as the Ḥijāz, and less comprehensive on ʿAlids in the West (especially North Africa and Spain). It may be argued that this suggests that the ʿAlids were of more importance in the Islamic East, or developed a clearer consciousness as a group there;[6] however, I would caution against rushing to such a conclusion, as it relies heavily on the surviving source material, which is clearly not all there was.

3 Chase F. Robinson, *Islamic Historiography* (Cambridge, 2003), p. 56.

4 Al-ʿUbaydalī, *Tahdhīb*, p. 21. Abū al-Ghanāʾim al-Dimashqī is an important source for a number of works, including al-Rāzī's *Shajara* and Ibn Funduq's *Lubāb*. Ibn Funduq lists three genealogists in Damascus by the name of Abū al-Ghanāʾim: The genealogist referred to here is the third, Abū al-Ghanāʾim ʿAbdallāh b. al-Ḥasan b. Muḥammad b. al-Ḥasan b. al-Ḥusayn b. ʿĪsā b. Yaḥyā b. al-Ḥusayn b. Zayd b. ʿAlī b. al-Ḥusayn b. ʿAlī b. Abī Ṭālib; see Ibn Funduq, *Lubāb al-ansāb*, pp. 631–2. For Abū al-Ghanāʾim's genealogy see also al-Rāzī, *al-Shajara*, p. 148, and al-ʿUmarī, *al-Majdī*, p. 380. A namesake, Abū al-Ghanāʾim Muḥammad b. ʿAlī, is the father of the genealogist al-ʿUmarī and frequently quoted in the *Majdī*; see, for example, al-ʿUmarī, *al-Majdī*, p. 205. For a number of other lost works, see the list of abbreviations for sources in Ibn Funduq, *Lubāb al-ansāb*, p. 719.

5 In the instances where al-ʿAqīqī is quoted in al-Bukhārī's *Sirr al-silsila*, for example, it is clear that a more detailed, or at least different, version of his work was used; see al-Bukhārī, *Sirr al-silsila*, pp. 20, 31 and 76.

6 See Scarcia Amoretti, 'A Historical Atlas on the ʿAlids', p. 111, who suggests: 'The ʿAlid diaspora appears as a meaningful phenomenon for the Eastern lands of the caliphate while the Maghrib seems to have been an almost accidental destination.'

Before turning to the specifically Ṭālibid genealogies, I will discuss briefly the historiographic context and lay out more clearly the relationship between the Ṭālibid and early Arab genealogies.

Genealogy and the Prophet

Genealogy is sometimes said to be a quintessentially Arab form of historiography, since it follows and preserves the tribal structure of the pre-Islamic Arabs.[7] It is said to satisfy an inherently Arab interest in lines of descent, an interest renewed or sustained by ʿUmar b. al-Khaṭṭāb's (r. 13–23/634–44) introduction of the *dīwān* system, in which the distribution of soldiers' salaries and the division of booty were done according to tribe: The adoption of a genealogical principle in organising the early Islamic state is thus central to the development of the discipline of genealogy.[8] Curiously, in al-Ṭabarī's lengthy account of ʿUmar's decision to introduce military registers, the practice is ascribed to a Byzantine precedent: al-Walīd b. Hishām b. al-Mughīra says to the caliph, 'I have been to Syria and seen how the rulers there have instituted a military roll and set up a regular army. You should do the same.'[9] And so the caliph did. Of course, this does not explain why the *dīwān* was organised according to tribe; however, the system itself, at least according to this account, did not continue a pre-Islamic Arab practice.

Whatever its roots, the aims of Arabic genealogy as it emerged in the second/eighth and third/ninth centuries can perhaps be more easily identified. I will not enter into a discussion on authenticity here, as it matters little for the present argument whether the genealogies were real or imagined.[10] What is important is that the genre

7 See, for example, Ignaz Goldziher, *Muslim Studies*, ed. S. M. Stern, trans C. R. Barber and S. M. Stern, 2 vols (London, 1967–71), vol. I, p. 179: '[The genealogical genre's] roots are, as we have repeatedly seen, among the most authentic impulses of Arab genius.' See also Ibn al-Kalbī, *Ǧamharat al-nasab: Das genealogische Werk des Hisām ibn Muḥammad al-Kalbī*, ed. Werner Caskel, 2 vols (Leiden, 1966), vol. I, pp. 27–31, and Caskel, 'Nasab', *EI2*. On social organisation in pre-Islamic Arabia, see most recently Robert G. Hoyland, *Arabia and the Arabs: From the Bronze Age to the Coming of Islam* (London, 2001), pp. 131–8, and Eva Orthmann, *Stamm und Macht: Die arabischen Stämme im 2. und 3. Jahrhundert der Hiğra* (Wiesbaden, 2002), pp. 208–21.

8 Morimoto, 'Formation and Development', p. 542, cites the compilation of *dīwāns* as 'a significant stimulus for the prevalence of genealogical consciousness, and the development of knowledge of genealogies'; see also ʿAbd al-ʿAzīz al-Dūrī, *The Rise of Historical Writing Among the Arabs*, ed. and trans. Lawrence I. Conrad (Princeton, 1983), p. 21: 'This [the *dīwān* system] gave genealogies new importance and provided further incentives for studying them', and pp. 50–3; Zoltán Szombathy, 'The Nassāba: Anthropological Fieldwork in Medieval Islam', *Islamic Culture* 73 (1999), pp. 98–9.

9 See al-Ṭabarī, *Taʾrīkh*, vol. I, p. 2,750; again in Jalāl al-Dīn al-Suyūṭī, *Taʾrīkh al-khulafāʾ*, ed. Ibrāhīm Ṣāliḥ (Beirut, 1997), p. 173. The account is also mentioned in Hugh Kennedy, 'From Oral Tradition to Written Record in Arabic Genealogy', *Arabica* 44 (1997), p. 540 (with a slightly different translation: 'I came to Syria and saw that its rulers had set up a *dīwān* and organised *ğunds*, so set up a *dīwān* and organise *ğunds*.').

10 See Ahmed, *Religious Elite*, p. 4, who argues that the genealogies are relatively more reliable than other kinds of early Islamic historiography. Although a certain amount of fabrication ('genealogical reshuffling', n. 11) did take place, it was generally limited to a mythological past. Elsewhere he writes that 'due to

be seen as part of the larger formation of Islamic historiography.[11] While Werner Caskel and others have suggested that genealogies were fixed in writing of some kind already in pre-Islamic times – and various pre-Islamic inscriptions from the Arabian peninsula attest to this – the genre of genealogical writing in the second/eighth and third/ninth centuries reflects a desire to contextualise and legitimise a new conquest elite.[12] Thus, the genealogies partly seek to explain the origins of the Arabs. They also give to an emerging Islamic Arab society an organisational structure, which is expressed in bipolar tribal terms: Everyone's genealogy can be traced back to either ʿAdnān or Qaḥṭān.[13] Significantly, the whole arrangement is built around the Prophet and Islam. What counts is a tribe's (or a tribe member's) role in the events of Islam and a tribe's (or a tribe member's) relationship to the Prophet. As Franz Rosenthal put it, early genealogical works were written precisely in order to 'fix the place of newly important families in relation to the Prophet'.[14]

The early genealogical works differ in the extent to which they emphasise one or another of the aims of the genre. Moreover, the surviving examples – such as the *Jamharat al-nasab* of Ibn al-Kalbī, the *Kitāb Ḥadhf min nasab Quraysh* of Muʿarrij b. ʿAmr al-Sadūsī (d. 195/810), the *Kitāb Nasab Quraysh* of Muṣʿab b. al-Zubayrī (d. 236/851), his nephew al-Zubayr b. Bakkār's (d. 256/870) *Jamharat nasab Quraysh wa-akhbārihā*, the *Jamharat ansāb al-ʿarab* of Ibn Ḥazm (d. 456/1064) or the *Kitāb al-Munammaq* and the *Kitāb al-Muḥabbar* of Muḥammad b. Ḥabīb (d. 245/860)[15] –

patterns of emerging alliances under Islam, tribes came to claim membership in a northern or southern block on the basis of their alleged descent from a common ancestor. Fictive genealogies for historical figures are generally rare, although it cannot be ruled out for all cases.' See Asad Ahmed, 'Prosopography and the Reconstruction of Ḥijāzī History for the Early Islamic Period: The Case of the ʿAwfī Family', in Katharine Keats-Rohan (ed.), *Prosopography Approaches and Applications: A Handbook* (Oxford, 2007), pp. 415–58.

11 Robinson, *Islamic Historiography*, does not discuss the genealogical genre in his division of Islamic historiography into biography, prosopography and chronography. However, genealogy fits well into the category of prosopography: People are grouped according to their alleged tribal or family origins, in the same way in which scholars are classified according to their schools. For the similarities between *ṭabaqāt* and *nasab*, see Tarif Khalidi, *Arabic Historical Thought in the Classical Period* (Cambridge, 1994), p. 49.

12 For developments in the early Islamic period, see Caskel, 'Nasab', *EI2*, and M. J. Kister and M. Plessner, 'Notes on Caskel's Ǧamharat an-nasab,' *Oriens* 25–26 (1976), pp. 50–4; see also Zoltán Szombathy, *The Roots of Arabic Genealogy: A Study in Historical Anthropology* (Budapest, 2003), pp. 91–5. I am grateful to Evrim Binbas for this reference. For inscriptions in pre-Islamic Arabia, see, for example, A. F. L. Beeston, 'Epigraphic South Arabian Nomenclature', *Raydan* 1 (1978), pp. 13–21, where he emphasises that the South Arabian tribe has to be understood not as a genealogical group but as an economic and socio-political unit.

13 See Orthmann, *Stamm und Macht*, p. 210–17. She suggests that this polarity, also found in the distinction between nomads and settlers, is perhaps best understood as an expression of a particular worldview, which is not specifically Arab but is also found in classical antiquity.

14 Franz Rosenthal, *A History of Muslim Historiography*, 2nd rev. edn (Leiden, 1968), p. 95. Even so, according to Ibn Qutayba (d. 276/889): '[T]he noblest do not know their descent and the best know nothing of their ancestors; Qurayshites are often ignorant of the point in their descent which links them genealogically to the Prophet.' Cited in Goldziher, *Muslim Studies*, vol. I, pp. 172–3.

15 Ibn al-Kālbī, *Ǧamharat an-nasab*; also as *Jamharat al-nasab*, ed. Maḥmūd Firdaws al-ʿAẓm, 3 vols (Damascus, 1982–6), and *Jamharat al-nasab*, ed. Nājī Ḥasan, 2 vols (Beirut, 1986); Muṣʿab al-Zubayrī

differ greatly in detail and scope. For example, Ibn al-Kalbī's monumental *Jamharat al-nasab* attempts to present a comprehensive genealogy of the Arabs, and it thus stands in contrast to al-Zubayr b. Bakkār's 'family history', focused on the Zubayrids within the Banū Asad b. ʿAbd al-ʿUzzā b. Quṣayy.[16]

The ʿAlids in the general works and the beginning of Ṭālibid genealogy

Unsurprisingly, given their close relation to the Prophet, the ʿAlids and other Ṭālibids take a prominent place in the Arab genealogies. They tend to be discussed towards the beginning of the works, but after the ʿAbbāsids: This order reflects their closeness to the heart of the Quraysh, yet emphasises the claims of the second dynasty of Islam as the legitimate heir to the Prophet. As the genealogies are part of the historiographic production of the ʿAbbāsid period, the authors' decision to place the ʿAbbāsids before the ʿAlids is not surprising. As for the content, in general terms information on the ʿAlids in the earlier works agrees with information in the later Ṭālibid ones, and details on marriages and the numbers and names of descendants concur for the first few generations of Islam. Indeed, the early Ṭālibid authors draw upon some of the main sources of genealogy: Abū Yaqẓān (d. 170 or 190/786 or 805) and al-Wāqidī (d. 207/823), for example, are among the main sources for al-Bukhārī in his work on the genealogy of the ʿAlid family.[17] However, despite the common source material and congruent information for the first few generations of ʿAlids, there are some important differences between the general and the Ṭālibid works. Genealogies of the general kind disappear after the third/ninth century (except in the case of Spain), around the time when the Ṭālibid works begin to emerge. The former focus on larger kinship groups, whereas the latter treat only one branch of the Banū Hāshim, the Ṭālibids, or even only the ʿAlids. Beyond this narrowing in the scope of the genealogies, there is also a change in the way in which they discuss their subjects:

(d. 236/851), *Kitāb Nasab Quraysh*, ed. É. Lévi-Provençal (Cairo, 1953); al-Zubayr b. Bakkār, *Jamharat nasab Quraysh wa-akhbārihā*, ed. Maḥmūd Muḥammad Shākir (Cairo, 1381/1961), vol. I; Ibn Ḥazm, *Jamharat ansāb al-ʿarab*, ed. É. Lévi-Provençal (Cairo, 1948); Ibn Ḥabīb, *Kitāb al-Muḥabbar*, ed. Ilse Lichtenstädter (Hyderabad, 1942); Ibn Ḥabīb, *Kitāb al-Munammaq fī akhbār Quraysh*, ed. Khurshīd Aḥmad Fāriq (Hyderabad, 1964); and Muʾarrij al-Sadūsī, *Kitāb Ḥadhf min nasab Quraysh*, ed. Ṣalāḥ al-Dīn al-Munajjid (Cairo, 1960).

16 Stefan Leder has argued that one should furthermore distinguish between more 'technical' works, such as Ibn al-Kalbī's *Jamharat al-nasab* or al-Zubayrī's *Kitāb Nasab Quraysh*, where the main concern is with lines of descent, and works such as al-Zubayr b. Bakkār's *Jamharat nasab Quraysh wa-akhbārihā*, which is more narrative in style (and survives only in part). For the latter works it may be more useful to speak of genealogy as an organisational principle of historical writing; another good example is al-Balādhurī's (d. 279/892) *Ansāb al-ashrāf*. See Stefan Leder, 'al-Zubayr b. Bakkār', *EI2*.

17 Al-Bukhārī draws on an unusually wide range of sources, genealogical and historical, and cites even the geographer Ibn Khurradādhbih (d. c. 300/912); see al-Bukhārī, *Sirr al-silsila*, p. 75. For a discussion of his sources, see Morimoto, 'Formation and Development', p. 546. The *Sirr al-silsila* is recorded in the library of the Shiʿite scholar Ibn Ṭāwūs (d. 664/1266) under the title *Kitāb Sirr al-ansāb al-ʿAlawiyyīn*; see Etan Kohlberg, *A Medieval Muslim Scholar at Work: Ibn Ṭāwūs and His Library* (Leiden, 1992), p. 333 (no. 548).

While the general Arab works attempt to place the various lineages in an alleged past, the Ṭālibid works are mainly concerned with taking stock of contemporary progeny.

The first genealogy focused specifically on the Ṭālibids as the descendants of the Prophet is attributed to the Ḥusaynid Yaḥyā b. al-Ḥasan al-ʿAqīqī.[18] Al-Ṭūsī records that al-ʿAqīqī wrote a *Kitāb Nasab āl Abī Ṭālib* as well as a *Kitāb Masjid al-nabī* and a *Kitāb al-Manāsik*, and he is also said to have been the author of a (now lost) *Taʾrīkh al-Madīna*.[19] Al-ʿAqīqī was one of the main sources for al-Iṣfahānī's *Maqātil al-Ṭālibiyyīn*,[20] but he is mostly remembered for his genealogy, which was used also by the Zaydī imām al-Nāṭiq bi-l-Ḥaqq (d. 424/1032–3) and quoted by all later Ṭālibid genealogists.[21]

Al-ʿAqīqī lived in Medina, and he was a contemporary of the genealogist al-Zubayr b. Bakkār. Neither mentions the other in his work, but they may well have met: As Stefan Leder has noted, Ibn al-Athīr (d. 630/1233) reports that Ibn Bakkār left his native Medina for Baghdad for a time because of a quarrel with the ʿAlids. According to this account, Ibn Bakkār had harmed the ʿAlids, and his uncle Muṣʿab b. ʿAbdallāh, the genealogist, urged him to make peace with them, referring to him as uncivil in this regard (*inna al-Zubayr fīhi jahl*).[22]

Despite his later importance, we know little about al-ʿAqīqī aside from the titles of his books. Nothing is known about his father, but his grandfather Jaʿfar is said to have been an imām of the Zaydiyya, with a following that called him 'al-Ḥujja'.[23]

18 Al-ʿAqīqī's full name is Abū al-Ḥusayn Yaḥyā b. al-Ḥasan b. Jaʿfar b. ʿUbaydallāh b. al-Ḥusayn b. ʿAlī b. al-Ḥusayn b. ʿAlī b. Abī Ṭālib; see, for example, al-ʿUmarī, *al-Majdī*, p. 406. Al-ʿAqīq is a place near Medina; see Yāqūt al-Ḥamawī, *Muʿjam al-buldān*, 20 vols in 5 (Beirut, 1955–7), vol. IV, pp. 138–41. There were probably other near-contemporary genealogies as well as earlier ones. Al-Bukhārī, for instance, cites (at pp. 37, 67 and 99) one Aḥmad b. ʿĪsā b. ʿAbdallāh b. Muḥammad b. ʿUmar, known as al-ʿUmarī al-Nassāba or 'al-ʿUmarī the genealogist', whose father is known to have been a child at the time of al-Nafs al-Zakiyya's uprising in 145/762–3, and thus Aḥmad probably lived towards the end of the second/eighth century; see Modarressi, *Tradition and Survival*, p. 294, and Nagel, 'Früher Bericht', p. 252.

19 Mentioned by al-Sakhāwī, as quoted in Rosenthal, *History*, p. 475. The *Taʾrīkh Madīna* is also mentioned in ʿUmar b. Shabba's work of the same title; see ʿUmar b. Shabba (d. 262/875), *Kitāb Taʾrīkh al-Madīna al-munawwara*, 2 vols (Beirut, 1996).

20 In the *Maqātil*, al-ʿAqīqī's work is mostly transmitted by the Kufan Aḥmad b. Saʿīd al-Hamdānī (d. 333/944); see Sebastian Günther, *Quellenuntersuchungen zu den 'Maqātil aṭ-Ṭālibiyyīn' des Abū 'l-Farağ al-Iṣfahānī (gest. 356/967): Ein Beitrag zur Problematik der mündlichen und schriftlichen Überlieferung in der mittelalterlichen arabischen Literatur* (Hildesheim, 1991), pp. 127 and 226; Wilferd Madelung, *Der Imam al-Qāsim ibn Ibrāhīm und die Glaubenslehre der Zayditen* (Berlin, 1965), p. 59, n. 102.

21 Al-Ṭūsī, *Tusy's list of Shiʿa Books* (Calcutta, 1853), p. 360, says that the book was transmitted by Aḥmad b. ʿAbdūn from Abū Bakr al-Dūrī from Abū Muḥammad Akhī Ṭāhir from his grandfather Yaḥyā b. al-Ḥasan, and from Abū ʿAlī b. Shādhān from Ibn Akhī Ṭāhir from his grandfather. For the Zaydī source, see al-Nāṭiq bi-l-Ḥaqq, *al-Ifāda fī taʾrīkh aʾimmat al-Zaydiyya*, ed. Muḥammad Yaḥyā Sālim (Ṣanʿāʾ, 1996), pp. 42, 58 and 116.

22 Ibn al-Athīr (d. 630/1233), *al-Kāmil fī al-taʾrīkh*, ed. C. J. Tornberg (Leiden, 1851–76); reprinted 13 vols (Beirut, 1965–7), vol. IV, p. 526, cited in Leder, 'al-Zubayr b. Bakkār', *EI2*. The genealogist al-Marwazī mentions an ʿAlid he saw in Baghdad in 598/1201 who 'was learning the *Kitāb Nasab Quraysh* of al-Zubayr b. Bakkār by heart'; see al-Marwazī, *al-Fakhrī*, p. 119. He also says that this man was a boon companion to the caliph al-Nāṣir li-Dīn Allāh for seventeen years.

23 Al-Bukhārī, *Sirr al-silsila*, pp. 71–2. He continues that the Zaydī al-Qāsim b. Ibrāhīm al-Rassī called

According to the genealogist al-Bukhārī, he was imprisoned in Medina for eighteen months by the governor Abū al-Bakhtarī Wahb b. Wahb.[24] But the family had not always been at odds with the authorities. Jaʿfar's father ʿUbaydallāh received a land grant from the first ʿAbbāsid caliph al-Saffāḥ (r. 133–6/750–4) near al-Madāʾin worth 80,000 dinars a year; he did not join the ʿAlid uprising led by al-Nafs al-Zakiyya.[25] According to one report reproduced by al-Iṣfahānī, he was poisoned by Abū Muslim (d. 140/757), the leader of the Hāshimiyya in Khurāsān. Al-Iṣfahānī doubts this report because the family's genealogist Yaḥyā b. al-Ḥasan does not mention it; and Yaḥyā, al-Iṣfahānī says, is the authority (*al-ʿanāya*) on matters of the family.[26]

We do not know why al-ʿAqīqī turned to writing about his family's relations.[27] A number of Ṭālibid genealogies followed al-ʿAqīqī's. The ones used here include al-Bukhārī's *Sirr al-silsila*, the *Tahdhīb al-ansāb wa-nihāyat al-aʿqāb* of Shaykh al-Sharaf al-ʿUbaydalī, the *al-Majdī fī ansāb al-Ṭālibiyyīn* of Abū al-Ḥasan al-ʿUmarī (d. 450/1058), the *Muntaqilat al-Ṭālibiyya* of Ibn Ṭabāṭabā, the *Lubāb al-ansāb* of Ibn Funduq al-Bayhaqī (d. 565/1169), the *al-Shajara al-mubāraka fī ansāb al-Ṭālibiyya* of Fakhr al-Dīn al-Rāzī (d. 606/1209), the *al-Fakhrī fī ansāb al-Ṭālibiyyīn* of al-Marwazī (d. after 614/1217), the *al-Aṣīlī fī ansāb al-Ṭālibiyyīn* of Ibn al-Ṭiqṭaqā (d. 708/1308) and the *ʿUmdat al-ṭālib* of Ibn ʿInaba.[28] The first systematic attempt at studying these works as a group was made by Kazuo Morimoto in an article published in 1999 with the title 'The Formation and Development of the Science of Ṭālibid Genealogies in the 10th and 11th Century Middle East'. As is clear from the title, Morimoto argues for the existence of a 'science' of genealogical writing, which

---

Jaʿfar b. ʿUbaydallāh an *imām min aʾimmat āl Muḥammad* (an *imām* from the family of the Prophet). According to Madelung, *Imām al-Qāsim*, p. 147, the Zaydī imām al-Hādī and the later Zaydī writers do not mention him.

24 Al-ʿAqīqī, in the published genealogy, gives his lineage up to his grandfather, whose mother he gives as Umm Ḥammāda bt. ʿAbdallāh b. Ṣafwān b. ʿAbdallāh b. Ṣafwān b. Umayya b. Khalaf al-Jumaḥī; so her ancestor was a non-Hāshimite Qurashī and descendant of an important Meccan family. ʿAbdallāh b. Ṣafwān b. Umayya was a well-known supporter of ʿAbdallāh b. al-Zubayr; see al-Ṭabarī, *Taʾrīkh*, vol. II, p. 513, and vol. II, pp. 797 and 852, and Wilferd Madelung, *The Succession to Muḥammad: A Study of the Early Caliphate* (Cambridge, 1997), p. 158. For Abū al-Bakhtarī Wahb b. Wahb, who was governor of Medina for Hārūn al-Rashīd (r. 169-193/786-809), see Ibn al-Jawzī (d. 597/1200), *al-Muntaẓam fī taʾrīkh al- mulūk wa al-umam*, eds Muḥammad and Muṣṭafā ʿAbd al-Qādir ʿAṭā, 18 vols (Beirut, 1992–3), vol. X, pp. 81–91. According to Modarressi, he was a judge in Medina; see Modarressi, *Tradition and Survival*, p. 389, where he describes him as 'a Sunnī transmitter of *ḥadīth* notorious for his unreliability and forgery'. He is mentioned in a number of Shiʿite rijāl works; see, for instance, Ibn Shahrāshūb, *Maʿālim al-ʿulamāʾ*, ed. ʿAbbās Iqbāl (Tehran, 1934), p. 114 (no. 832).

25 Al-Bukhārī, *Sirr al-silsila*, p. 70, and al-ʿUmarī, *al-Majdī*, p. 397. ʿUbaydallāh had a Zubayrid mother called Umm Khālid bt. Ḥamza b. Muṣʿab al-Zubayrī; see al-ʿAqīqī, *Kitāb al-Muʿaqqibīn*, p. 97.

26 Al-ʿAqīqī says that his great-grandfather ʿUbaydallāh died during the lifetime of his father; see Abū al-Faraj al-Iṣfahānī, *Kitāb Maqātil al-Ṭālibiyyīn*, ed. Aḥmad Ṣaqr, 2 vols (Beirut, 1949), vol. I, p. 170.

27 The work covers the Ḥasanids and Ḥusaynids up to the sixth generation after ʿAlī, and also includes brief discussions of the descendants of Muḥammad b. al-Ḥanafiyya, ʿUmar b. ʿAlī, ʿAbbās b. ʿAlī, Jaʿfar b. Abī Ṭālib and ʿAqīl b. Abī Ṭālib.

28 For bibliographical references, see n. 1 in this chapter. For a very detailed list of Ṭālibid genealogists over the centuries, see the introduction by al-Marʿashī in Ibn Funduq, *Lubāb al-ansāb*, pp. 7–144.

he suggests emerged as an independent discipline in the second half of the third/ninth century.[29] He shows clearly that there was a network among the Ṭālibid genealogists, many of whom were themselves ʿAlids. While the genealogist al-Bukhārī still draws on a variety of sources, al-Marwazī in the sixth/twelfth century cites in his *al-Fakhrī fī ansāb al-Ṭālibiyyīn* only other Ṭālibid genealogists, mainly from the fourth/tenth and fifth/eleventh centuries. Morimoto thus argues that the science of Ṭālibid genealogy 'reached its maturity by the end of the eleventh century'.[30]

The *nassāba* and genealogical registers

The Ṭālibid genealogies provide some evidence on how genealogical control was exercised and how information on the various lineages was collected, updated and tested for truth or falsity. The first important step was to record the state of each lineage, whether it continued and through whom (*wa-l-ʿaqab min . . ./lahu wuld fī saḥḥ . . .*), or whether it had died out (*maḍā/inqaraḍa/wa-lā baqiyya lahu*). Al-Rāzī in the *Shajara* always indicates how many lineages there are: al-Ḥusayn b. Zayd al-Shahīd, for instance, has true offspring (*ʿaqibuhu al-ṣaḥīḥ*) from three sons, Yaḥyā, al-Ḥusayn and ʿAlī. There were another three, Iṣḥāq, Muḥammad and al-Qāsim, but their lineages eventually died out; indeed, he says, there are many among al-Ḥusayn's offspring whose lineages died out or who only left female offspring (*kāna lahum ʿaqibun illā innahum inqaraḍū, wa-l-dārijūn min awlād al-Ḥusayn kathīr*).[31] Al-ʿUbaydalī finishes almost every paragraph throughout his work with a statement that either affirms the continued existence of a lineage (sometimes specifying where) or declares it to have died out. For example, of the descendants of ʿAli b. ʿĪsā b. Yaḥyā b. Zayd al-Shahīd, he says that ʿAbdallāh b. ʿAlī had progeny in Baghdad and Mosul (*lahu baqiyya bi-l-Baghdād wa-l-Mawṣil*); al-Ḥasan had descendants (*lahu aʿqāb*), Abū al-Ḥusayn Zayd had offspring (*lahu ʿaqib*), and al-Ḥusayn had children (*lahu wuld*).[32] The authors were taking stock of who was around and part of the family, and thus entitled to the privileges that accompanied Prophetic descent.

Moreover, collecting reliable information on the various lineages was clearly central to the endeavour to establish boundaries. As we know from the genealogist of the Saljūq period Ibn Funduq al-Bayhaqī, there was a *nassāba* (genealogist) in most major towns by the sixth/twelfth century.[33] His *Lubāb al-Ansāb* focuses on eastern Iran, so his information is most detailed for this area; he lists a *nassāba* for

29 Morimoto, 'Formation and Development', pp. 541–70.

30 Morimoto, 'Formation and Development', pp. 547–8. Similarly, Wasim Dahmash, in an article on the *sayyids* of medieval Ramlah, argues that '*ʿilm ansāb al-Ṭālibiyyah* only became a discipline beginning in the fourth[/tenth] century'; see Wasim Dahmash, 'On Sādāt in Medieval Ramlah', *Oriente Moderno*, n.s., 18 (1999), p. 443.

31 Al-Rāzī, *al-Shajara*, p. 142. The '*dārijūn*' are those who left no male offspring.

32 Al-ʿUbaydalī, *Tahdhīb*, p. 195, and throughout the work.

33 For a discussion of the *Lubāb al-ansāb*, see Kazuo Morimoto, 'Putting the *Lubāb al-ansāb* in Context: *Sayyids* and *Naqībs* in Late Saljuq Khurasan', *Studia Iranica* 36 (2007), pp. 163–83.

Rayy, Damascus, Qā'in (in Khurāsān), Marw, Iṣfahān, Hamadān, Astarābād, Egypt, Baghdad, Nishapur, Bayhaq and Khwārazm, as well as for smaller places elsewhere.[34] He often says that he travelled in order to obtain genealogical information, sometimes in the company of another genealogist, and sometimes visited other genealogists to gather material.[35] Some information was of course drawn from earlier written works: al-ʿUbaydalī, for instance, one of the genealogists of Baghdad in the early fifth/eleventh century, is frequently quoted in the *Lubāb*.[36]

Information was also gathered orally. Ibn Funduq often writes that 'so-and-so dictated his genealogy to me in this order (*amlā ʿalayya nasabahu ʿalā hādhā al-tartīb*)',[37] or that 'such-and-such an ʿAlid came to me and dictated his genealogy (*dakhala ʿalaynā rajul/ʿalawī wa-amlā nasabahu*)'.[38] Some ʿAlids thus also came to the *nassāba* to register themselves or their descendants.

The gathered information was then compiled into books or registers (*jarīda*, pl. *jarā'id*), which could be organised either by place or by family.[39] The genealogist Abū al-Ghanā'im, who was well known for his extensive travels, reportedly met an ʿAlid in Nishapur and recorded the names of his children (*wa-kataba asāmī awlādihi*), so that they were listed in his book (*masṭūr fī kitāb Abī al-Ghanā'im*).[40] Ibn Funduq refers to the registers of the genealogists in all countries (*jarā'id al-nassābīn fī-kull balad*), and mentions registers for Rayy, Nishapur, Ṭabaristān and Iṣfahān as well as the names of their respective compilers.[41] He also says that he found a certain lineage, not mentioned by any of the other genealogists, in the '*jarīda* of the *qāḍī* (judge) al-Wanakī (?) in al-Rayy'.[42] Often books and registers were kept by the *naqīb*: al-ʿUbaydalī, for example, says that al-Bukhārī could not find a certain lineage in the *jarā'id al-nuqabā'*; and Abū al-Ghanā'im verified the genealogies of some ʿAlids

34 For the genealogists, see Ibn Funduq, *Lubāb al-ansāb*, pp. 630–48.

35 He sometimes also travelled in the company of *ʿAlids*; see Ibn Funduq, *Lubāb al-ansāb*, p. 676 (on a journey to Bayhaq in 548/1148) and p. 668 ('[H]is grandson dictated to me and to the Sayyid al-Imām Shams al-Dīn, the *nassāba* of Khurāsān').

36 Al-ʿUbaydalī's full name is given as Shaykh al-Sharaf al-Ṣandūq Abū al-Ḥasan Muḥammad b. Muḥammad b. ʿAlī b. al-Ḥusayn b. ʿAlī b. Ibrāhīm b. ʿAlī b. ʿUbaydallāh b. al-Ḥusayn al-Ṣaghīr; see Ibn Funduq, *Lubāb al-ansāb*, p. 635. His work is quoted under the title *Kitāb Nihāyat al-aʿqāb*, most frequently to authenticate or add information about lineages in the section on the *nuqabā'* of various places; see, for example, p. 544 (*naqīb* Arrajān), p. 551 (*naqīb* Āba wa-Mayyāfāriqīn), p. 556 (*naqīb* Ahwāz), p. 565 (*naqīb* Shīrāz), p. 573 (*naqīb* Tarmad) and p. 611 (*naqīb* Rayy wa-Qum).

37 See, for example, Ibn Funduq, *Lubāb al-ansāb*, pp. 672 and 668.

38 Ibn Funduq, *Lubāb al-ansāb*, p. 656.

39 The term *jarīda* was also used for a kind of tax register in fifth-/eleventh-century Muslim Sicily; see Jeremy Johns and Alex Metcalfe, 'The Mystery at Churchuro: Conspiracy or Incompetence in Twelfth-Century Sicily', *Bulletin of the School of Oriental and African Studies* 62 (1999), pp. 226–59, where these lists of tax-payers are mentioned in the context of a study of administrative documents of the Norman period.

40 Ibn Funduq, *Lubāb al-ansāb*, p. 646; al-ʿUmarī, *al-Majdī*, p. 380 for his travels. That the genealogists travelled is a well-known practice also in earlier times; see Szombathy, 'The Nassāba', pp. 81–3.

41 Ibn Funduq, *Lubāb al-ansāb*, pp. 719–21. Al-ʿUmarī mentions the *jarā'id* of Basra; see al-ʿUmarī, *al-Majdī*, p. 39.

42 Ibn Funduq, *Lubāb al-ansāb*, p. 668.

in Tabrīz and Marāgha through the written register (*al-jarīda al-mudawwana*) in the house of the *naqīb* of the region.[43]

It is unclear how comprehensive these registers were, how frequently they were updated and how much of the material the author-genealogists chose to include or exclude. It appears, however, that the extant Ṭālibid genealogies are to a large part based on such registers, which probably simply took the form of long lists of names, sometimes adding information on places. Certain sections of the genealogies still employ this format.[44]

References to other authorities

As we have seen, the authors used the works of other genealogists, whom they often quote.[45] To copy information from earlier authorities, edit it and update it with new material was, of course, common practice among all kinds of authors, including historians and geographers. However, a particular consciousness of writing within an already existing tradition to which reference should be made is explicit in a section at the end of Ibn Funduq's *Lubāb al-ansāb*. This section reads like an index to the trade, or a manual for other genealogists, with the author even indicating which abbreviations stand for which author, work or method of transmission. He says, for example, that 's-r' stands for information that the *nassāba* has collected from whoever dictated it. In citing other authors, 'ṣ-ḥ' is given as the shorthand for the well-known genealogist Shaykh al-Sharaf al-ʿUbaydalī, 'b-sh-f' for Shaykh al-Sharaf al-Dīnawarī (d. c. 480/1087) and 'y-ṭ' for Abū Ghanāʾim al-Dimashqī.[46]

The genealogists quote other authorities sometimes to confirm a particular genealogy (*qāla* or *thabata/athbata fulān*), and at other times to give a variant opinion.[47] In fact, other authorities seem to be cited most often when there was disagreement over a lineage. Whether this shows that there were different kinds of legitimising projects among the genealogists, with individual genealogists consciously affirming certain lineages and denying others, is difficult to ascertain. It is clear, however, that lineages were selectively revived, and some declared extinct by one

43 Al-ʿUbaydalī, *Tahdhīb*, p. 39; Ibn Funduq, *Lubāb al-ansāb*, p. 696. On the relationship between *nassāba* and *naqīb*, see Morimoto, 'Formation and Development', pp. 557ff. and Chapter 3 below.

44 Ibn Funduq, *Lubāb al-ansāb*, pp. 672–3, and al-ʿUbaydalī, *Tahdhīb*, pp. 282 and 299. It seems that such lists simply meant to indicate which lines survive and where they settled.

45 Ibn Funduq, *Lubāb al-ansāb*, p. 672: 'I copied (*naqaltu min khaṭṭ*) from Muḥammad b. ʿAbd al-Ṣamad al-Hāshimī, the *nassāba* in Medina.' For more examples, see al-Marwazī, *al-Fakhrī*, p. 137, 'I copied down his genealogy from his hand' (*katabtu nasabahu ʿan khaṭṭihi*); or Ibn Ṭabāṭabā, *Muntaqila*, p. 26 (*raʾaytu bi-khaṭṭ* . . .), on a lineage about which there was disagreement.

46 Ibn Funduq, *Lubāb al-ansāb*, pp. 720–1. The abbreviation 's-r' is also used in al-Bukhārī's *Sirr al-silsila*, albeit in a different manner. This work, at least the edited version, was transmitted by one ʿAbd al-Raḥmān, and the abbreviation probably indicates information originally transmitted from al-Bukhārī. The majority of the accounts introduced by 's-r' give either updates or opinions on the authenticity or otherwise of a particular lineage; see, for example, al-Bukhārī, *Sirr al-silsila*, pp. 2 and 73; for ʿAbd al-Raḥmān, p. 42 and the introduction, p. 9.

47 See, for example, al-ʿUbaydalī, *Tahdhīb*, p. 115, and Ibn Ṭabāṭabā, *Muntaqila*, p. 29 (on a Jaʿfarid).

genealogist but affirmed by another. Al-Rāzī, for example, frequently juxtaposes the opinion of the fourth-/tenth-century genealogist al-Bukhārī with those of later authorities, such as Abū al-Ghanā'im, Ibn Ṭabāṭabā and Abū al-Ḥasan al-Buṭḥānī in his *Shajara*.[48]

One good example of this practice is the section on the descendants of al-Ḥasan b. Zayd b. al-Ḥasan b. ʿAli, who was appointed *amīr* of Medina in 150/767–8 for the caliph al-Manṣūr (r. 136–58/754–75).[49] Al-Rāzī relies on al-Bukhārī as a major source for this section, quoting some passages verbatim.[50] He mentions a number of instances where al-Bukhārī contests the continued existence of a particular branch of the family. For example, al-Rāzī quotes al-Bukhārī as saying that there was disagreement over the line of ʿAbd al-ʿAẓīm b. ʿAbdallāh b. ʿAlī,[51] but according to al-Rāzī, genealogists otherwise agreed on this lineage. Al-Bukhārī continues that Ṭāhir b. Zayd b. al-Ḥasan had no male offspring, although he had seen people in the Ḥijāz and in Basra claiming descent from him;[52] by contrast, al-Rāzī confirms the authenticity of these lineages, quoting Abū al-Ghanā'im, who says that Ṭāhir had two sons.[53]

Clearly, genealogists at times affirmed the existence of lineages that had been declared extinct by others. Ibn Ṭabāṭabā once claimed that a genealogist in Baghdad, Abū Ḥarb Muḥammad b. al-Muḥsin al-Dīnawarī, was guilty of not checking his information properly. Accordingly, a Ḥusaynid by the name of Muḥammad b. Aḥmad went in 405/1014 from Qum to Baghdad, where al-Dīnawarī confirmed his genealogy (*athbata nasabahu*), even though it had been known in Qum that the man was not in fact an ʿAlid. Ibn Ṭabāṭabā complains that al-Dīnawarī had acted without knowing anything about the circumstances of the man, whom he calls a *daʿī kādhib fāsiq*.[54] Elsewhere, however, Ibn Ṭabāṭabā himself reportedly refused to accept a

48 I am grateful to Asad Ahmed for bringing this to my attention.

49 Al-Ṭabarī, *Ta'rīkh*, vol. III, p. 358. He remained governor of Medina until 155/772; see al-Ṭabarī, *Ta'rīkh*, vol. III, p. 377.

50 Compare, for example, al-Rāzī, *al-Shajara*, pp. 55 and 81 to al-Bukhārī, *Sirr al-silsila*, pp. 22 and 25, respectively. Al-Rāzī also adds much of the later material, particularly for the descendants of Muḥammad al-Buṭḥānī and ʿAbd al-Raḥmān al-Shajarī. In the *Sirr al-silsila*, al-Bukhārī discusses the branch of al-Ḥasan b. Zayd in some detail and grants the account particular credibility by giving his source for the whole account at the end: 'Abū Naṣr read (*qara'a*) this on the authority of ʿAbdallāh b. ʿAlī Abū Zayd. Those are the seven descendants of al-Ḥasan b. Zayd'; see al-Bukhārī, *Sirr al-silsila*, p. 28.

51 Al-Bukhārī, says that al-ʿUmarī confirms it, while Abū Yaqẓān says it died out; see al-Bukhārī, *Sirr al-silsila*, p. 24.

52 Al-Bukhārī cites another ʿAlid genealogist, Aḥmad b. ʿĪsā b. al-Ḥusayn b. ʿAlī b. al-Ḥasan, who reportedly heard Ṭāhir say on his deathbed that he had no descendants; see al-Bukhārī, *Sirr al-silsila*, pp. 23–4.

53 There is another opinion according to which he had only one son, called either Muḥammad or al-Ḥasan, but nothing more is known of either of them; see al-Rāzī, *al-Shajara*, p. 79. It is certainly noteworthy that al-Rāzī draws attention to these disagreements, sometimes even in an exaggerated manner (compare, for instance, *al-Shajara*, p. 81, with *Sirr al-silsila*, p. 25), while other genealogists, such as al-ʿUbaydalī in the *Tahdhīb*, simply pass over them. Whether al-Rāzī's presentation was merely a consequence of reading and quoting faithfully from al-Bukhārī or whether he intended to make a point with it we can only guess.

54 The man's full name was Muḥammad b. Aḥmad b. ʿAbdallāh b. Mahmūd b. ʿUmar b. Muḥammad b. Mūsā b. Muḥammad b. ʿAlī al-Riḍā; see Ibn Ṭabāṭabā, *Muntaqila*, p. 254. Al-ʿUmarī, *al-Majdī*, p. 313, similarly

lineage as extinct. Al-Bukhārī had declared that the Ḥusaynid Ibrāhīm b. Mūsā al-Kāẓim had descendants only through his sons Mūsā and Jaʿfar, not through a third son, Ismāʿīl, and that 'anyone who claims descent from someone other than those two is a false claimant (*daʿī kadhdhāb*)'.[55] But according to al-Rāzī, Ibn Ṭabāṭabā countered vehemently that al-Bukhārī's claim exceeded all proper bounds and violated the faith (*innahu iṭlāq al-qawl mimmā yuksibu al-ithm wa-yakhruju ʿan al-dīn*).[56] Despite efforts to clarify and verify descent from the Prophet, disagreements remained among genealogists over the state of a number of lineages, which facilitated the work of false claimants.

False claimants

The case of the false Ḥusaynid from Qum, whose genealogy had even been erroneously confirmed in Baghdad, was no isolated incident. Ibn ʿInaba explicitly discusses the ubiquity of false claimants to a Prophetic genealogy, and decries the difficulty of distinguishing genuine claims from false ones.[57] Clearly, the genealogists were aware of the problem, which (perhaps unsurprisingly) seems to have occurred with increasing frequency with the rise of the family of the Prophet and their dispersal to all parts of the Islamic world.

The Ṭālibid works record an ever-growing number of false claimants (*daʿī kādhib* or *daʿī kadhdhāb*), or at least report them with increasing frequency. Already al-ʿAqīqī's third-/ninth-century work is, as its title claims, a *Kitāb al-Muʿaqqibīn* – a genealogy of those branches of the family that have offspring. Al-Bukhārī, as has been noted, tells us a century later not only which branches have survived and which ones have died out, but in addition mentions a number of false claimants, that is, people who pretended to be of ʿAlid or Ṭālibid descent. He clearly states at the beginning of his work that there are only a few surviving branches of the Banū Hāshim, and whoever claims descent from any other branch is a liar (*daʿī mubṭil*). Among the sons of Abū Ṭālib, he says, ʿAqīl had offspring only through his son Muḥammad, and whoever claims descent from anyone other than Muḥammad b. ʿAqīl is a false claimant (*muddaʿin*).[58] He also mentions some people who claim

records a supposed descendant from Mūsā al-Kāẓim who came to Baghdad between 410/1019 and 420/1029 and turned out to be a false claimant (*mubṭil daʿī kadhdhāb*) 'despite having been confirmed in the register in Baghdad' (*ghayra annahu thubita fī jarīdat Baghdād*).

55 Al-Bukhārī, *Sirr al-silsila*, p. 43.

56 Al-Rāzī, *al-Shajara*, pp. 96 and 101. Al-ʿUmarī, *al-Majdī*, p. 262, records another disagreement between Ibn Ṭabāṭabā and al-Bukhārī, regarding the descendants of Muḥammad b. Aḥmad b. Ibrāhīm b. Aḥmad Ṭabāṭabā.

57 Ibn ʿInaba, *ʿUmdat al-ṭālib*, ed. Nizār Riḍā (Beirut, 1963?), p. 236, quoted in Zoltán Szombathy, 'Techniques of Genealogical Forgery and Procedures of Genealogical Verification in the Mediaeval Middle East' (unpublished manuscript).

58 Al-Bukhārī, *Sirr al-silsila*, pp. 3–4. He goes on to say that Jaʿfar b. Abī Ṭālib only had descendants from his son ʿAbdallāh. At the end of the book he also treats Muḥammad b. al-Ḥanafiyya and his descendants (p. 85), and mentions a potential false claimant (*daʿī kadhdhāb*).

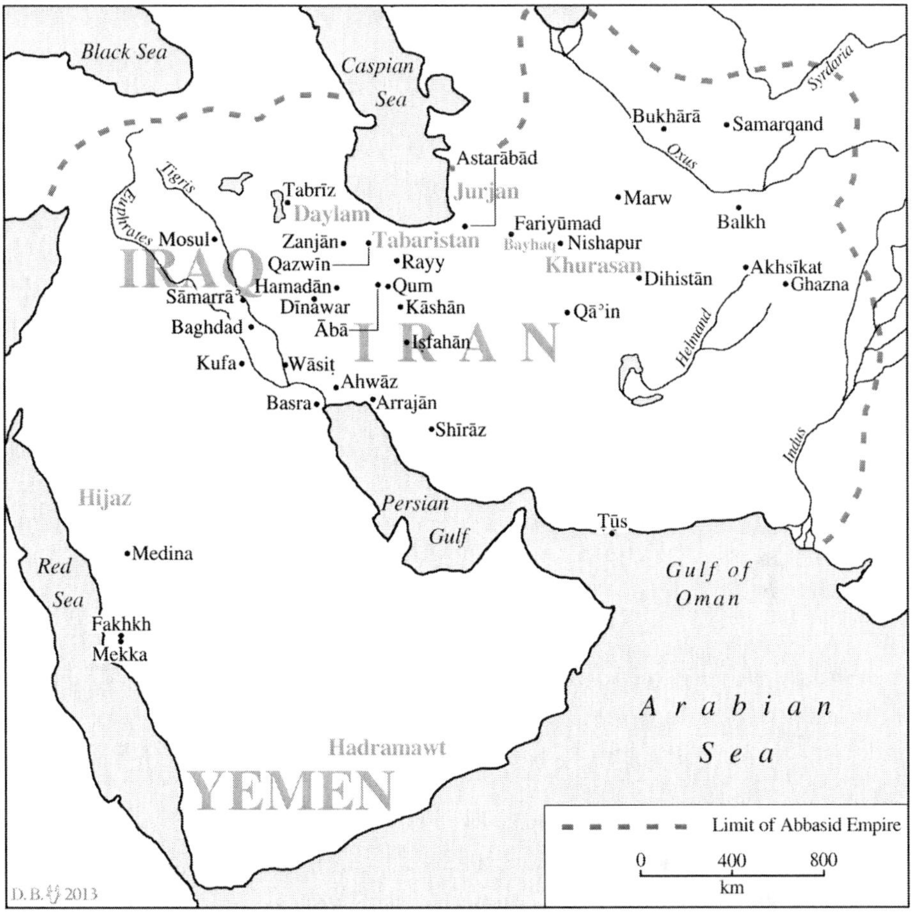

Figure 2.1 Eastern Islamic world, with main places of settlement of the ʿAlids

descent from extinct lines in places such as Egypt, Rayy, Hamadān, Khurāsān and Kufa.[59]

As Zoltán Szombathy notes, forging a Prophetic genealogy was no mean feat. One major way to do it was to attach oneself to an ancestor who was thought to have died childless. In this way, there was less risk of refutation and exposure, at least from living kin. As we have seen, later genealogists often affirmed the continued existence of lineages that earlier ones such as al-Bukhārī had declared extinct, thus possibly approving fraudulent individuals and branches. To address this issue, Ibn Funduq has a long list of individuals whose lineages died out; and there were even

59 Al-Bukhārī, *Sirr al-silsila*, p. 51: a group in Egypt who claim descent from ʿAbdallāh b. Aḥmad b. Ismāʿīl b. Muḥammad b. ʿAbdallāh al-Bāhir; p. 37: in Arrajān from Zayd b. ʿAlī b. Jaʿfar b. Zayd b. Mūsā al-Kāẓim; p. 38: in Rayy and Hamadān from Hārūn b. Mūsā al-Kāẓim; and p. 86: in Kufa and Khurāsān from al-Ḥasan b. ʿAlī al-ʿAriḍī, and in Kufa from Muḥammad b. al-Ḥanafiyya. See Szombathy, 'Motives and Techniques', n. 36, for more references to supposedly extinct branches.

books that listed not the *muʿaqqibūn* but rather the *munqariḍūn*, those who left no descendants.[60]

Geographical distance was another way to increase one's chances of having a false genealogy accepted.[61] Passing as someone else was of course easier away from one's own community and locality. This fact is also reflected in the genealogies, which display a growing concern with locations. If we compare al-ʿAqīqī's work with the *Sirr al-silsila* of al-Bukhārī, we find that al-ʿAqīqī very rarely mentions place names, except occasionally to note the locations where early ʿAlids died, such as Karbalāʾ and Fakhkh.[62] Al-Bukhārī, in contrast, often says where a certain ʿAlid lived, where he moved, and which lineage is to be found where. For example, he specifies that the Ḥusaynid Aḥmad b. al-Ḥusayn b. Jaʿfar, one of the few recorded early ʿAlid Sufis, arrived in Balkh in 332/943 from Qazwīn. He went on to Bukhārā and Samarqand and stayed there until his death in 355/965. He left a son called al-Ḥasan in Jurjān, and three daughters in Samarqand. The son of his brother Abū al-Qāsim ʿAbdallāh moved to Nishapur and married the daughter of a local notable there.[63] By the fifth/eleventh century, geographical information had become so important that Abū Ismāʿīl al-Ṭabāṭabāʾī arranged his genealogy alphabetically by place: He says in his introduction that this method of organisation should help to identify more easily whether someone's claim to a certain genealogy was genuine or not (*fa-in wajad dhalika fa-huwa ṣādiq fī daʿwatihi, wa-illā fa-huwa daʿī khādhib*).[64]

The ʿAlids' whereabouts thus became an important piece of information for keeping track of this ever-dispersing family. These geographical records also give readers a sense of the mobility and the geographic spread of the family. Even within one generation and one family, it became increasingly common to have sons, daughters or cousins settled in a number of different cities. Biancamaria Scarcia Amoretti has recently proposed that this kind of information may be used to produce a historical atlas of the ʿAlids, shedding light on 'the historical significance of the ʿAlid diaspora'. She suggests using the geographical references in the genealogies as the building blocks and then complementing these with other sources, such as local histories.[65] That the latter can help to track the ʿAlids' geographic mobility is illustrated by works such as the *Tārīkh-i Qum*, which has a chapter on the *sādāt* in Qum that provides much information not found elsewhere.[66] The ʿAlids in the city

60 Ibn Funduq, *Lubāb al-ansāb*, pp. 439–72, and p. 721 for a *Kitāb al-Dārijīn wa-l-munqariḍīn*; al-ʿUbaydalī, *Tahdhīb*, p. 32, mentions another *Kitāb al-Munqariḍīn*.

61 Szombathy, 'Motives and Techniques'.

62 Al-ʿAqīqī, *Kitāb al-Muʿaqqibīn*, pp. 63, 69, 70 and 131 (Fakhkh); pp. 58 and 109 (Karbalāʾ).

63 See al-Bukhārī, *Sirr al-silsila*, p. 47. The full name of this Ḥusaynid was Aḥmad b. al-Ḥusayn b. Jaʿfar b. Muḥammad b. ʿAlī b. Muḥammad b. ʿAlī b. Mūsā b. Jaʿfar (al-Ṣādiq) b. Muḥammad b. ʿAlī b. al-Ḥusayn b. ʿAlī.

64 Ibn Ṭābāṭabā, *Muntaqila*, pp. 2–3.

65 See Scarcia Amoretti, 'A Historical Atlas on the ʿAlids', pp. 92–122.

66 The Arabic original of this work, known as *Kitāb Taʾrīkh Qum*, was written in 378/988–9 by al-Ḥasan b. Muḥammad b. al-Ḥasan al-Qummī; the surviving Persian translation dates to 805–6/1403, and it was made by al-Ḥasan b. ʿAlī b. al-Ḥasan b. ʿAbd al-Malik al-Qummī (published as *Taʾrīkh-i Qum*, ed. Sayyid Jalāl

are listed according to family groups, the most important ones being the Mūsawiyya and the ʿArīḍiyya.[67] Many of the *sādāt* who came to Qum, we gather from the chapter, did not stay there: Some went further east to Nishapur or Dīnawar while others returned to the places where they had come from, such as Baghdad or Rayy.[68]

The family's geographical dispersal made it more difficult to keep track of all its branches, and thus the certification of a lineage became a serious matter. Ibn Funduq records the story of an ʿAlid by the name of Ibrāhīm b. ʿAlī b. Muḥammad b. Aḥmad b. Muḥammad b. al-Ḥusayn b. Ibrāhīm b. Ibrāhīm b. Mūsā al-Kāẓim b. Jaʿfar al-Ṣādiq, who claimed to belong to a little-known lineage of Ḥusaynids and said that he lived in Rayy (*anā sākin fī maḥallat al-Rayy, wa-anā Ibrāhīm* . . .). The man knew his genealogy well, and he also gave information about the names of his forefathers and where they had lived. In 544/1149 the matter went before the *naqīb al-nuqabāʾ* in Baghdad, Muḥammad b. ʿAlī al-Murtaḍā, the son of the Sharīf al-Murtaḍā (d. 436/1044). He acknowledged Ibrāhīm as an ʿAlid, and four years later the lineage was confirmed also by the *nassāba al-mashriq* (genealogist of the East) Abū Jaʿfar Muḥammad b. ʿAlī b. Hārūn b. Muḥammad al-Mūsawī.[69] Elsewhere Ibn Funduq gives other examples of how claims to an ʿAlid descent were established; the evidence was mostly based on the accounts of witnesses (*ʿudūl*) and judged by either a *qāḍī* or a *naqīb*.[70] Before someone was let into the fold, a number of steps had to be observed.

The genealogists also tell us something about the punishments that were meted out when a false genealogical claim was discovered. Ibn Funduq's work includes a chapter on 'those who had their heads shaven by the *nuqabāʾ* of Ghazna, Khwārazm and Nishapur', apparently an appropriate punishment for such charlatans. In two other instances the false claimant first had his head shaven and was then exiled; once Ibn Funduq was even a witness to the banishment (*wa-ashhadu ʿalā nafīhi*).[71] A false claimant in Khwārazm, who turned out to be a Nubian slave, was punished rather visibly: He not only had his head shaven but he also had his forehead branded

al-Dīn al- Ṭīhrānī [1313s/1353/1934]). According to the index, there were twenty chapters in the original, but only five survive. Jürgen Paul suggests that 'perhaps this was all that was ever written'; see Jürgen Paul, 'The Histories of Herat', *Iranian Studies* 33 (2000), p. 98; see also the discussion in Andreas Drechsler, *Die Geschichte der Stadt Qom im Mittelalter (650–1350)* (Berlin, 1999), p. 22, where he argues that all twenty chapters probably did exist at some point.

67 The Mūsawiyya are Ḥusaynids, descendants of Mūsā al-Kāẓim b. Jaʿfar al-Ṣādiq; for some of the family's branches, see al-ʿUbaydalī, *Tahdhīb*, pp. 100–71. The ʿArīḍiyya are also Ḥusaynids, descendants of ʿAlī al-ʿArīḍī b. Jaʿfar al-Ṣādiq; see, for example, al-ʿUbaydalī, *Tahdhīb*, pp. 175–80, and Ibn Funduq, *Lubāb al-ansāb*, p. 280, where he explains that the *nisba* refers to a place near Medina.

68 Al-Qummī, *Tārīkh-i Qum*, pp. 210 and 228–9. For a short discussion of the ʿAlids' movements in the *Tārīkh-i Qum* see also Scarcia Amoretti, 'A Historical Atlas on the ʿAlids', pp. 104–11.

69 Ibn Funduq, *Lubāb al-ansāb*, p. 657.

70 Ibn Funduq, *Lubāb al-ansāb*, pp. 724–5. Whether the testimony of the *ʿudūl* was based on written records is not indicated; in fact, it may well have been oral. For the use of oral testimonies to confirm the lineages of *ashrāf* in the Maghreb, see Powers, *Law, Society and Culture*, pp. 167–205. See also Ibn al-Ṭiqṭaqā, *al-Aṣīlī*, p. 42, for instructions on the different ways in which a lineage may be authenticated.

71 Ibn Funduq, *Lubāb al-ansāb*, p. 727.

with a hot iron (*mikwāh*).[72] In the modern period, things apparently went even further: Amir Taheri suggests that in recent times someone falsely claiming *sayyid* descent became *mahdūr al-dam* (one whose blood could be shed), and that there was no need for a trial to do so.[73]

The financial rewards of ʿAlid descent

The false claimants, as well as the various attempts of the genealogists to control the ʿAlid lineage and to monitor the family's whereabouts, suggest that there were significant interests at stake. In addition to access to the honour and respect associated with ʿAlid descent, there were financial benefits to being part of the Prophet's family, which were at times substantial. By the mid-third/ninth century, at least some ʿAlids seem to have expected to receive financial support on account of their descent. The reports of the ʿAlid Yaḥyā b. ʿUmar's uprising in 250/864, for instance, suggest that Yaḥyā was not given a grant (*ṣila*) or an allowance (*rizq*) in spite of repeated requests; he was so outraged by this that he started a rebellion in Kufa, where he was killed by the Ṭāhirid Muḥammad b. Ṭāhir.[74]

As is well known, the family of the Prophet was frequently exempted from various kinds of taxes, and it was entitled to a share of the *khums*, usually understood as one-fifth of the spoils of war and other specified resources. Some information on this income can be gleaned from the legal discussions on tax payments, in particular the discussions on *khums*, *zakāt* (obligatory alms) and *ṣadaqa* (optional charity). Roy Mottahedeh has recently analysed Qurʾānic commentaries on the so-called *khums* verse (VIII:41), which provides the basis for the family's claims, and shown the extent to which Sunnis and Shiʿites differ over the question of who was to administer these taxes and the definition of what actually constituted them.[75] A major point of contention was of course the question of who was eligible: For some it was just the descendants of Ḥasan and Ḥusayn, for others the Banū Hāshim, or the Banū Hāshim and their allies (*ḥulafāʾ*) the Banū Muṭṭalib, or even all members of the Quraysh. In very general terms, there is agreement that *khums* is reserved for the

72 Ibn Funduq, *Lubāb al-ansāb*, p. 723; see also p. 724 for another case of branding with a hot iron. Morimoto suggests that the shaving of the hair was an appropriate punishment because it was the hair, maybe the forelocks, which distinguished the ʿAlids; see Morimoto, 'Formation and Development', p. 563. The shaving of the hair or beard was quite a common punishment; see, for example, Ibn Qayyim al-Jawziyya, *Aḥkām ahl al-dhimma*, ed. Yūsuf ibn Aḥmad al-Bakrī and Shākir ibn Tawfīq al-ʿĀrūrī, 3 vols (Beirut, 1997), vol. I, p. 183; Tamer el-Leithy, 'Public Punishment in Mamluk Society' (MPhil thesis, Cambridge University, 1997), p. 24; see also Chase F. Robinson, 'Neck Sealing in Early Islam', *Journal of the Economic and Social History of the Orient* 48 (2005), p. 410, and n. 39 for further references.

73 Amir Taheri, *The Spirit of Allah: Khomeini and the Islamic Revolution* (London, 1985), p. 26. I am grateful to Rowena Abdul Razak for sending me this reference.

74 Al-Ṭabarī, *Taʾrīkh*, vol. III, pp. 1516–23; see al-Iṣfahānī, *Maqātil*, pp. 639–64. This episode is interesting for a number of reasons, in particular for its possible connection with the origins of the *niqāba*; see Chapter 3.

75 Roy Parviz Mottahedeh, 'Qur'ānic Commentary on the Verse of *khums* (al-Anfāl VIII:41)', in Morimoto (ed.), *Sayyids and Sharifs in Muslim Societies*, pp. 37–48.

ahl al-bayt – however broadly defined – and *ṣadaqa* and *zakāt* are prohibited to them.[76]

Unfortunately, the theoretical discussions tell us little about the actual financial situation of the kinsfolk of the Prophet, and it is unclear how much tax was actually paid, how frequently and to whom. More insightful are reports in the historical and genealogical literature of actual revenue payments to the family. One interesting example that shows the late inclusion of members of the ʿAbbāsid family in the category of *ahl al-bayt* comes from Ibn Funduq's *Lubāb al-ansāb*. He has a brief section on those *sadāt* who received income and endowment yields (*al-arzāq wa-ruyūʿ al-awqāf*) from the *dīwān* of Ghazna and its environs. He details who the recipients were, starting with the descendants of Muḥammad b. al-Ḥanafiyya; then he goes on to list other Ṭālibids, before turning to some descendants of the ʿAbbāsid caliphs al-Manṣūr. Finally, he says that there were about one hundred descendants of ʿUmar b. ʿAlī in Ghazna – and all of them received a pension from the *dīwān*.[77] In medieval Ghazna at least, a *sayyid* who qualified for a stipend could be anyone from the Banū Hāshim.

Despite the relative scarcity of such reports, we do know that the kinsfolk of the Prophet received payments and gifts from caliphs and local rulers.[78] One example of a generous courtly patron is the Būyid vizier al-Ṣāḥib Ismāʿīl b. ʿAbbād (d. 381/991). Ibn ʿAbbād was famously well inclined towards the kinsfolk of the Prophet, who gathered around him to receive lavish gifts and money. His daughter was married to an ʿAlid, one ʿAlī al-Uṭrūsh b. Ḥusayn, an alliance that, according to the literateur Thaʿālibī (d. 429/1038), pleased Ibn ʿAbbād: He was proud (*muṣāhara*) of the marriage relationship and honoured (*muwāṣala*) by the connection with the ʿAlid, and he encouraged his court poets to celebrate it.[79] However, the vizier was also critical of at least some of his in-laws, describing those who arrived from the the Ḥijāz to receive his stipends as 'beetles, scarabs, chameleons and ravens'.[80] Nonetheless, Ibn ʿAbbād paid the ʿAlids handsomely and was also a benefactor of

76 For more details, see the following excellent studies in *EI2*: A. Zysow and R. Gleave, 'Khums'; A. Zysow, 'Zakāt'; and T. H. Weir and A. Zysow, 'Ṣadaqa'. See also Norman Calder, 'Zakāt in Imāmī Shīʿī Jurispridence, from the Tenth to the Sixteenth Century A.D.', *Bulletin of the School of Oriental and African Studies* 44 (1981), pp. 468–80, and Norman Calder, 'Khums in Imāmī Shīʿī Jurispridence, from the Tenth to the Sixteenth Century A.D.', *Bulletin of the School of Oriental and African Studies* 45 (1982), pp. 39–47.

77 Ibn Funduq, *Lubāb al-ansāb*, p. 728. It appears that there is an error in the genealogy of the descendant of al-Manṣūr. Either way, he is an ʿAbbāsid, apparently known as Abū Ṭālib al-Fawshaḥī (?).

78 See Szombathy, 'Motives and Techniques', for references to payments to the family of the Prophet by the Fāṭimids, Marīnids, the sultanate of Kilwa in East Africa and some Shiʿite tribes in southern Iraq.

79 Al-Thaʿālibī, *Tatimmat yatīmat al-dahr* (Beirut, 1983), p. 296. In the genealogies ʿAlī al-Uṭrūsh (ʿAlī b. al-Ḥusayn b. ʿAlī b. al-Ḥusayn b. al-Ḥasan b. al-Qāsim b. Muḥammad al-Buṭḥānī b. al-Qāsim b. al-Ḥasan b. Zayd b. al-Ḥasan b. ʿAlī) is explicitly called the son-in-law (*khatan*), see Ibn Funduq, *Lubāb al-ansāb*, p. 560; al-Rāzī, *al-Shajara*, p. 60; and al-Marwazī, *al-Fakhrī*, p. 136. For Ibn ʿAbbād and the 'ʿAlid network', see Maurice Pomerantz, 'Licit Magic and Divine Grace: The Life and Letters of al-Ṣāḥib ibn ʿAbbād (d. 385/995)' (PhD dissertation, University of Chicago, 2010), pp. 104–26.

80 Al-Tawḥīdī, *Akhlāq al-wazīrayn*, ed. Muḥammad b. Ṭāwīt al-Tanjī (Damascus, 1965; reprinted Beirut, 1992), p. 295. I am grateful to Zoltán Szombathy for the reference.

ʿAlid shrines. According to al-Qummī (fl. 378/988), the author of the *Tārīkh-i Qum*, a structure (*turba*) was erected at an ʿAlid tomb in Jurjān on Ibn ʿAbbād's orders in 374/984.[81] Like the royal courts, these shrines became focal points for *sayyid*s and *sharīf*s, as *waqf*s and other endowments set up for and by the family were frequently associated with such places.[82]

However, the general impression given by the sources is that official pension payments to the family of the Prophet were less regular and comprehensive than is generally assumed. Moreover, the example of the caliph al-Muʿtaḍid's (d. 289/902) budget shows that even when there was a state pension, it was subject to change at any time. According to the budgetary entry for the pensions (*jārī*) of the Hāshimites, payments had been made monthly in the amount of one dinar; this was reduced to a quarter of a dinar under al-Muʿtaḍid.[83] Perhaps because of this reduction, the Zaydī ruler of Ṭabaristān Muḥammad b. Zayd is said to have sent large amounts of money to the *sayyid*s in Kufa and Baghdad in about the year 282/895.[84]

Arguably more important than official stipends and institutional taxes were the many informal contributions and offerings by individual Sunnis and Shiʿites. Such payments were most significant in helping to confirm the kinsfolk of the Prophet as a distinct and distinguished social group, not only because of the money they actually brought in, but also because of their symbolic character. Innumerable reports, anecdotes and traditions detailing financial contributions, large and small, by ordinary Muslims show how engrained the special treatment of the kinsfolk of the Prophet became. Of course, this was not pure altruism: As Graham notes: 'There are . . . a large number of traditions that urge [this] affection, represent it as proof of faith or deference against Hellfire, promise in return for it the *shafāʿa* of the Prophet on the Day of Resurrection and reward in the next world.'[85] In view of such traditions, it may indeed be advisable to express some affection for the *sayyid*s and *sharīf*s in the form of a small monetary contribution.

Many examples could be given to illustrate the role of ordinary Muslims in the financial making of the *ahl al-bayt*. Clearly, all kinds of ʿAlids – rich and poor, honourable and wicked – profited from informal donations. According to one account in the *Lubab al-ansāb*, the ʿAlid Abū Muḥammad Yaḥyā from the Zubāra family in

81 Al-Qummī, *Tārīkh-i Qum*, pp. 223–4; Thomas Leisten, *Architektur für Tote: Bestattung in architektonischen Kontext in den Kernländern der islamischen Welt zwischen 3./9. und 6./12. Jahrhundert* (Berlin, 1998), p. 33.

82 See, for instance, Ibn Funduq, *Lubāb al-ansāb*, p. 562; al-ʿUmarī, *al-Majdī*, p. 462; and Teresa Bernheimer, 'Shared Sanctity: Some Notes on *Ahl al-Bayt* Shrines in the Early Ṭālibid Genealogies', *Studia Islamica* (forthcoming), for further references. There are early references to *wuqūf rasūl Allāh* and to *ṣadaqat ʿAlī*, but these cannot be understood as sources of income for the kinsfolk of a Prophet as a whole. See, for instance, al-Ṭabarī, *Taʾrīkh*, vol. II, 1672, or vol. II, p. 1,668, for *ṣadaqat rasūl Allāh*.

83 The budget is preserved in the *Kitāb al-Wuzarāʾ* of Hilāl al-Ṣābiʾ (d. 448/1056m–7). See Heribert Busse, 'Das Hofbudget des Chalifen al-Muʿtaḍid billāh (279/892–289/902)', *Der Islam* 43 (1967), pp. 27–8. This is another example that includes a reference to payments to the *Banū Hāshim* as a whole.

84 Al-Ṭabarī, *Taʾrīkh*, vol. III, pp. 2,147–8.

85 Van Arendonk and Graham, 'Sharīf', *EI2*.

Nishapur went on the *ḥajj* accompanied by 700 men, *sādāt* and *ʿulamāʾ* (scholars); he was clearly a prominent man. A *wakīl* (proxy) was in charge of the provisions. When they were ready to return home after completing the *ḥajj* rituals, the remaining funds were insufficient for the journey. Abū Muḥammad Yaḥyā decided to sell one of his slave girls to raise funds, and the *wakīl* was reportedly offered a price of 1,000 dinars for her. The *sayyid*, however, decided after all against selling the girl, and instead let her go free. His *wakīl* asked in astonishment what they would now do with all the *sādāt* and *ʿulamāʾ* in the entourage, and the *sayyid* told him not to despair, but to have faith in God. Soon a man came to tell him about a rich merchant from Khurāsān who lay dying in the neighbourhood; he wished to see the *sayyid* in order to make him heir to his property. When he died, the merchant bequeathed to Abū Muḥammad Yaḥyā seven of his cargo loads (*aḥmāl*) worth 7,000 dinars.[86]

In another account, a Kufan flour merchant time and again gave his flour for free to members of the Prophet's family, who could not or would not pay for it. After complaining about the lack of payment, the merchant was told in a dream to put the payment 'on the Prophet's account', which he did, until he himself was impoverished. He died soon after, and was reportedly rewarded lavishly in the afterlife for his good deeds to the Prophet's kin. The anecdote is recorded in an interesting group of works, recently studied by Kazuo Morimoto, which preserve trans-sectarian traditions recommending unconditional respect for the kinsfolk of the Prophet, regardless of their behaviour.[87] Whatever the historicity of this story and the many similar ones scattered throughout the literature, they reflect not only the special treatment offered by both Sunnis and Shiʿites to (and sometimes demanded by) the family of the Prophet, but also the way in which their elevated status could be cashed in for money and other material benefits.

Conclusion

The appearance of Ṭālibid genealogies from the third/ninth century onwards reflects the increasing efforts of the family of the Prophet to define its boundaries and guard its interests: Being part of this elite group was not only an honour, it also came with privileges, tangible and intangible, which had to be protected against impostors and pretenders. The frequent references to cases of attempted fraud in the genealogies give the impression that claiming an ʿAlid genealogy became quite an industry; and despite the attempts on the part of the genealogists to uncover such claims and to record the state and whereabouts of the various lineages, questions about the authenticity of some branches remained. The belief in the special position of the Prophet's family became so thoroughly confirmed, however, that it was deemed better to let one fraudster slip through the net than to offend a true *sayyid*.

86 Ibn Funduq, *Lubāb al-ansāb*, pp. 498–9. A similar story follows.

87 See Kazuo Morimoto, 'How to Behave toward *Sayyids* and *Sharīfs*: A Trans-sectarian Tradition of Dream Accounts', in Morimoto (ed.), *Sayyids and Sharifs in Muslim Societies*, pp. 26–7.

3

Shifting Hierarchies and Emphasising Kinship: ʿAlid Marriage Patterns

In 1905, the Islamic reformer Rashīd Riḍā published in his journal *al-Manār* a response to a question posed to him by a reader in Singapore. It concerned the marriage of a *sayyida* from the Ḥaḍramī community in South East Asia. The marriage had been publicly denounced by the Ḥaḍramī ʿAlids because of its unsuitability: The groom was an Indian Muslim of non-*sayyid* descent. Rashīd Riḍā sanctioned the marriage, arguing that there was nothing in Islamic law to prohibit it. Riḍā's opinion was strongly contradicted by the leading Ḥaḍramī scholar of the time, Sayyid ʿUmar al-ʿAṭṭās, who declared that a marriage between a *sayyida* and a non-*sayyid* was unlawful, because descent was the basic criterion for suitability in marriage (*kafāʾa*). He identified four levels of *kafāʾa*: Arabs must not marry non-Arabs; Qurashīs must not marry non-Qurashīs; Hāshimites must not marry non-Hāshimites; and descendants of Ḥasan and Ḥusayn must not marry anyone other than Ḥasanids or Ḥusaynids.[1] The discussion went back and forth for some time and eventually sparked a power struggle in the overseas Ḥaḍramī communities that had long adhered to a rigid system of social stratification based on descent. People began to question openly the centuries-long domination of the *sayyid*s, their status and their system of social control, setting in motion events that arguably led to the Yemeni revolution and the abolition of the Zaydī imāmate in 1962. In the early twentieth century, then, marriage relations provided a means to question the special status of the kinsfolk of the Prophet.

When this special status was being formulated in the early Islamic period, marriage relations became a critical way to emphasise it. While the genealogical works on the Ṭālibids show the growing eagerness of the family of the Prophet to define its boundaries, the ʿAlids' marriage patterns reflect their increasing sense of themselves as the First Family of Islam. Of course, the ʿAlids belonged to an Islamic

1 The last level is worth emphasising, since none of the early scholars seem to make this distinction. A translation of the response is given in Engseng Ho, *The Graves of Tarim: Genealogy and Mobility across the Indian Ocean* (Berkeley and Los Angeles, 2006), pp. 174–6. See also Abdalla S. Bujra, 'Political Conflict and Stratification in Ḥaḍramaut – I', *Middle Eastern Studies* 3 (1967), pp. 355–75. For a recent discussion with extensive references, see Yamaguchi Motoki, 'Debate on the Status of *sayyid/sharīf*s in the Modern Era: The ʿAlawī-Irshādī Dispute and Islamic Reformists in the Middle East', in Morimoto (ed.), *Sayyids and Sharifs in Muslim Societies*, pp. 49–71.

elite from the earliest period of Islam. From the second/eighth to the sixth/twelfth centuries, however, the criteria that determined who else was part of this elite were gradually narrowed as well as shifted. This is evident in the changing marriage patterns: ʿAlid daughters were no longer given away in marriage to other families, whether Arab or non-Arab, but rather were married off only to other ʿAlids, or sometimes other Ṭālibids. Increasingly, only a *sayyid* or *sharīf* was considered a suitable partner for a *sayyida* or *sharīfa*. Of course, there must have been exceptions, but the sources rarely record them. The men also married increasingly within the family; if they married out of the family, they took wives from other elite families, often non-Arabs. As marriage is an expression of at least some measure of shared identity and hierarchic rank, these changes in marriage patterns reflect shifting notions of the status of the family within the social hierarchy of medieval Islamic society more generally.[2] Interestingly, an examination of the legal sources shows that the narrowing of the spectrum of possible marriage relations must be considered primarily a matter of social praxis, because it is not reflected in the theory of the law. In fact, early Imāmī works even explicitly sanctioned the marriage of ʿAlid women to non-ʿAlid men, an example of a disengagement of ʿAlids and Shiʿites: Although a high regard for the family of the Prophet was certainly central to Shiʿite dogma, this did not result in the family's unconditional elevation in all matters.

Endogamy and exogamy

Already in the first two centuries of Islam, the genealogical data show that the ʿAlids frequently married endogamously, or within the family. Ḥasanids married other Ḥasanids, Ḥusaynids married other Ḥusaynids, or Ḥasanids and Ḥusaynids married each other. As Scarcia Amoretti notes, although the two branches of the ʿAlid family are discussed separately in the sources, the family is clearly conceived of as a whole, 'with no impediments to marriage between the two branches'.[3]

For all ʿAlids, the most common choice was first- or second-cousin marriage, a pattern found in many societies throughout history. There have been a number of studies on the phenomenon of cousin marriage, and various explanations have been offered: strengthening of the bonds of kinship, social and political solidarity among clan members, protection of the honour of the women, and preservation of property. Endogamous marriage ensured that a family's inheritance was maintained intact: Rather than adding to the wealth of another family, a woman's share would be kept among her relations. For an ʿAlid daughter marrying a cousin was desirable also because she would not be required to join a group of strangers but rather would remain within her extended kinship group, where a loss of status was

2 For a similar argument, see Michael H. Fisher, 'Political Marriage Alliances at the Shiʿi Court of Awadh', *Comparative Studies in Society and History* 24 (1983), pp. 593–616.

3 Biancamaria Scarcia Amoretti, 'Genealogical Prestige and Matrimonial Politics among the Ahl al-Bayt: Status Quaestionis', in Sarah Savant and Helena de Felipe (eds), *Genealogy and Knowledge in Muslim Societies: Understanding the Past* (Edinburgh, forthcoming).

less likely. In the case of the descendants of the Prophet, such was an important consideration.[4]

A close analysis of the ʿAlids' marriage patterns gives us some insight into the family's different socio-political programmes.[5] A striking example in the crucial late Umayyad and early ʿAbbāsid periods concerns two of the main lines of Ḥasanids and Ḥusaynids, that is, the lines of ʿAbdallāh b. al-Ḥasan b. al-Ḥasan b. ʿAlī and of Muḥammad b. ʿAlī b. al-Ḥusayn b. ʿAlī. Politically, the behaviour of the two lines diverged quite dramatically: The Ḥasanids sparked a series of ʿAlid rebellions in the second/eighth and third/ninth centuries (ʿAbdallāh was the father of Muḥammad al-Nafs al-Zakiyya, Ibrāhīm, Yaḥyā and Idrīs, whose rebellions were mentioned in the introductory chapter), whereas the Ḥusaynid line produced the quietist Twelver imāms.[6] In terms of marriage relations, the Ḥasanids had been taking wives from within the family or from other prominent Arab families, thereby extending their networks, on which they could draw for rebellious support.[7] From the generation of ʿAbdallāh's children, that is, from the IV generation after ʿAlī,[8] the Ḥasanids began

4 The anthropological literature on cousin marriage is extensive. See, for instance, Burton Pasternak, *Introduction to Kinship and Social Organisation* (Englewood Cliffs, NJ, 1976); Martin Ottenheimer, 'Complementarity and the Structure of Parallel Cousin Marriage', *American Anthropologist* 88 (1986), pp. 934–9; Robert F. Murphy and Leonard Kasdan, 'The Structure of Parallel Cousin Marriage', *American Anthropologist* 61 (1959), pp. 17–29; and Dale Eickelman, *The Middle East and Central Asia: An Anthropological Approach*, 4th edn (Upper Saddle River, NJ, 2002), pp. 163–78, for further references. In a study on the Arab tribes in the second/eighth and third/ninth centuries, Eva Orthmann shows that the bond with the *ʿamm* (paternal uncle) and *ibn ʿamm* (son of a paternal uncle) is described as particularly close and important; particularly desirable are parallel cousin marriages, that is, a man marrying his *bint ʿamm*, the daughter of his father's brother. Orthmann points out, however, that the emphasis on this relationship should be treated with some caution, since the ʿAbbāsids emphasised their right to the caliphate through al-ʿAbbās, the *ʿamm* of the Prophet; see Orthmann, *Stamm und Macht*, p. 226.

5 See Ahmed, *Religious Elite*, especially chapter V at pp. 137–8 (emphasis in original). Although the ʿAlids present a special case, their marriage patterns seem to be comparable to those of other prominent early Islamic Arab families: 'In several ways, the kinship patterns of the descendants of ʿAlī match those of the descendants of Saʿd, ʿAbd al-Raḥmān, and Ṭalḥa. They can also be contrasted with the trends noted for the ʿUthmānids. For example, like the former set, socially and politically some of the most notable descendants of ʿAlī were born to daughters of southern tribes or to the elite who had a presence and influence in Iraq and northeast Arabia; and unlike the ʿUthmānids, his progeny to the Meccan old aristocracy enjoyed limited prosperity. Yet the ʿAlids were an exception to all the families studied in the previous chapters in that their successful lines *frequently* maintained some association with the ʿAlīd descendants of Fāṭima, the favourite daughter of the Prophet. Ties with this religious royalty guaranteed longevity to the various ʿAlīd lines born to the tribal elite.'

6 However, it must be noted that the identification of the branches as the 'quietist Ḥusaynids' and the 'activist Ḥasanids' was not clear-cut, as certain Ḥusaynids were more associated with the activist Ḥasanids, and the line of Zayd b. al-Ḥasan b. ʿAlī more with the quietist Ḥusaynids.

7 ʿAbdallāh b. al-Ḥasan's grandmother was Khawla al-Fazāriyya, the daughter of a Fazārī chief, who was first married to Muḥammad b. Ṭalḥa. As her sister was married to a Zubayrid, she brought with her kinship ties to both Ṭalḥids and Zubayrids; see Ahmed, *Religious Elite*, chapter III. ʿAbdallāh's mother was Fāṭima bt. al-Ḥusayn, and he was thus called *al-Mahd* for his pure lineage on both his mother's and his father's side; see al-Isfahānī, *Maqātil*, p. 179, for Fāṭima's maternal ancestors.

8 I have followed Morimoto in using Latin numerals to refer to the generation numbers, generation I being the first generation after ʿAlī, that is, the generation of al-Ḥasan and al-Ḥusayn; see Morimoto, 'Diffusion', p. 14.

to marry mainly endogamously. ʿAbdallāh b. al-Ḥasan's three daughters, Zaynab, Fāṭima and Ruqayya, were all married to paternal cousins, as was their brother Muḥammad and a great number of Ḥasanids after them.[9] The Ḥusaynids, in contrast, were predominantly endogamous already in the IV generation. As we shall see in more detail below, a number of their exogamous marriages were contracted with the ʿAbbāsids. Interestingly, from the VI generation onwards, all imāms were born to *umm walad*s (slaves), which limited the influence of a potentially powerful maternal clan.[10] The Ḥusaynid daughters continued to be married outside the family; the Ḥusaynids' relations with the ʿAbbāsids seem to have generally prevented them from joining the uprisings led by their Ḥasanid cousins. As Asad Ahmed concludes, the Ḥusaynids' marriage patterns in this period 'are a fair testament to the general quietism of the Twelver line'.[11]

Of course, the conclusions are not always so clear, but overall, the growing perception of the ʿAlids as the First Family of Islam is indicated both by increasing endogamy and by changes in the choice of exogamous partners, of which we will explore some examples below. In general terms, the exogamous marriage patterns can be summarised as follows: In the early period, marriages outside of the family were contracted with other Qurashīs and sometimes, although more rarely, with members of other Arab tribes. Both men and women inter-married with these families. However, as the examples of marriages with the Banū Makhzūm and the Banū ʿAbbās show, the ʿAlids were increasingly in a position of relative strength vis-à-vis the other families, as they 'took in' women but 'gave out' only men. Thus, they accepted Makhzūmī brides, but rarely married their daughters to the Banū Makhzūm. As one only gives one's daughters in marriage to one's equals or superiors, this seems to indicate on the one hand a shared identity but on the other the superior status of the ʿAlids. In the ʿAbbāsid case, certain ʿAlid lineages married their daughters to the ʿAbbāsids, indicating closeness between the families, particularly around the time of the ʿAbbāsid Revolution. Notably, however, the ʿAlids took few ʿAbbāsid brides.

From the late second/eighth century onwards, the ʿAlids married almost exclusively within the family. Endogamous marriage came to be prescribed for ʿAlid women and recommended for ʿAlid men. As discussed in more detail in the next chapter, the main duties of the *naqīb* explicitly included the supervision of ʿAlid women's marriages: According to the jurist al-Māwardī (d. 450/1058), the *naqīb al-ashrāf* must

9 Fāṭima married Abū Jaʿfar b. ʿAbdallāh b. al-Ḥasan b. al-Ḥasan b. al-Ḥasan b. ʿAlī and Ruqayya married Isḥāq b. Ibrāhīm b. al-Ḥasan b. al-Ḥasan b. ʿAlī (after she had been married to two Umayyads and one ʿAbbāsid; see Ibn Ḥabīb, *Kitāb al-Muḥabbar*, p. 437). Muḥammad al-Nafs al-Zakiyya was married to Umm Salama bt. Muḥammad b. al-Ḥasan b. al-Ḥasan b. ʿAlī; see al-Zubarī, *Nasab Quraysh*, pp. 51–6.

10 Scarcia Amoretti has linked the new predominance of *umm walads* to the lineage's move from Medina to Iraq, where alliances with the tribes were less important; see Scarcia Amoretti, 'Genealogical Prestige'. An alternative explanation may be that once this Ḥusaynid line was singled out as the Imāmī line, they were prevented from making strong alliances with potentially rebellious ʿAlids.

11 Ahmed, *Religious Elite*, p. 183.

> prevent their single women, whether divorced or widowed, from marrying any but those of compatible birth, owing to their superiority to other women, in order to protect their purity of descent and maintain inviolability against the indignity of being given away by someone other than a legal guardian or of being married to unsuitable men.[12]

The Saljūq genealogist Ibn Funduq al-Bayhaqī adds that the *naqīb* should furthermore 'prohibit the men from marrying common women (*al-ʿāmmiyyāt*), so that no daughters of the Prophet remain unmarried'.[13]

The evidence of the sources, both genealogical and narrative, indicates that these prescriptions were generally followed well into the modern period. Of course, as we will see below, there were some notable exceptions. However, if the ʿAlids married out, it was generally the men who took brides from other families. From the third/ninth century onwards, the families from which these brides came were no longer necessarily Arab. Indeed, as the ʿAlids left the Ḥijāz and settled in cities all over the Islamic world, their marital, political and scholarly relations reflected the changing makeup of the Islamic empire. From the second/eighth to the sixth/twelfth centuries, social hierarchies changed considerably in Muslim societies all over the Islamic world, and these societies came to include an increasing number of non-Arabs.[14] So, too, did the population of the ʿAlids' wives.

Mothers, wives and matrilineality

As is customary for Arab genealogy (and many other kinds of genealogy, for that matter), the records follow a patrilineal definition of genealogy, that is, a child is part of the family of the father, not of the mother, and lines of descent are followed through the father's side.[15] Information on women is therefore patchy: Women appear if they are listed as wives or daughters of a given ʿAlid, but the daughters' lineages are not followed. The sixth-/twelfth-century genealogist Fakhr al-Dīn al-Rāzī, for instance, lists all twenty-seven daughters of Jaʿfar al-Kadhdhāb (a brother of al-Ḥasan al-ʿAskarī), but none of them reappear elsewhere in the text.[16] Perhaps

12 Al-Māwardī, *al-Aḥkām*, p. 81; translation adapted from W. H. Wahba, *The Ordinances of Government* (Reading, 1996), p. 107.

13 Ibn Funduq, *Lubāb*, p. 722.

14 The geographical dispersal itself may have contributed to the increase in endogamy. Such an explanation has been suggested for the case of Jews in twentieth-century America, who married overwhelmingly within their community. Goldstein and Goldschneider argue that in the face of geographic mobility, restricting marriages to the Jewish community was a means of self-preservation. See Sidney Goldstein and Calvin Goldschneider, 'Social and Demographic Aspects of Jewish Intermarriages', *Social Problems* 13 (1966), pp. 386–99. One may add that being an ʿAlid entitled one to certain privileges, which was not the case for the Jews. Yet in both cases the restrictions guarded an identity.

15 For the patrilineal definition of genealogy, see, for example, Orthmann, *Stamm und Macht,* p. 205. For a modern study, see Gideon Kressel, *Descent through Males: An Anthropological Investigation into the Patterns Underlying Social Hierarchy, Kinship, and Marriage among Former Bedouin in the Ramla-Lod Area* (*Israel*) (Wiesbaden, 1992).

16 Al-Rāzī, *al-Shajara*, p. 93.

– although this is unlikely – none of the daughters were married, or perhaps none of them had children; even an ʿAlid woman would usually not be mentioned as a wife if the alliance did not produce any (male) offspring.[17] To give some sense of the disproportional nature of the material, the index in al-Rāzī's published *al-Shajara al-mubāraka fī ansāb al-Ṭālibiyyīn* may be helpful: The section on women runs to five pages, whereas the men occupy 136 pages.

Moreover, not only are women only mentioned as mothers and wives if at all, the information is more plentiful for the earlier generations than the later ones. For the earlier period, often corresponding to the generations covered by the early genealogical works on the Arabs or the Quraysh, the names of the wives or mothers of ʿAlids are generally given. Sometimes there is an explicit focus on the marriages of prominent women: Some of the earlier works have short sections on 'multi-marrying women', but these cover only the first generations of the Islamic period.[18] For the later generations covered in the Ṭālibid genealogies, there is much less information on mothers, whether or not they were ʿAlids themselves. This decrease in information on women may simply reflect a pragmatic decision: There was an ever greater number of people to cover, so the authors were no longer able to include everyone. Rather than giving a complete account of all the offspring of the kinsfolk of the Prophet, what mattered more was to record the lineages that survived, so no one could falsely claim to be a member of the Prophet's family.

However, there may also be another reason for the apparent decline in interest in women, suggested recently by Asad Ahmed. Ahmed convincingly argues for the importance of cognate relationships in the early period of Islam: 'Until the early ʿAbbāsid period, matrilineality still counted for much, not just in practical socio-politics . . . but also as an abstract principle of legitimacy and authority.' He suggests that the decrease in information on women in the genealogies may reflect changing notions of legitimacy, which in the early ʿAbbāsid period 'had begun to shift drastically in favor of exclusive patrilineal claims'.[19] There is some indication in the

17 Of course, there are some exceptions. Ibn Ḥazm, *Jamhara*, pp. 35–6, for instance, mentions that al-Ḥasan b. al-Ḥasan b. ʿAlī married three of his cousins: a daughter of Ibn al-Ḥanafiyya, a daughter of ʿUmar b. ʿAlī, and Fāṭima bt. al-Ḥusayn. More usually, however, only the marriage to Fāṭima is mentioned in the sources, because al-Ḥasan apparently had children only with her.

18 See al-Madāʾinī, 'Kitāb al-Murdifāt', in ʿAbd al-Salām Muḥammad Hārūn (ed.), *Nawādir al-makhṭūṭāt* (Beirut, 1991), vol. I, pp. 57–80 and Ibn Ḥabīb, *Kitāb al-Muḥabbar*, pp. 435–55 (al-Madāʾinī is said to have written a number of books on women and marriages; see Ibn al-Nadīm, *The Fihrist of al-Nadīm*, trans. Bayard Dodge, 2 vols [New York, 1970], vol. I, pp. 220–1). These are essentially lists of women from the Quraysh who married two or more times. In the *Kitāb al-Muḥabbar* of Ibn Ḥabīb the bar is even raised slightly, as his section is entitled 'accounts of women who married three or more times'. In some of the cases a woman's husband died, but often it is not clear why she married again; the text simply says *khalafa ʿalayhā*. Divorce seems to have been fairly common among some elites in early Islam.

19 Ahmed, *Religious Elite*, p. 136, and n. 735, where he notes that an alternative interpretation is that matrilineality came into focus only briefly in the early Islamic period because the rival claims to legitimacy were so similar in patrilineal terms. He rejects this possibility, because matrilineality seems to have played a greater role for all recorded Arab families, not just ʿAlids and ʿAbbāsids, in the *jāhiliyya* and early Islamic period, and a lesser role later on.

sources, most explicitly in the letters exchanged between the caliph al-Manṣūr and Muḥammad al-Nafs al-Zakiyya, that the relative weight of female descent mattered a great deal in ʿAlid–ʿAbbāsid arguments over legitimacy and the rightful succession to the Prophet. As al-Nafs al-Zakiyya reportedly wrote to al-Manṣūr, 'no one from the Banū Hāshim has the sort of bonds we can draw upon through kinship, precedence and superiority. We are the descendants of the [fore]mother of God's Messenger, Fāṭima bt. ʿAmr, in the *jāhiliyya* (pre-Islamic period) and descendants of his daughter Fāṭima in Islām.' Al-Manṣūr answered with a denial of the importance of the maternal line: 'You [the ʿAlids] are the descendants of his daughter [Fāṭima], which is a close kinship. But it does not legitimate inheritance, nor does it bequeath the *wilāya*, neither does it confer the *imāma* on her. So how could it be inherited from her?'[20] For the descendants of the Prophet, their relation to Fāṭima continued to be crucial and was variously emphasised, whereas the ʿAbbāsids used arguments such as these to discount any claims based on maternal descent.[21]

Perhaps the reason for the decrease in information on women was the ʿAbbāsids' dismissal of the importance of the female line in legitimising authority; after all, the genealogies are products of ʿAbbāsid historiography, in that they were in the very least composed within the broader framework of an ʿAbbāsid worldview. However, as noted above, the information on the later generations is less comprehensive in general, not just in terms of information on women. The Ṭālibid genealogies usually give relatively full description of the lineages up to generation VII or VIII after ʿAlī, and this information corresponds largely to the material found in the earlier general works of genealogy. But after that, the Ṭālibid genealogies focus on particular branches and no longer provide a complete account of the family. While the authors certainly always made choices about whom to include or omit, the earlier genealogical works give the impression of recording all possible lines of descent, including many women; this is no longer the case in the Ṭālibid genealogies. The extant works not only record mostly the branches of the family that settled in the Islamic East but also focus their attention decidedly on the surviving male lineages.[22]

At the present stage of the scholarship on the issue, we cannot be sure of the reasons for the changes in genealogical record keeping, that is, the reduction in information on women and the shifts in the selection of recorded lineages. An important consequence for a study on marriage patterns is that the genealogical 'data

20 Al-Ṭabarī, *Taʾrīkh,* vol. III, pp. 208–15; see also the introduction and extensive additional references in Amikam Elad, 'The Correspondence Between al-Manṣūr and Muḥammad b. ʿAbdallāh', in Elad, *The Rebellion of Muḥammad al-Nafs al-Zakiyya.*

21 The ʿAbbāsids eventually based their own claims to authority on their relation to the Prophet's uncle al-ʿAbbās; see Moshe Sharon, *Black Banners from the East: The Establishment of the ʿAbbāsid State; Incubation of the Revolt* (Jerusalem and Leiden, 1983), pp. 92–3. For the ʿAbbāsids' changing arguments for the legitimacy of their rule, see Martin Hinds, 'The Early ʿAbbāsid Caliphs and Sunna', paper presented at the Colloquium on the Study of Hadith (Oxford, 1982).

22 See the discussion in the previous chapter. As Morimoto ('Diffusion', p. 12) rightly says, 'the generation up to which such full descriptions are made is by no means uniform within a single work, or among different works'.

set' is much less complete than one would wish. Not only is information on women limited, generally attached to male lineages and increasingly rare, but even the records for men are patchy. Nevertheless, given that my findings are largely based on Ṭālibid genealogies, which were often written by (and perhaps mainly for) the Ṭālibids themselves, they at the very least provide a picture that the family itself sought to preserve and to convey. Let us now turn to some examples.

Marriages with the Banū Makhzūm

The Banū Makhzūm were an important clan of Quraysh. Some of the clan's members are said to have been among the Prophet's adversaries in Mecca, but it seems that the differences between the families were soon overcome. There were ʿAlid–Makhzūmī relations from the earliest Islamic period, particularly involving the Ḥasanid branch: Fākhita bt. Abī Ṭālib, a sister of ʿAlī, was married to Hubayra b. Abī Wahb al-Makhzūmī, a warrior and poet who never converted to Islam and eventually died in Najrān.[23] Their son Jaʿda b. Hubayra married Umm al-Ḥasan bt. ʿAlī (a first-cousin marriage through the mother's side), and Jaʿda and his sons are later mentioned as supporters of ʿAlid claims in Kufa.[24]

Relations between Makhzūmīs and Ḥasanids intensified in the late Umayyad and early ʿAbbāsid periods, but only in the form of ʿAlid men taking Makhzūmī brides; I have found no example of an ʿAlid woman being married off to a Makhzūmī after the mid-second/eighth century. In the late Umayyad period, ʿAbdallāh b. al-Ḥasan married the Makhzūmī ʿĀtika bt. ʿAbd al-Malik b. al-Ḥārith b. Khālid b. al-ʿĀṣī b. Hishām b. Mughīra, the mother of Idrīs b. ʿAbdallāh, the founder of the Idrīsid dynasty in North Africa. ʿAbdallāh's brother Ibrāhīm married Rabīḥa bt. Muḥammad b. ʿAbdallāh b. Abī Umayya b. Mughīra. In the two generations that followed there are at least four more marriages contracted between Ḥasanid men and Makhzūmī women.[25]

Even though the Banū Makhzūm's relations with the Ḥasanids were particularly close, there are also some examples of Ḥusaynid–Makhzūmī marriages. Umm Ibrāhīm bt. Ibrāhīm b. Hishām b. Ismāʿīl b. Hishām b. al-Walīd b. al-Mughīra al-Makhzūmī, for instance, was married to Ismāʿīl b. Jaʿfar b. Muḥammad b. ʿAlī b. al-Ḥusayn; according to al-Bukhārī, their son ʿAlī was known as Ibn al-

23 See al-Ṭabarī, *Taʾrīkh*, vol. III, p. 2,465; see also Ibn Ḥabīb, *Kitāb al-Munammaq*, pp. 457, 519 and 528, describing Hubayra as one of the *fursān Quraysh*.

24 After al-Ḥasan died, the Kufan Shīʿa expressed their support for al-Ḥusayn, and Jaʿda, or his sons, conveyed a letter of support; see Ibn Ḥabīb, *Kitāb al-Muḥabbar*, pp. 437–8. According to Ibn Ḥabīb, Fākhita was subsequently married to Jaʿfar b. ʿAqīl, who was killed with al-Ḥusayn, and then to ʿAbdallāh b. al-Zubayr b. ʿAwwām.

25 Al-Bukhārī, *Sirr al-silsila*, pp. 18, 23 and 25: Ibrāhīm b. Ismāʿīl al-Ṭabāṭabā married Umm al-Zubayr bt. ʿAbdallāh al-Makhzūmī; Sulaymān b. Dāwūd b. al-Ḥasan married Asmāʾ bt. Isḥāq b. Ibrāhīm [b. Yaʿqūb] b. Salama al-Makhzūmī; Zayd b. al-Ḥasan b. Zayd b. al-Ḥasan b. ʿAlī married Asmāʾ bt. Ibrāhīm b. Mūsā b. ʿAbd al-Raḥmān b. ʿAbdallāh b. Abī Rabīʿa b. al-Mughīra al-Makhzūmī; and Muḥammad b. Zayd b. ʿAbdallāh married a Makhzūmī woman, whose name is not known.

Makhzūmiyya.[26] Muḥammad b. Zayd b. ʿAlī b. al-Ḥusayn was married to Hunāda bt. Khalaf from the Āl Ḥurayth al-Makhzūmī, a family that had gained some wealth early in the conquest in Kufa and who had become quite important there.[27]

The reasons for the strong marriage connections between the ʿAlids and the Makhzūmīs cannot easily be discerned from the sources. During the Umayyad period the Banū Makhzūm were mostly supporters of the 'fiercely anti-ʿAlid family of al-Zubayr', as Madelung described them,[28] with whom the ʿAlids incidentally had marriage relations throughout this period. After the ʿAbbāsid Revolution, there are some Makhzūmīs among the supporters of Muḥammad al-Nafs al-Zakiyya, which was probably a consequence of the Ḥasanid–Makhzūmī alliances.[29] The Makhzūmī women came from a number of different families, although mainly from the al-Mughīra branch, which Martin Hinds identified as the most important one in the early Islamic period.[30] The evidence suggest that the change in the marriage pattern, whereby the ʿAlids no longer gave their daughters in marriage to the Makhzūmīs after a certain point in the mid-second/eighth century, reflects a shift in the social hierarchy or in the relative status of the two families – particularly given that there clearly had been such inter-marriages in earlier times. In other words, as the Makhzūmīs became less prominent in the ʿAbbāsid period, the ʿAlids no longer married their daughters to them. The shift also suggests that the ʿAlids, after the successful coming to power of their ʿAbbāsid cousins and their own repeated failure to wrest that power from them, increasingly sought to bolster their own clan solidarity. Boundaries were beginning to be drawn around the kinsfolk of the Prophet.

Marriages with the Banū al-ʿAbbās

Most ʿAlid–ʿAbbāsid marriages took place between Ḥusaynids and ʿAbbāsids, eclipsing ʿAlid marriages with the Banū Makhzūm. Certainly, there are some

26 Al-Bukhārī, *Sirr al-silsila*, p. 35; al-Zubayrī, *Nasab Quraysh*, p. 65, as well as p. 246 (for her father); see also Martin Hinds, 'Makhzūm', *EI2*.

27 Al-Zubayrī, *Nasab Quraysh*, p. 71, where she is called ʿAnāda bt. Khalaf b. Ḥafṣ b. ʿUmar b. ʿAmr b. Ḥurayth b. ʿAmr b. ʿUthmān b. ʿAbdallāh b. ʿUmar b. Makhzūm. For ʿAmr b. Ḥurayth b. ʿAmr b. ʿUthmān b. ʿAbdallāh b. ʿUmar al-Makhzūmī, see al-Zubayrī, *Nasab Quraysh*, p. 333. He is said to have been the first Qurashī to make a lot of money in Kufa (*iʿtaqada bi-l-Kūfa mālan*).

28 Wilferd Madelung, 'Yaḥyā b. ʿAbdallāh', *EI2*.

29 See for instance al-Ṭabarī, *Taʾrīkh*, vol. III, p. 226, and al-Balādhurī, *Kitāb Ansāb al-ashrāf*, ed. Maḥmūd Firdaws al-ʿAẓm, 20 vols (Damascus, 1996–), vol. II, p. 429. For ʿAbdallāh b. ʿAbd al-Raḥmān b. al-Ḥārith b. ʿAbdallāh b. ʿAyyāsh, who went out to rebel with Muḥammad b. ʿAbdallāh in Medina and was killed by al-Manṣūr, see al-Zubayrī, *Nasab Quraysh*, p. 315; al-Balādhurī, *Ansāb al-ashrāf*, ed. al-ʿAẓm, vol. VIII, p. 309, calls him Abū Salama ʿAbdallāh b. ʿAbd al-Raḥmān and says that he rebelled with Muḥammad b. ʿAbdallāh b. al-Ḥasan and was taken prisoner and killed by al-Manṣūr. There were also a number of Zubayrids on the side of the ʿAbbāsids, such as ʿAbd al-ʿAzīz b. al-Muṭṭalib b. ʿAbdallāh b. al-Muṭṭalib b. Ḥanṭab. He was the *qāḍī* in Medina during the reigns of al-Manṣūr and al-Mahdī; see al-Zubayrī, *Nasab Quraysh*, p. 341.

30 Martin Hinds, 'Makhzūm', *EI2*: '[T]here are in addition indications that in the early ʿAbbāsid period Makhzūmī links with the ʿAlids, notably the Ḥasanids, became closer.'

examples of Ḥasanid women married to ʿAbbāsid men, particularly in the first generations of Islam;[31] in the later Umayyad and early ʿAbbāsid periods, however, especially the Ḥusaynid daughters were married off to the ʿAbbāsids. There are very few instances of ʿAbbāsid women being offered as brides to ʿAlids. One famous example is that of the caliph al-Maʾmūn: He gave two of his daughters in marriage to the Ḥusaynids, one to ʿAlī al-Riḍā (d. 203/818), the later eighth imām of the Imāmī Shiʿites, and the other to the latter's son Muḥammad. In view of the rarity of such marriages in the preceding generations, the gesture is significant. Not only had the caliph named ʿAlī al-Riḍā as his successor, but he also forged ties of kinship to underline the connection.[32]

The list of Ḥusaynid–ʿAbbāsid marriages is long and clearly reflects the alliances identified by Ahmed as the 'ʿAbbāsid–Ḥanafiyya–Ḥusaynid coalition', which may well explain, at least partly, the Ḥusaynids' quietism.[33] Indeed, the alliances include two daughters of Jaʿfar al-Ṣādiq, both of whom were married, one after the other, to Muḥammad b. ʿAbdallāh b. Muḥammad b. ʿAlī b. ʿAbdallāh b. al-ʿAbbās, the son of the first ʿAbbāsid caliph al-Saffāḥ.[34] Muḥammad b. Ibrāhīm also had other Ḥusaynid wives, such as Fāṭima bt. al-Ḥusayn b. Zayd b. ʿAlī b. al-Ḥusayn. After he died, Fāṭima married a son of al-Manṣūr, but he divorced her (*fāraqahā*).[35] The caliph Hārūn al-Rashīd (r. 169–193/786–809) also married a Ḥusaynid, if only very briefly: He divorced Zaynab bt. ʿAbdallāh b. al-Ḥusayn b. ʿAlī b. al-Ḥusayn b. ʿAlī after just one night, which earned her the nickname 'Zaynab laylatin' ('Zaynab of one night') among the people of Medina.[36]

An example of a Ḥasanid woman who was married to an ʿAbbāsid is Zaynab bt. Muḥammad, the daughter of the rebel Muḥammad al-Nafs al-Zakiyya.[37] She was married to Muḥammad b. ʿAbdallāh, the son of al-Saffāḥ, shortly after her father had

31 See, for instance, al-Zubayrī, *Nasab Quraysh*, pp. 26 and 28. Umm Kulthūm bt. al-Faḍl b. al-ʿAbbās was married to al-Ḥasan b. ʿAlī. She bore him Muḥammad, Jaʿfar, Ḥamza and Fāṭima, but the line continued only through Fāṭima (*darijū*). Al-Ḥasan divorced Umm Kulthūm, and she was then married to Abū Mūsā b. ʿAbdallāh b. Qays. Another example is Lubāba bt. ʿUbaydallāh b. ʿAbbās, for whom see al-Zubayrī, *Nasab Quraysh*, p. 32: She was first married to al-ʿAbbās b. ʿAlī b. Abī Ṭālib, and after he was killed with al-Ḥusayn she married al-Walīd b. ʿUtba b. Abī Sufyān, at the time *wālī* of Mecca and Medina. They had a son, al-Qāsim, and when al-Walīd died, Lubāba married Zayd b. al-Ḥasan b. ʿAlī, with whom she had a daughter, Nafīsa. Nafīsa also had a number of husbands, ʿAbbāsid and Ḥasanid, as well as an Umayyad, al-Walīd b. ʿAbd al-Malik b. Marwān; see al-Bukhārī, *Sirr al-silsila*, p. 29.

32 For an excellent recent discussion of ʿAlī al-Riḍā, see Tamima Bayhom-Daou, 'ʿAlī al-Riḍā', in *Encyclopaedia of Islam*, 3rd edn (henceforth *EI3*).

33 Ahmed, *Religious Elite*, p. 193; see also pp. 168–81 for a detailed discussion of the *Ḥusaynid* marriages.

34 Al-Zubayrī, *Nasab Quraysh*, pp. 63–5. Muḥammad b. Ibrāhīm also married Fāṭima bt. al-Ḥusayn b. Zayd b. ʿAlī b. al-Ḥusayn and Khadīja bt. Isḥāq b. ʿAbdallāh b. ʿAlī b. al-Ḥusayn b. ʿAlī, after she separated from her first husband; al-Zubayrī, *Nasab Quraysh*, pp. 65 and 67.

35 Al-Zubayrī, *Nasab Quraysh*, pp. 65–6.

36 Al-Zubayrī, *Nasab Quraysh*, p. 73. Before Hārūn, there had been another ʿAlid woman married to an ʿAbbāsid caliph, namely, the daughter of Abū ʿAbdallāh al-Ḥusayn b. Zayd b. ʿAlī b. al-Ḥusayn b. ʿAlī, who was married to the caliph al-Mahdī (d. 169/785); see al-Bukhārī, *Sirr al-silsila*, p. 62.

37 Al-Zubayrī, *Nasab Quraysh*, p. 54; Ibn Ḥabīb, *Kitāb al-Muḥabbar*, p. 438. See Ahmed, *Religious Elite*, p. 161 for more references.

been killed by the ʿAbbāsids. According to al-Balādhurī, the marriage was initiated when al-Saffāḥ was still alive, but it was not consummated, presumably because Zaynab was still a minor. After Muḥammad al-Nafs al-Zakiyya was killed in 145/762–3, Muḥammad, the groom, wrote to the aunt of Zaynab bt. Muḥammad, asking that the girl be sent to him; the aunt was outraged over this demand and wrote to Muḥammad's uncle ʿIsā b. Mūsā, 'yesterday you killed her father and today he will marry her (*qad qataltum abāhā bi-l-ams wa yuʿarrisa bihā al-yawm*)'. ʿIsā apologised for Muḥammad, scolded him and called him an imbecile for having demanded the girl so soon after her father's death.[38] Eventually, however, Zaynab did go to live with Muḥammad. Later she was married again a number of times, to at least two more ʿAbbāsids.[39]

To what extent the ʿAlids were coerced to marry their daughters to the ʿAbbāsids is not known. According to Abū Naṣr al-Bukhārī's account of the one-night marriage between the caliph Hārūn and Zaynab bt. ʿAbdallāh, Zaynab did not want to be married to the ʿAbbāsid. Trouble was anticipated already ahead of time: On the wedding night (*laylat al-dukhūl*), a slave came to Zaynab, intending to bind her with a rope so that she would 'not be unapproachable' for Hārūn; but when the slave approached her, she kicked him so hard that she broke two of his ribs. Hārūn let her go without having consummated the marriage, but he still sent her 4,000 dinars each year for her maintenance.[40] We should probably read these alliances as conciliatory gestures. Marriages such as the one between Zaynab bt. Muḥammad al-Nafs al-Zakiyya and Muḥammad b. ʿAbdallāh, who had even taken an active part in the defeat of his father-in law's revolt, were probably a way to display the ʿAbbāsid victory over the ʿAlids (also indicated by the fact that no ʿAbbāsid daughters were married to the Ḥasanids), while also attempting to draw the Ḥasanids closer to the ʿAbbāsids. The latter strategy does not seem to have been particularly successful, as the ʿAlids reacted by taking a clear turn towards strengthening the cohesion of their own clan through endogamous marriages; and they continued to revolt.

38 ʿĪsā b. Mūsā's reaction is meant to emphasise the unease of the ʿAbbāsids in killing members of the family of the Prophet. Al-Ṭabarī, *Taʾrīkh,* vol. III, pp. 264–5, for instance, reports that ʿĪsā b. Mūsā made a prostration before he cut off the head of Muḥammad al-Nafs al-Zakiyya. Although he was enlisted by al-Manṣūr to lead the forces against Muḥammad and Ibrāhīm b. ʿAbdallāh, he reportedly spent some time trying to persuade leading members of the ʿAlid family and of other Medinese families to break away from Muḥammad al-Nafs al-Zakiyya. For another account of the ʿAbbāsids' unease in killing ʿAlids, see al-Ṭabarī, *Taʾrīkh,* vol. III, pp. 223 and 225, where Hārūn al-Rashīd exclaims: 'By God, were it not for sparing the blood of the Hāshimites, I would cut off your head!'

39 Ibn Ḥabīb, *Kitāb al-Muḥabbar*, p. 449. Another example of a Ḥasanid–ʿAbbāsid marriage is that of Umm Kulthūm bt. Muḥammad b. al-Ḥasan b. al-Ḥasan b. ʿAlī and ʿĪsā b. ʿAlī b. ʿAbdallāh b. al-ʿAbbās; see al-Zubayrī, *Nasab Quraysh*, p. 53. Her father, Muḥammad, played no particular role in the historical events, and he does not appear in the historical sources. Ahmed also notes that a daughter of Mūsā b. ʿAbdallāh b. al-Ḥasan b. al-Ḥasan b. ʿAlī was married to a son of al-Manṣūr after the Ḥasanid uprising; Ahmed, *Religious Elite*, p. 61.

40 Al-Bukhārī, *Sirr al-silsila,* p. 61.

Marriages in the third/ninth century and after

As ʿAlid–ʿAbbāsid relations continued to deteriorate and status relations began to shift during the second/eighth century, inter-marriages between the two families decreased sharply. This was the case also for the ʿAlids' marriages with all other non-Ṭālibid families. Indeed, from the early third/ninth century onwards, the ʿAlids married overwhelmingly within their own family. A good example of the changes in the later generations is provided by the Buṭḥānīs, a Ḥasanid family that rose to prominence in various cities in the East. Richard Bulliet examined the branch that settled in Nishapur in his *Patricians of Nishapur*.[41]

The Buṭḥānīs were descendants of al-Ḥasan b. Zayd b. al-Ḥasan b. ʿAlī, one of the few ʿAlids who continued to support the ʿAbbāsids after their rise to the caliphate. Al-Ḥasan was governor of Medina for the caliph al-Manṣūr and 'the first to wear black among the ʿAlids', black being the colour of the ʿAbbāsids; he allegedly died in 168/784 at the age of 80.[42] His grandson Muḥammad b. al-Qāsim b. al-Ḥasan was the eponymous al-Buṭḥānī.[43] By the end of the third/ninth century, Buṭḥānī Ḥasanids had spread to many parts of the Muslim world: There were still distinguished members of the family in Medina, but they had also established themselves in Egypt (one Buṭḥānī was a genealogist in the *maḥḍar* incident of the Fāṭimids, where an official document was drawn up to disclaim their ʿAlid descent) and in Ṭabaristān (there are two well-known Buṭḥānī supporters of the *dāʿī* al-Ḥasan b. Zayd, also the authors of important Zaydī works), as well as in various cities in the East. In Nishapur they rose to particular prominence, taking over the *niqāba* from a rival Ḥusaynid family, the Āl Zubāra, in 395/1004. They then held the office for at least 120 years. Most surprisingly, perhaps, the Buṭḥānīs may have been Sunni. They made marriage alliances with elite families of the scholarly community, taking wives from both of the rival Ḥanafī and Shāfiʿī factions: In generation IX, the Buṭḥānī Abū Muḥammad Ḥamza married al-Ḥurra bt. al-Imām al-Muwaffaq Hibat Allāh b. al-Qāḍī ʿUmar b. Muḥammad, chief of the Shāfiʿīs (*muqaddam aṣḥāb al-Shāfiʿī*). Incidentally, the Shāfiʿīs in particular supported the transfer of the *niqāba* to the Buṭḥānī family. As Ibn Funduq says, 'the followers of the Imām Muṭṭalibī Shāfiʿī, may God be pleased with him, considered it advisable to help the sons of the Sayyid Abū ʿAbdallāh [the Buṭḥānīs], and the *niqāba* passed from this line to the other one'.[44] But the Buṭḥānīs did not keep all their eggs in one basket: A generation later, Abū al-Ḥasan ʿAlī is described as the son-in-law (*khatan*) of the prominent Ḥanafī *shaykh* al-Ṣandalī.[45]

41 Bulliet, *Patricians*, pp. 234–45.

42 Al-Bukhārī, *Sirr al-silsila*, pp. 21–2. See also al-Ṭabarī, *Taʾrīkh*, vol. III, pp. 144–5 and 149–50; and al-Khaṭīb al-Baghdādī (d. 463/1071), *Taʾrīkh Baghdād*, 14 vols (Cairo, 1931, vol. VII, pp. 309–13.

43 There is some discussion over the correct form of his *laqab*; see, for instance, al-ʿUmarī, *al-Majdī*, pp. 203–5.

44 Ibn Funduq, *Tārīkh-i Bayhaq*, p. 55, translated in Clifford E. Bosworth, *The Ghaznavids: Their Empire in Afghanistan and Eastern Iran, 994–1040* (Edinburgh, 1963), p. 197. The episode is also mentioned in Ibn Funduq, *Lubāb*, pp. 608–9.

45 Ibn Funduq, *Lubāb*, p. 604.

Overall, the marriages of this Ḥasanid family conform to the pattern described above: Most of the recorded marriages were contracted within the family, with other ʿAlids or Ṭālibids. But there were some notable exogamous marriages as well. One early Buṭḥānī married a woman from the Banū Thaqīf, another Arab tribe; and in the mid-second/eighth century, there was a marriage between an ʿAbbāsid and a granddaughter of al-Ḥasan b. Zayd, the *amīr* in Medina (she was a daughter of al-Ḥasan's son ʿAbd al-Raḥmān al-Shajarī, the brother of Muḥammad al-Buṭḥānī).[46] Information on the later generations pertains almost exclusively to ʿAlid men; when they did not marry endogamously, they took wives from among the local notables or from other prominent families, not necessarily Arabs. Like ʿAlī al-Uṭrūsh b. al-Ḥusayn, a paternal cousin of the Buṭḥānīs in Hamadān who married the daughter of al-Ṣāḥib b. ʿAbbād,[47] prominent ʿAlids continued to take wives from elite families. But the new elites were Persians and Turks or, in the case of North Africa, sometimes Berbers; and like the old elites in the earlier centuries, they gave their daughters in marriage to *sayyid*s and *sharīf*s so that their offspring would be part of the kinsfolk of the Prophet.

Marriage regulations in the law: *Kafāʾa* and descent

While the evidence from the genealogies and narrative histories suggests that there were fewer and fewer families with whom the ʿAlids inter-married and to whom they gave their daughters as brides, such restrictions were not reflected in the law. There are of course some general regulations: Although in theory a Muslim adult male can freely chose his wife, the law books give a series of rules and stipulations regarding marriage (*nikāḥ* or *zawāj*). The section of the *Kitāb al-nikāḥ* usually opens with a discussion of those marriage choices that are prohibited, including through relations of affinity or consanguinity – a man is generally not allowed to marry his female ascendants or descendants, his sisters, the female descendants of his siblings, or his aunts and great-aunts; much of this is understood to be based on the Qurʾān, sūra IV.[48] There are further restrictions regarding relationships of fosterage and religion: A woman is always prohibited from marrying an infidel, whereas a man is in principle allowed to do so. According to Joseph Schacht, however, the permission for men to marry even women of the *ahl al-kitāb* (people of the book) is, 'at least by the Shāfiʿīs, so restricted by conditions as to be prohibited in practice'.[49] Number is another factor: A free man can take up to four wives at the same time, a woman of course only one husband. The *Kitāb al-nikāḥ* goes on to discuss a variety of other topics, such as the role of a woman's guardian (*walī*), the amount of the dower

46 Al-ʿUmarī, *al-Majdī*, p. 215.

47 Ibn ʿAbbād was probably of Iranian descent, although the family had been Muslim for some time; see Maurice Pomerantz, 'Al-Ṣāḥib Ismāʿīl b. ʿAbbād (d. 385/995): A Political Biography', *Journal of the American Oriental Society* (forthcoming), n. 13.

48 The relevant verses are Qurʾān IV: 20–5.

49 Joseph Schacht, 'Nikāḥ', *EI2*.

(*mahr*), when and how the dower must be paid and prescriptions regarding sexual intercourse.

The most important discussion for the present purposes centres on *kafāʾa*, equality or suitability in marriage, and its emphasis on descent (*nasab*). According to the *Lisān al-ʿArab*, *kafāʾa* in marriage means that a husband must be equal to his wife in terms of honour (*ḥasab*), religion (*dīn*), descent (*nasab*) and family (*bayt*), as well as in other respects (*wa-ghayr dhālika*).[50] *Kafāʾa* is thus intended to regulate the choice of a husband for a woman; it is the woman who may not marry beneath herself. The husband can marry quite freely (within the limits set by the prohibitions), because he 'raises' his wife to his station. As Ibn Funduq noted, there were recommendations for ʿAlid men also, but these are not reflected in the law; *kafāʾa* as a legal term is generally understood to refer to the marital choices of women only.

The legal schools differ regarding the categories and regulations of *kafāʾa* as well as its overall importance. The regulations were elaborated in most detail by some Ḥanafī scholars, who specified that in addition to parity in descent and religion, other criteria involving freedom, means (*māl* or *yasār*), piety (*diyāna*) and profession (*ḥirfa*) must likewise be met at the time of the marriage.[51] Early Ḥanbalī and Shāfiʿī works also emphasise the importance of the regulations of *kafāʾa*; Muḥammad b. Idrīs al-Shāfiʿī (d. 204/820), for example, discusses *kafāʾa* in general terms but insists that women be married according to the requirements of *kafāʾa*. Abū al-Ḥasan al-Māwardī lists seven possible determinants of *kafāʾa,* namely religion/piety, descent, freedom, means, earnings/livelihood (*kasb*), age (*sinn*, that is, reaching puberty) and freedom from physical deficiencies (*salāma min al-ʿuyūb*).[52] At the other end of the spectrum, the Mālikīs are considered to have given *kafāʾa* relatively little consideration, placing the highest emphasis on piety or religion (*dīn*). Mālik b. Anas (d. 179/795) is reported to have explicitly authorised the marriage of non-Arab men to Arab women and to have said that a previously married woman should be able to choose her husband regardless of his *sharaf* or *ḥasab*.[53] However, as Amalia Zomeño has recently shown, there was considerable development in the Mālikī school, too, towards an acceptance of descent as a factor in *kafāʾa*, and although *nasab* never became one of the formal criteria included in theoretical legal discussions, it did become a factor in legal rulings. A *fatwā* from fifteenth-century Fez seeks to dissolve a marriage primarily on the grounds of descent.[54]

50 Ibn Manẓūr, *Lisān al-ʿArab*, 20 vols in 10 (Cairo, 1880–9), vol. I, p. 134.

51 Y. Linant de Bellefonds, *Traité de droit musulman comparé*, 3 vols (Paris and La Haya, 1965), vol. II, p. 171.

52 Al-Māwardī, *al-Ḥāwī al-kabīr*, 24 vols (Beirut, 1414/1994), vol. IX, pp. 100–8.

53 Saḥnūn (d. 240/854), *al-Mudawwana al-kubrā*, 16 vols in 4 (Cairo, 1323/1905), vol. IV, p. 13. A virgin girl, however, needs a guardian; see Farhat Ziadeh, 'Equality (Kafāʾah) in the Muslim Law of Marriage', *American Journal of Comparative Law* 6 (1957), p. 505. See also the Imāmī view in Ibn Bābūya, *al-Muqniʿ wa-'l-Hidāya*, ed. Muḥammad Ibn Mahdī al-Wāʿiẓ (Tehran, 1377/1957), p. 68 (*al-Hidāya*).

54 Amalia Zomeño, '*Kafāʾa* in the Maliki School: A *Fatwā* from Fifteenth Century Fez', in Robert Gleave and Eugenia Kermeli (eds), *Islamic Law: Theory and Practice* (London, 1997), p. 95. She says that 'this appearance of the *nasab* criterion could be interpreted as reflecting a social and political situation that

The differences between the schools with regard to the determinants of *kafāʾa* have been tentatively explained as stemming either from the social circumstances at the time of their elaboration,[55] or alternatively from different developments within the respective legal schools. Linant de Bellefonds suggests that the importance attached to *kafāʾa* depends on the role assigned to the guardian. The Mālikī school, in which *kafāʾa* is the least important, demands the presence of a guardian in most types of marriage contract, thus providing a safeguard for the interests of the bride and her family without articulating further explicit rules. Ḥanafī law, by contrast, gives an adult woman greater freedom to choose a husband without the assistance of a guardian, but in compensation it contains very complex *kafāʾa* regulations. Thus the presence of the guardian ensured suitability in the marriage laws of the Mālikī school, while the Ḥanafīs placed less importance on the guardian but more on *kafāʾa*.[56] However, both Shāfīʿis and Ḥanbalīs insist on the guardian as well as on *kafāʾa*; thus, even though both regulations – the requirement of a guardian and insistence on *kafāʾa* – were certainly intended to limit a woman's choice for a husband, one did not exclude the other.

The Mālikīs generally exclude the notion of descent (*nasab*) from theoretical legal discussions, but as noted above, there is evidence that it did matter in practice.[57] Other schools are more explicit even in theory: The Imāmī scholar Muḥammad b. al-Ḥasan al-Ṭūsī (d. 460/1067) ascribes to Abū Ḥanīfa (d. c. 150/767) the statement, 'All of the Quraysh are equal (*akfāʾ*); but the Arabs are not equal to the Quraysh.'[58] Al-Ṭūsī further says that there is a disagreement between Ḥanafīs and Shāfīʿīs, as the latter add that 'non-Arabs (*ʿajam*) are not suitable for the Arabs, the Arabs are not equal to the Quraysh, and the Quraysh are not equal to the Banū Hāshim'.[59] This is repeated by al-Māwardī, who says that the disagreement is between the 'school of the Basrans' and the 'school of the Baghdadis':[60] the former say that all of the Quraysh are equal in marriage, whereas the latter insist that the Banū Hāshim are preferred (*ashraf* or *afḍal*) on account of their closer relation with the Prophet. He argues that this is reflected in the *dīwān* of ʿUmar: The Banū Hāshim and the Banū

could change the general meaning of the Mālikī theory on *kafāʾa*'. See also Powers, *Law, Society and Culture*, p. 167.

55 According to Ziadeh, 'Equality', p. 508, 'there is very little in the Arab background but much in the Persian background, to constitute an origin for the doctrine of *kafāʾa*'.

56 Linant de Bellefonds, 'Kafāʾa', *EI2*; see also the summary in Zomeño, '*Kafāʾa*', p. 87, and Louise Marlow, *Hierarchy and Egalitarianism in Islamic Thought* (Cambridge, 1997), p. 31.

57 There is some indication that descent was discussed even in Mālikī works on substantive law. Zomeño cites the opinion of Khalīl b. Isḥāq al-Jundī (d. 776/1374) from his *Mukhtaṣar* that 'a man without noble origin (*ghayr sharīf*) is not suitable for a noble woman (*sharīfa*)'; see Zomeño, '*Kafāʾa*', p. 91.

58 Abū Bakr b. Masʿūd al-Kāsānī (d. 587/1189) cites this with minor alteration as a *ḥadīth* of the Prophet; see Abū Bakr b. Masʿūd al-Kāsānī, *Bidāyat al-ṣanāʾiʿ fī tartīb al-sharāʾiʿ*, 7 vols (Cairo, 1327–8), vol. II, p. 319.

59 Al-Ṭūsī, *Kitāb al-Khilāf*, 4 vols (Qum, 1413), vol. IV, pp. 271–2. See also al-Ṭūsī, *al-Mabsūṭ*, 8 vols in 7 (Tehran, 1352/1968), vol. II, p. 178, where he repeats this disagreement with some elaboration, but does not ascribe it.

60 I am not sure whether this refers to different schools among the Shāfiʿīs, or to Basrans versus Muʿtazilites.

al-Muṭṭalib were equal (*akfāʾ*), because the Prophet had placed them in the same category with regard to their tax portion (*sahm dhāwī al-qurbā*).[61] However, beyond these discussions, the Sunni schools are noticeably quiet on the question of ʿAlid or Hāshimite marriages.

The Shiʿite view

Given the importance of the descendants of the Prophet in Shiʿite doctrine, it is surprising that the Shiʿites also do not single out the ʿAlids as requiring special *kafāʾa* in marriage on account of their genealogy. Indeed, not only do early Imāmī works fail to restrict ʿAlid marriages; contrary to what one may expect, some works even explicitly state that marriages between non-ʿAlid men and ʿAlid women are allowed. Thus, according to the great Imāmī authority of the Būyid period, the Sharīf al-Murtaḍā (d. 436/1044), the marriage of a non-ʿAlid to an ʿAlid woman – called explicitly *imraʾa ʿAlawiyya Hāshimiyya* – may be seen as reprehensible in terms of governance and custom (*siyāsa wa-ʿāda*), but 'it is not forbidden as far as the religion is concerned (*lam yakun maḥẓūran fī al-dīn*)'.[62] Al-Murtaḍā's friend and student al-Ṭūsī similarly states in the *Nihāya*:

> The believers are of equal worth to one another in terms of marriage, just as they are equal in terms of lives, even if they differ in terms of lineage (*nasab*) and honour (*sharaf*). If a believer asks another for the hand of his daughter, has the means to support her, is satisfactory in religion and faith (*dīnuhu wa-īmānuhu*) and has not committed any crime, he [the father] is sinning against God and going against the *sunna* of the Prophet if he does not marry him to her, even if he [the suitor] is of low origin *(ḥaqīr fī nasabihi*).[63]

The early Imāmī scholars thus do not support regulations regarding *kafāʾa* in the same way as do some of their Sunni counterparts. Descent and honour are not important factors; it is only a suitor's faith and his ability to provide maintenance (*nafaqa*) that must be considered.[64] This is also the view expressed in the *Kāfī* of Muḥammad b. Yaʿqūb al-Kulīnī (d. 329/941): Jaʿfar al-Ṣādiq is reported to have said that the two criteria for suitability in marriage are virtue and means (*al-kufūʾ an yakūna ʿafīfan wa-ʿindahu yasār*).[65] Half a century later, Ibn Bābūya (d. 381/991) says that if a man is good enough in religion, morality and faith (*dīnuhu wa-khuluquhu wa-īmānuhu*), he should be accepted for marriage; Ibn Bābūya further cites a Qurʾānic

61 Al-Māwardī, *al-Ḥāwī al-kabīr*, pp. 102–3.

62 Al-Sharīf al-Murtaḍā (d. 436/1044), *Rasāʾil al-Sharīf al-Murtaḍā*, ed. Mahdī al-Rajāʾī, 3 vols (Qum, 1405/1984–85), vol. I, p. 300.

63 Al-Ṭūsī, 'Bāb al-kafāʾa fī al-nikāḥ wa-ikhtiyār al-azwāj', in *al-Nihāya fī mujarrad al-fiqh wa-l-fatāwā* (Tehran, 1954), p. 470; see also al-Ṭūsī, *Kitāb al-Khilāf*, vol. IV, p. 272.

64 Al-Ṭūsī, *Kitāb al-khilāf*, vol. IV, p. 272; see also Ziadeh, 'Equality', p. 507.

65 Al-Kulīnī (d. 329/941), *Uṣūl min al-Kāfī*, ed. ʿAlī Akbar Ghaffārī, 8 vols (Tehran, 1375–81/1955–61), vol. V, p. 347.

verse to say that means matter little.[66] There is nothing about descent in either the *Hidāya* or the *Muqniʿ*, but he does elaborate on the question a little in his *Iʿtiqādāt fī dīn al-Imāmiyya*. There he argues that devotion to the descendants of the Prophet is obligatory, because it is the recompense for the Prophetic message; to substantiate his point he cites Qurʾān XLII:23, '*Qul lā asʾalukum ʿalayhi ajran illā al-mawadda fī al-qurbā*', 'Say: I ask of you no reward for it except the love of kin'. There is nothing more explicit on marriages. Regarding *nasab*, he cites Jaʿfar al-Ṣādiq as having said that his devotion (*walāya*) to the Prophet was dearer to him than his descent from him.[67] What does matter is good moral behaviour. According to al-Ṭūsī, it is reprehensible (*makrūh*) that a man should marry his daughter to a wine drinker or an openly immoral person; however, if he does, the contract is nonetheless valid (*māḍiyan*), even if it passes over a more qualified suitor (*al-afḍal*).[68]

To the Imāmīs, then, piety and good deeds were more important than family relations. Again, this is surprising: One would have expected the Imāmīs to elevate the family of the Prophet more explicitly. What it shows is that the disengagement of ʿAlidism and Shiʿism went both ways: Not only could one be a supporter of the ʿAlids without being a Shiʿite, one could also be a Shiʿite without proposing any special treatment for the ʿAlids. Moreover, we may see the rejection of the importance of *nasab* as an attempt on part of the Imāmī scholars to assert their authority against and over the ʿAlids or, put differently, to refute any possible claims to authority by descendants of the Prophet. After the disappearance of the last imām, scholarship was more important than descent for the purposes of authority. The Imāmīs had singled out one holy lineage, the line of the twelve Ḥusaynid imāms; beyond that, all believers, including the rest of the ʿAlids and other Hāshimites, were to be equal.

Both the Ismāʿīlīs and the early Zaydīs (judged by the views ascribed to Zayd b. ʿAlī) agreed with the Imāmīs in rejecting descent as a criterion of *kafāʾa*. Asked for his opinion, Zayd b. ʿAlī reportedly answered that all people are equal, whether Arab, non-Arab (*ʿajamī*), Qurashī or Hāshimī, 'if they confess to Islam and believe (*idhā aslamū wa-āmanū*), so their religion is one (*fa-dīnuhu wāḥid*)'.[69] Egalitarianism as far as descent is concerned therefore seems to have been shared by all early Shiʿites.[70]

66 Ibn Bābūya, *al-Muqniʿ*, p. 101; he cites Qurʾān XXIV:32, 'If they are poor, God will make them rich through His mercy.'

67 Ibn Bābūya al-Qummī, *al-Iʿtiqadāt fī dīn al-Imāmiyya* (Qum, 1412), p. 86; I am grateful to Kazuo Morimoto for sending me a copy of this text. See also Asaf A. A. Fyzee, *A Shiʿite Creed* (Calcutta, 1942), pp. 114–15; reprint (Tehran, 1982), p. 100.

68 Al-Ṭūsī, *al-Nihāya*, p. 470.

69 [Pseudo] Zayd b. ʿAlī, *Muṣnad al-Imām Zayd* (Beirut, 1991), p. 275; [Pseudo] Zayd b. ʿAlī, *Corpus iuris di Zaid b. ʿAlī*, ed. E. Griffini (Milan, 1919), p. 199. For the authenticity of the work, see Wilferd Madelung, 'Shiʿi Attitudes toward Women as Reflected in Fiqh', in Afaf Lutfi al-Sayyid-Marsot (ed.), *Society and the Sexes in Medieval Islam, Sixth Giorgio Levi Della Vida Conference* (Malibu, CA, 1979), p. 76; and Josef van Ess, *Theologie und Gesellschaft im 2. und 3. Jahrhundert Hidschra: Eine Geschichte des religiösen Denkens im frühen Islam*, 6 vols (Berlin and New York, 1991–7), vol. I, p. 262.

70 Patricia Crone points out that early Shiʿism comes across in the sources as egalitarian in the sense of being

Later works by Yemeni Zaydīs, however, agree with the majority of the Sunni schools and emphasise the importance of *kafāʾa*; they single out *dīn* and *nasab* as the two most important determinants.[71] This is consistent with Madelung's findings in other fields of law; Madelung says: '[W]ith one exception, all the Zaydī schools rejected the Imāmī deviations in the law of marriage, divorce and inheritance and adopted the positions also supported by the Sunni schools.'[72] This later development corresponds to the major difference between the Zaydīs on the one hand and the Imāmīs and Ismāʿīlīs on the other: With regard to the imāmate, the latter two had chosen their lineage, whereas the former kept open the possibility of leadership for any able and active member of the Ḥasanid and Ḥusaynid lineages. If the lineage for the imāmate is defined but not finally determined, it is less possible to make all Muslims equal, also in marriage.

Despite this rejection of genealogy as a criterion of equality in marriage, descent from the Prophet was an issue for the Imāmīs on related questions. In a tradition ascribed to Jaʿfar al-Ṣādiq, discussed in an article by Robert Gleave, the imām is asked about the legality of a man being married to two descendants of Fāṭima (that is, to two Ḥasanids or Ḥusaynids; the question may also include the descendants of Fāṭima's daughters). The *imām* replies that 'it is not permitted for a man to join with two women descended from Fāṭima, for it affects her and causes her distress'.[73] The statement thus makes it clear that a man should be married to only one descendant of Fāṭima at a time. As is evident from the genealogical data, however, ʿAlids and ʿAbbāsids were sometimes married to two or more descendants of Fāṭima at the same time, at least in the early period. Even two daughters of Jaʿfar al-Ṣādiq were married to an ʿAbbāsid, who was also married to other ʿAlid women at the same time.[74]

---

against Arabism; see Patricia Crone, 'Mawālī and the Prophet's Family: An Early Shīʿite View', in M. Bernards and J. Nawas (eds), *Patronate and Patronage in Early and Classical Islam* (Leiden 2005), p. 183; see also Asma Afsaruddin, *Excellence and Precedence: Medieval Islamic Discourse on Legitimate Leadership* (Leiden, 2002), p. 179.

71 See Yaḥyā b. al-Ḥusayn b. Hārūn al-Nāṭiq bi-l-Ḥaqq (d. 424/1032–3), *Kitāb al-Taḥrīr*, ed. Muḥammad Yaḥyā Sālim, 2 vols (Ṣanʿāʾ, 1418/1997), vol. I, p. 232, where *kafāʾa* is understood as consisting of *dīn* and *nasab* together. The main question discussed here, however, is whether or not the marriage regulations can be waived. The answer is yes, if the woman so chooses and the guardians do not disagree. I am grateful to Patricia Crone and Aron Zysow for discussion and references on this point.

72 Madelung, 'Shiʿi Attitudes', p. 75.

73 This indicates that the question is really about the status of Fāṭima, which perhaps confirms that the answer relates to questions of Shiʿite doctrine more generally; Robert Gleave, 'Marrying Fāṭimid Women: Legal Theory and Substantive Law in Shīʿī Jurisprudence', *Islamic Law and Society* 6 (1999), pp. 38–68. Gleave's intention in his study is to demonstrate the relationship between legal theory (*uṣūl al-fiqh*) and substantive law with reference to their relative usage in Akhbārī and Uṣūlī discourse in the seventeenth century; he thus does not discuss the two points of interest here. The *khabar* is found in al-Ṭūsī, *Tahdhīb al-aḥkām*, 10 vols (Tehran, 1390/1970), vol. VII, p. 463, no. 1,855, and in Ibn Bābūya al-Qummī, *ʿIlal al-sharāʾiʿ* (Najaf, 1383/1963), p. 590, no. 38.

74 They were both married to Muḥammad b. Ibrāhīm b. Muḥammad b. ʿAlī b. ʿAbdallāh b. al-ʿAbbās. He also married Fāṭima bt. al-Ḥusayn b. Zayd b. ʿAlī b. al-Ḥusayn b. ʿAlī and Khadīja bt. Isḥāq b. ʿAbdallāh b. ʿAlī b. al-Ḥusayn b. ʿAlī; see al-Zubayrī, *Nasab Quraysh*, pp. 63–7.

Perhaps the tradition was a later consideration projected back to an early authority; or perhaps it indicated an early elevation of the female descendants of Fāṭima. Either way, the statement does not specify who the men are who may or may not marry two Fāṭimid women. It simply says that 'it is not permitted for anyone (*lā yuḥill li-aḥad*)'; that is, ʿAlid women may be married to anyone considered of suitable status, not just to other ʿAlids.

Indeed, a recent study of some of the most important *sayyid* families in contemporary Iraq shows that today's practice conforms to the Imāmīs' view that ʿAlid daughters do not have to be married endogamously. As Raffaele Mauriello shows in his study on the Baḥr al-ʿUlūm, al-Ṣadr, Ḥakīm and Khūʾī families, very prominent *sayyid*s consciously married their daughters to non-ʿAlid members of the religious establishment in order to build scholarly and political alliances. The three sisters of Sayyid Muḥammad al-Ṣadr, for example, were all married to prominent *ʿulamāʾ*, two of whom were not *sayyid*s. According to Muḥammad al-Ṣadr, 'his father, Ayatollah Sayyid Reza al-Sadr, had insisted that his daughters marry members of the religious establishment but had not required that they be *sayyid*s, despite attaching value to *sayyid* descent'.[75] Overall, Mauriello's analysis shows that even though there is still a preference for intra-family and inter-ʿAlid relations (like in the early period, second-cousin marriages being the predominant pattern), marriages with non-ʿAlid *ʿulamāʾ* and other important families do occur.[76] The explicit sanction, if not preference, for marriages with the non-*sayyid* elite does not only attest to the importance of the religious scholars in Shiʿism; it also accords with the view of the medieval Shiʿite sources that *nasab* was not a necessary (and certainly not an exclusive) criterion for suitability in marriage.

Conclusion

Despite examples to the contrary from the contemporary Imāmī context, for most of Islamic history social convention made it very difficult for a *sayyida* to marry outside of the family. Al-Murtaḍā called it reprehensible in terms of governance and custom, and it remains so in many Muslim societies, as the example of the southeast Asian Ḥaḍramī community mentioned at the beginning of this chapter shows. If not a union of love (which arguably few marriages were before the modern period), a marriage alliance may be seen as the result of a cost–benefit calculation. For the ʿAlids, much could be lost by marrying daughters to men outside of the family: Such marriages would 'commonise' them and compromise the family's special status, on which claims to privileges and social exceptionalism were based. Endogamy, which became the predominant form of marriage for the kinsfolk of the Prophet, not only strengthened the bonds of kinship but also ensured that the family's interests and status were protected.

75 Raffaele Mauriello, 'Genealogical Prestige'. For more examples, see Mauriello, *Descendants of the Family of the Prophet*.

76 Mauriello, 'Genealogical Prestige'.

4

The *Niqāba*, the Headship of the ʿAlid Family

The emergence of the *niqāba*, the 'headship' of the ʿAlid (or Ṭālibid) family, was a clear indication that the kinsfolk of the Prophet had come to be perceived as deserving special treatment on account of their genealogy. Within 100 years of their initial appearance in the late third/ninth century, *nuqabāʾ* (sing. *naqīb*) were found all over the Islamic world. In various ways, the office gave the family a certain self-determination over its affairs, not least in administering its privileges. No other social group could claim such exceptions and exemptions. While Morimoto has traced the rapid dispersion of the *niqāba* across the Islamic world, the origins and functions of the office are still poorly understood;[1] moreover, there has been little discussion of the extent of a *naqīb*'s power, his autonomy from the authorities or his duties towards the ʿAlids.[2]

Part of the reason for the scarcity of studies on the establishment of the *niqāba* lies in the relative lack of information in the sources: Accounts concerning the appointment of the first ever *naqīb* and names and dates in office of early *nuqabāʾ* are virtually absent from the historical literature.[3] This is perhaps not surprising. The non-ʿAlid and non-Shiʿite sources may not have cared much for this innovation or, if they did, may not have advertised it. Why these accounts appear so late in the Ṭālibid genealogies and why there are no ʿAlid claims to the first *niqāba* is more puzzling. There may have been some ambiguity or even controversy attached to the post in the early period, because it may have been seen as a mode of government service and thus as cooperation with an often hostile regime. But if this was the case,

1 Morimoto, 'Diffusion', pp. 3–42.

2 For brief discussions of the *niqāba* in the secondary literature, see Mez, *Die Renaissance des Islāms*, p. 145; van Arendonck and Graham, 'Sharīf', *EI2*; Havemann, 'Naḳīb al-ashrāf', *EI2*; and Tyan, *Histoire de l'organisation judicaire*, pp. 550–8. There are more thorough studies on the *niqāba* in Ottoman Egypt; see Michael Winter, 'The *Ashrāf* and *Niqābat al-Ashrāf* in Egypt in Ottoman and Modern Times', *Asian and African Studies* 19 (1985), pp. 17–41, and Michael Winter, *Egyptian Society under Ottoman Rule, 1517–1798* (London, 1992), pp. 185–98, and Michael Winter, *'The ashrāf* and *naqīb al-ashrāf* in Ottoman Egypt and Syria: A Comparative Analysis', in Kazuo Morimoto (ed.), *Sayyids and Sharifs in Muslim Societies*, pp. 139–157; see also Rüya Kılıç, 'The Reflection of Islamic Tradition on Ottoman Social Structure: The *sayyids and sharīfs*', in Kazuo Morimoto (ed.), *Sayyids and Sharifs in Muslim Societies*, pp. 123–138; and H. L. Bodman, *Political Factions in Aleppo, 1760–1826* (Chapel Hill, NC, 1963), pp. 85–6. For an example from Central Asia, see Devin DeWeese, 'The Descendants of *Sayyid* Ata and the Rank of *Naqīb* in Central Asia', *Journal of the American Oriental Society* 115 (1995), pp. 612–34.

3 Evidence for the pre-Būyid period in particular is scant, which has led some scholars to suggest that the *niqāba* was founded in the Būyid period; see Kabir, *Buwayhid Dynasty*, p. 187.

there is little trace of it in the sources. The evidence of the genealogies shows that it is clearly the families of the *nuqabāʾ* and the *ruʾasāʾ* (sing. *raʾīs,* head, leader) that are treated as the most distinguished.[4] Ibn Funduq in the *Lubāb*, for instance, organises his genealogical discussion of various ʿAlid families by *niqāba*; he thus gives first the name of the *naqīb* of a certain place and then the genealogies of his forefathers, sometimes adding relevant narrative accounts.[5] Expressions such as '*min al-sādāt al-nuqabāʾ*' are found frequently in the genealogies.

Moreover, even though the *naqīb* was sometimes appointed by the ruler, the *niqāba* was probably not a state office like the judgeship. The *naqīb*'s authority and responsibilities varied considerably over place and time, and they generally depended more on the status and standing of the *naqīb* locally and among other ʿAlids, rather than on his formal investiture. The early *nuqabāʾ* are often said to have been genealogists too, and the supervision of the lineages remained an essential part of the *naqīb*'s duties; further duties followed, such as the distribution of pensions and the supervision of all members of the family. Whether Ṭālibid or ʿAlid, the *niqāba* spread with the dispersal of the family to many different places, and the Ṭālibid genealogies in particular contain numerous references to *nuqabāʾ* from Damascus to Akhsīkat, places that varied greatly in size and ʿAlid population.[6]

Before returning to the question of the origins of the *niqāba*, I will examine what the office comprised, a topic on which one finds little information in the primary literature. Even the genealogies with their numerous references to the *nuqabāʾ* do not provide much information on the *naqīb*'s duties; only Ibn Funduq gives a brief list of five rules (*ādāb*) of the *niqāba*.[7] Indeed, the most comprehensive but almost lone account of the theoretical duties of the *naqīb* is given by al-Māwardī in his *al-Aḥkām al-sulṭāniyya*.[8] Examining the duties of the *naqīb* as outlined by al-Māwardī and

4 The genealogies frequently mention that the *naqīb* in a given town was also the *raʾīs* (*naqīb wa-raʾīs*); there are numerous examples, for instance al-Bukhārī, *Sirr al-silsila*, p. 64. It seems that in some cases at least the *raʾīs* was a representative of his family branch or of the *sayyids* in a given locality, much like the *naqīb*; see, for example, al-Marwazī, *al-Fakhrī*, p. 67 (*raʾīs al-Ṭālibiyyīn*), and al-Nāṭiq bi-l-Ḥaqq, *al-Ifāda*, p. 179 (*raʾīs ashrāf Baghdād*). For the *raʾīs* in the sense of mayor, see Axel Havemann, 'Raʾīs, 1. In the Sense of "Mayor" in the Central Arab Lands', *EI2*; C. E. Bosworth, 'Raʾīs, 2. In the Sense of "Mayor" in the Eastern Islamic Lands', *EI2.* In his discussion of a Ḥasanid family in Nishapur, Bulliet also notes that 'the exact distinction between the two [titles *naqīb* and *raʾīs*] is unclear'; see Bulliet, *Patricians*, p. 235.

5 Ibn Funduq, *Lubāb*, p. 589. The *naqīb* in Zanjān, for instance, was *al-sayyid al-naqīb* Abū al-Ḥasan b. Zayd b. Muḥammad b. Aḥmad b. Muḥammad b. al-Ḥusayn b. ʿĪsā b. Muḥammad al-Buṭḥānī, from the well-known Ḥasanid family discussed in the previous chapter. Ibn Funduq goes on to give genealogies for Abū al-Ḥasan's forefathers, who had settled in Dīnawar, Qazwīn, Zanjān, Hamadān and Astarābād. He also lists Buṭḥānī *nuqabāʾ* in Hamadān and Nishapur. See Ibn Funduq, *Lubāb*, p. 561 (Hamadān) and p. 602 (Nishapur).

6 For Akhsīkat, see Guy Le Strange, *The Lands of the Eastern Caliphate* (Cambridge, 1905), pp. 477–8. Morimoto, 'Diffusion', p. 37, estimates the date of appointment of the first *naqīb* there as 425/1033; see Ibn Funduq, *Lubāb*, p. 628, and al-Rāzī, *al-Shajara*, p. 169.

7 Ibn Funduq, *Lubāb al-ansāb*, p. 722.

8 Al-Māwardī, *al-Aḥkām*, pp. 81–4; *Ordinances of Government*, pp. 107–11. There is a second description by Abū Yaʿlā b. al-Farrāʾ (d. 458/1066) in his work of the same title that is very closely related to al-Māwardī's and therefore does not necessitate a separate discussion; for the relationship between the two works, see D. Little, 'A New Look at *al-Aḥkām al-Sulṭāniyya*', *Muslim World* 64 (1974), pp. 1–18.

setting these against new evidence from the genealogical literature makes clear that the role of the *naqīb* was ceremonial and social rather than judicial, and it demonstrates that the *niqāba* remained an important office under fiercely Sunni rulers such as the Ghaznavids and the Saljūqs. I will then explore the various accounts of its establishment in the late third/ninth century and discuss the example of the earliest *nuqabā*ʾ in Kufa.

The *niqāba* in al-Māwardī's *al-Aḥkām al-sulṭāniyya*

The context and intention of al-Māwardī's *Aḥkām* have been described and interpreted in various ways. Whether or not the work ought to be seen as a blueprint for caliphal restoration, it seems clear that it aimed to manifest, if not extend, state power.[9] Al-Māwardī's chapter on the *niqāba* may apply best to the situation in the Būyid period, when the Ṭālibids clearly benefited not only from Būyid attention but also from the advances of the ʿAbbāsid caliphs.[10] The fact that al-Māwardī describes the *niqāba* in the context of other state offices, such as the amirate, the vizierate and the judgeship, suggests that it was an important post in his time. Indeed, the influence of some ʿAlids, such as the Ḥusaynids al-Sharīf al-Raḍī (d. 406/1016) and al-Sharīf al-Murtaḍā (d. 436/1044), increased both socially and politically in this period: They were entrusted not only with the *niqāba* but also with the the leadership of the *ḥajj* and the supervision of the *maẓālim* courts, and some acted as envoys to the Fāṭimid and Ghaznavid courts.[11] As a representative of the ʿAlid family, the *naqīb* in this period clearly enjoyed particular authority and respect.

Despite its possible specificity, al-Māwardī's account provides a useful framework. The chapter is entitled 'Fī al-niqāba ʿalā dhawī al-ansāb', and al-Māwardī refers explicitly to a *naqīb al-Ṭālibiyyīn* and a *naqīb al-ʿAbbāsiyyīn*;[12] indeed, a *niqāba* in

9 The term 'caliphal restoration' is borrowed from Patricia Crone, *God's Rule*, p. 223. For the argument that al-Māwardī's *al-Aḥkām* was written for the caliph al-Qādir or the caliph al-Qāʾim and was intended to make the legitimising role of the caliph explicit, see H. A. R. Gibb, 'Al-Mawardi's Theory of the Khalifa', *Islamic Culture* 11 (1937), pp. 291–302; Franz Rosenthal, *Political Thought in Medieval Islam* (Cambridge, 1958), pp. 251–71; and Norman Calder, 'Friday Prayer and the Juristic Theory of Government: Sarakhsī, Shīrāzī, Māwardī', *Bulletin of the School of Oriental and African Studies* 49 (1986), p. 46. For al-Māwardī more generally, see Hanna Mikhail, *Politics and Revelation: Māwardī and After* (Edinburgh, 1995), and the foreword to Mikhail's work by Biancamaria Scarcia Amoretti. Some of the discrepancies in al-Māwardī's theoretical discussion and actual practice have been pointed out; see, for example, John Donohue, *The Buwayhid Dynasty in Iraq, 334 H./945 to 403 H./1012: Shaping Institutions for the Future* (Leiden, 2003), pp. 125–30 on the amirate, and H. F. Amedroz, 'The Office of the Kadi in the Ahkam al-Sultaniyya of Mawardi', *Journal of the Royal Asiatic Society*, n.s., 42 (1910), pp. 761–96 on the judgeship.

10 The role of the *niqāba* of both the ʿAbbāsids and the Ṭālibids in the Būyid period has recently been discussed by Donohue, *Buwayhid Dynasty*, pp. 303–14; see also Heribert Busse, *Chalif und Großkönig: Die Buyiden im Iraq (945–1055)* (Beirut, 1969), pp. 280–97, and Tamima Bayhom-Daou, *Shaykh al-Mufid* (Oxford, 2005), pp. 20–1.

11 The leadership of the *ḥajj* had thus far apparently been the right of the descendants of the ʿAbbāsid imām Ibrāhīm; see Massignon, 'Cadis et *naqībs*', p. 111. For an ʿAlid, see Ibn al-Jawzī, *al-Muntaẓam*, vol. XV, p. 95, and Ibn al-Athīr, *al-Kāmil*, vol. IX, p. 242. He was Muḥammad b. Muḥammad b. ʿUmar, Abū al-Ḥārith al-ʿAlawī, *naqīb* in Kufa, who died in 304/916.

12 Al-Samʿānī (d. 562/1166), in his *Ansāb*, also notes that the *naqīb* of the ʿAlids in Baghdad was called the

Baghdad is well documented for both families for the period of the fourth/tenth century and after.[13] As regards the purpose of the *niqāba*, al-Māwardī notes that it is 'intended to protect persons of noble descent from being governed by someone of lower origins and less honour than themselves'; presumably, al-Māwardī felt that such an official would be more solicitous for the welfare of the Prophet's family and his decisions would be more likely to be complied with.[14] He continues that the *niqāba* is recognised if it is granted in one of three ways: by the caliph, by one of his agents such as the vizier or *amīr*, or by the general *naqīb* (*naqīb ʿāmm*).

As in his better-known discussion of the amirate, al-Māwardī thus distinguishes between two kinds of *niqāba*, the special and the general (*khāṣṣa wa-ʿāmma*). For the special *niqāba*, he stipulates that the *naqīb* has no juristic functions. He may not judge or impose penalties, and he does not have to be learned. Al-Māwardī lists twelve responsibilities, which can be divided into three general areas: genealogical, social, and financial. The genealogical responsibilities include the keeping of genealogical records, clearly distinguishing the separate lineages and recording births and deaths, as well as the supervision of marriages, especially of those of the women.[15] The social responsibilities relate mainly to supervision of the members of the family with regard to their moral conduct: The *naqīb* must ensure that they behave in accordance with their noble descent and that they refrain from attempting to make improper financial gains, seeking wicked pursuits, committing evil acts or improperly exerting authority over the common people (*al-ʿāmma*) on account of their descent. Regarding financial matters, the *naqīb* is responsible for the families' monetary situation: He must ensure that the members are paid their dues (*fī al-fay wa-l-ghanīma*), and he should take care of their endowments (*wuqūf*) in order to protect and increase their yields.[16]

The general *niqāba* (*al-niqāba al-ʿāmma*) includes all of the duties of the special *niqāba* and adds five more: the general *naqīb* is to judge in disputes, take charge of the properties of orphans, impose penalties (*al-ḥudūd*) on criminals, marry the divorced or widowed women of the family who have no legal guardian or only an

naqīb al-Ṭālibiyyīn, and the *naqīb* of the ʿAbbāsids the *naqīb al-Hāshimiyyīn*; see al-Samʿānī, *Kitāb al-Ansāb*, 13 vols (Hyderabad, 1962–82), vol. IX, p. 7. There are a few examples of *nuqabāʾ* from other Ṭālibid families as well, such as the Jaʿfarids, the ʿAqīlīs, the ʿUmarīs and descendants of Muḥammad b. al-Ḥanafiyya, but the great majority were either Ḥasanids or Ḥusaynids. The sources sometimes also give the term *naqīb al-ʿAlawiyyīn*, but as elsewhere the terms 'ʿAlid' and 'Ṭālibid' seem to be used quite interchangeably, and *naqīb al-ʿAlawiyyīn* does not necessarily exclude other Ṭālibids. There is even one instance of a *naqīb al-Ḥasaniyyīn*, in Kufa; see al-Rāzī, *al-Shajara*, p. 78. For a *naqīb al-ʿAlawiyyīn*, see al-ʿUbaydalī, *Tahdhīb*, p. 90; for one example of a *naqīb* from the descendants of ʿUmar al-Aṭraf b. ʿAlī (in al-Nīl in Iraq), see al-Rāzī, *al-Shajara*, p. 205.

13 For different lists of the *nuqabāʾ* in Baghdad, see Massignon, 'Cadis et *naqībs*', pp. 106–15; ʿAbd al-Razzāq Kammūna al-Ḥusaynī, *Mawārid al-itḥāf fī nuqabāʾ al-ashrāf*, 2 vols, (Najaf, 1968), vol. I, pp. 45–116, and pp. 117–25 for the ʿAbbāsids; and Morimoto, 'Diffusion', p. 30, for an alternative list of early *nuqabāʾ* in Baghdad.

14 Al-Māwardī, *al-Aḥkām*, p. 82; *Ordinances of Government*, p. 107. See also Chapters 1 and 2.

15 Ibn Funduq also emphasises especially that men should marry ʿAlid wives; see Ibn Funduq, *Lubāb*, p. 722.

16 Al-Māwardī, *al-Aḥkām*, pp. 83–4.

unsuitable one, and determine the legal competence of individuals who are insane or have gone astray. For the general *niqāba*, al-Māwardī says, the candidate must be a scholar (*yakun ʿāliman min ahl al-ijtihād*) so that his judgements are correct. Indeed, in the remainder of the chapter he provides a long discussion on the respective areas of competence of the *qāḍī* and the *naqīb* and explains when the rulings of one or the other must be followed.[17]

The question of succession

How does al-Māwardī's theoretical discussion fit with the evidence from the genealogical literature? Let us begin with the succession arrangements. In short, the way in which the *niqāba* was conferred or passed on clearly varied considerably in time and place. The evidence for the *niqāba* in the Būyid period is unusually rich thanks to a number of extant investment deeds. They are preserved in the collection of writings of Abū Isḥāq Ibrāhīm al-Ṣābiʾ (d. 384/994)[18] and were all written for the famous Ḥusaynid family of Abū Aḥmad al-Ḥusayn b. Mūsā and his two sons, al-Sharīf al-Murtaḍā and al-Sharīf al-Raḍī, who held the *niqābat al-Ṭālibiyyīn* in Baghdad for more than a century.[19] As al-Māwardī had laid it out, the appointments are made by the Būyid *amīr*, or by the caliph upon the *amīr*'s recommendation; and indeed, the investment deed of 354/965 for Abū Aḥmad al-Ḥusayn b. Mūsā and a letter for the leadership of the *ḥajj* are written in the name of the caliph al-Muṭīʿ (r. 334–63/946–74).[20] According to Donohue, these are the only documents for this period written in the name of the caliph, apart from appointment letters of *amīr*s and judges.[21]

Regarding the earlier Būyid *nuqabāʾ*, the Zaydī source *Kitāb al-Ifāda* records that the *amīr* Muʿīzz al-Dawla (r. 334–54/945–67) appointed the Ḥusaynid Abū ʿAlī Aḥmad al-Kawkabī,[22] but the ʿAlids complained of his harshness towards them, so he was dismissed. Muʿīzz al-Dawla asked the ʿAlids to recommend someone else, and they chose Abū ʿAbdallāh Muḥammad b. al-Dāʿī,[23] who was eventually

17 Al-Māwardī, *al-Aḥkām*, pp. 84–6.

18 Klaus Hachmeier, *Die Briefe Abū Isḥāq Ibrāhīm al-Ṣābiʾs (st. 384/994 A.H./A.D.)* (Hildesheim, 2002), pp. 234 (nos. 23–4) and 237 (nos. 84–7). I am grateful to Klaus Hachmeier for sending me microfilm copies of letters 84–6.

19 See, for example, al-Rāzī, *al-Shajara*, pp. 97–8, or al-Marwazī, *al-Fakhrī*, p. 70.

20 Al-Ṣābiʾ, *Rasāʾil al-Ṣābiʾ wa-l-Sharīf al-Raḍī* (Kuwait, 1961), p. 217–22; for the *taqlīd al-ḥajj*, see pp. 223–6. The appointment of Abū Aḥmad al-Ḥusayn as *naqīb al-Ṭālibiyyīn* is also mentioned by Ibn al-Athīr for this year; see Ibn al-Athīr, *al-Kāmil*, vol. VIII, p. 565 (*niqābat al-ʿAlawiyyīn wa-imārat al-ḥajj*).

21 Donohue, *Buwayhid Dynasty*, p. 123. Donohue also draws attention to another letter, according to which al-Raḍī specifically asked that a second diploma for the jurisdiction over the *maẓālim* courts be written in the caliph's name; see Donohue, *Buwayhid Dynasty*, p. 124, n. 494.

22 For Abū ʿAlī al-Kawkabī, see, for example, al-Rāzī, *al-Shajara*, p. 134. Another al-Kawkabī, al-Ḥusayn b. Aḥmad b. Muḥammad b. Ismāʿīl b. Muḥammad al-Arqaṭ, rebelled in Qazwīn in 251/865 and was killed by the first *dāʿī* al-Ḥasan b. Zayd; see al-Bukhārī, *Sirr al-silsila*, p. 26; al-Iṣfahānī, *Maqātil*, p. 712; and Madelung, *Imām al-Qāsim*, p. 155.

23 He was the son of al-Ḥasan b. al-Qāsim al-Dāʿī al-Ṣaghīr, who succeeded al-Nāṣir al-Uṭrūsh as the ruler of Daylam in 304/917. For a discussion of the accounts of his rule, see Wilderd Madelung, 'Abū Isḥāq

confirmed, although only after he had been granted permission not to wear the black robes of the ʿAbbāsids.[24] The report in the *Ifāda* goes on to say that Abū ʿAbdallāh then appointed (*wallā*) deputies in Kufa, Basra, Wāsiṭ and Ahwāz.[25] The deputy in Basra was Abū Aḥmad al-Mūsawī, the later *naqīb al-Ṭālibiyyīn* in Baghdad.[26] Al-Māwardī's term *al-naqīb al-ʿāmm* is not used, neither here nor, as far as I have seen, elsewhere in the sources; nonetheless, this appointment of deputies in other cities corresponds to al-Māwardī's description of the general *naqīb*'s position.[27]

There is more evidence of a *naqīb* appointing deputies elsewhere. According to Ibn al-Jawzī, it was an innovation in 403/1012 that al-Raḍī was given the title *naqīb al-nuqabāʾ*, denoting the supervision of the *nuqabāʾ al-Ṭālibiyyīn* in the rest of the country (*niqābat nuqabāʾ al-Ṭālibiyyīn fī sāʾir al-mamālik*).[28] However, the investment deed of 354/965 for Abū Aḥmad al-Ḥusayn already says that he was to choose deputies (*al-khulafāʾ*) for the provinces (*fī al-bilād*),[29] and he seems to have instituted two of his brothers in Kufa and Wāsiṭ.[30]

As for the title *naqīb al-nuqabāʾ*, the genealogies show that more than one individual could carry the title at one time, and that the officeholder did not have to be based in Baghdad. For instance, according to Ibn Funduq, ʿAḍud al-Dawla appointed the Ḥusaynid Abū Isḥāq b. Ibrāhīm b. al-Ḥusayn b. ʿAlī b. al-Muḥsin to the *niqābat al-Ṭālibiyyīn* 'in his lands (*fī mamālikihi*)', probably meaning Fārs; Abū

al-Ṣābī on the ʿAlids of Ṭabaristān and Gīlān', *Journal of Near Eastern Studies* 26 (1967), pp. 34–41, and pp. 47–8 for Abū ʿAbdallāh b. al-Dāʿī. Ibn al-Dāʿī is one of the very few ʿAlids to appear in a biographical dictionary of the Ḥanafī school; see ʿAbd al-Qādir b. Muḥammad al-Qurashī (d. 776/1374 or 5), *Jawāhir al-muḍiyya fī ṭabaqāt al-Ḥanafiyya*, ed. ʿAbd al-Fattāḥ al-Ḥulw, 3 vols (Cairo, 1978), vol. III, pp. 127–8.

24 There is one other account of an ʿAlid chosen as *naqīb* by the ʿAlids in Baghdad. This ʿAlid, Abū Aḥmad Muḥammad b. Jaʿfar b. Muḥammad b. Jaʿfar b. al-Ḥasan b. Jaʿfar b. al-Ḥasan b. al-Ḥasan b. ʿAlī, seems to have refused the *niqāba*; see al-ʿUbaydalī, *Tahdhīb*, p. 97.

25 Al-Nāṭiq bi-l-Ḥaqq, *al-Ifāda*, pp. 181–2. Abū ʿAbdallāh appointed (*wallā*) Abū al-Ḥusayn b. ʿUbaydallāh to the *niqāba* of Kufa, Abū Aḥmad al-Mūsawī to the *niqāba* of Baṣra, Abū al-Ḥusayn al-Mūsawī to the *niqāba* of Wāsiṭ, and Abū al-Qāsim al-Zaydī to the *niqāba* of Ahwāz and its districts. This account is very similar to the one quoted in Donohue by al-Muḥallī, *al-Ḥadāʾiq al-wardiyya fī dhikr aʾimmat al-zaydiyya*; see Donohue, *Buwaydid Dynasty*, pp. 308 and 313. Madelung suggests that al-Muḥallī largely copied his account from the *Ifāda*; see Madelung, 'Abū Isḥāq al-Ṣābī', p. 47.

26 According to al-Bukhārī, *Sirr al-silsila*, p. 95, another ʿAlid from the descendants of al-ʿAbbās b. ʿAlī was the successor or deputy (*khalīfa*) of Abū ʿAbdallāh b. al-Dāʿī in Baghdad. His full name was Abū al-Ḥasan ʿAlī b. Yaḥyā b. ʿAlī b. Ibrāhīm b. al-Ḥasan b. ʿUbaydallāh b. al-ʿAbbās b. ʿAlī; see Ibn ʿInaba, *ʿUmdat al-ṭālib*, p. 358; al-Khaṭīb al-Baghdādī, *Taʾrīkh Baghdād*, vol. XII, p. 78; and Madelung, 'Abū Isḥāq al-Ṣābī', p. 48, n. 187.

27 One deed for the Sharīf al-Raḍī says that it is an *ahd bi-niqābat al-Ṭālibiyyīn khuṣūṣan*, referring probably not to the *niqāba al-khāṣṣ* of al-Māwardī but to the *niqāba* of the Ṭālibids in particular, as opposed to the one of the ʿAbbāsids. See Donohue, *Buwayhid Dynasty*, p. 313, and Hachmeier, *Briefe*, p. 237 (no. 86).

28 Ibn al-Jawzī, *al-Muntaẓam fī tārīkh al-mulūk wa al-umam*, 10 vols (Hyderabad, 1357–9[1938-40]), vol. VII, p. 260; the new edition (Beirut, 1992), vol. XV, p. 89, has only '*niqābat al-Ṭālibiyyīn fī sāʾir al-mamālik*'. Ibn al-Jawzī says that the *niqāba* was conferred to al-Raḍī by Bihāʾ al-Dawla and that al-Raḍī was the first Ṭālibid to wear the black robes of the ʿAbbāsids; see also Ibn al-Athīr, *al-Kāmil*, vol. IX, p. 242.

29 Al-Ṣābiʾ, *Rasāʾil*, vol. I, p. 153.

30 Al-Rāzī, *al-Shajara*, p. 97.

Isḥāq b. Ibrāhīm then took the title *naqīb al-nuqabāʾ*.[31] At about the same time, Abū al-Ḥusayn Muḥammad b. Aḥmad (d. 339/951) and his son Abū Muḥammad Yaḥyā (d. 376/986) from the Zubāra family held the title *naqīb al-nuqabāʾ* in Nishapur, as did the Ḥasanids who succeeded them.[32]

In which districts or towns the *naqīb al-nuqabāʾ* appointed deputies and to what extent the spheres of authority were clearly defined cannot be established from the sources. Perhaps the title was simply an added honorific, at least in some cases.

Generally, the information on who was appointed and how is much patchier for periods and areas other than Būyid Baghdad, although there are a few more examples of investment deeds: Maurice Pomerantz has recently drawn attention to a letter of appointment by al-Ṣāḥib b. ʿAbbād, which depicts the Būyid vizier appointing a *naqīb* in Rayy.[33] For the Saljūq period, one document is preserved in the *ʿAtabat al-kataba*, which names a certain Murtaḍā Jamāl al-Dīn Abū al-Ḥasan al-ʿAlawī as *naqīb* of Jurjān, Dihistān and Astarābād.[34] Al-Qalqashandī (d. 821/1418) also includes one template deed in his *Ṣubḥ al-aʿshā*.[35] Hossein Modarressi has suggested

31 This is recorded in the section for the '*naqīb* Shīrāz'; see Ibn Funduq, *Lubāb*, p. 566. Al-Rāzī says that he was the *naqīb* in Shīrāz. See al-Rāzī, *al-Shajara*, p. 99. ʿAḍud al-Dawla took over rule in Fārs in 338/949; see Donohue, *Buwayhid Dynasty*, p. 24.

32 See Ibn Funduq, *Lubāb*, pp. 603–9. Al-ʿUbaydalī calls the Buṭḥānī Ḥasanid Abū Muḥammad al-Ḥasan *naqīb al-nuqabāʾ bi-Khurāsān*; see al-ʿUbaydalī, *Tahdhīb*, p. 116. There are a number of other examples of a *naqīb al-nuqabāʾ*, including in Egypt (al-Rāzī, *al-Shajara*, p. 118), in Ghazna (al-Marwazī, *al-Fakhrī*, p. 63; according to al-Rāzī, *al-Shajara*, p. 168, and Ibn Funduq, *Lubāb*, p. 727, this *naqīb*'s two sons succeeded him in the *niqāba* there but were only called '*naqīb*')), in Medina (al-Rāzī, *al-Shajara*, p. 107: Abū al-Ḥusayn ʿAlī, a descendant of Mūsā al-Kāẓim, was first the *amīr* in Wādī al-Qurrā and then became *naqīb al-nuqabāʾ* in Medina [*thumma ṣāra naqīb al-nuqabāʾ bi-l-Madīna*]), in Āmul (al-Rāzī, *al-Shajara*, p. 70), in Balkh (al-Marwazī, *al-Fakhrī*, p. 119) and in Basra (al-Marwazī, *al-Fakhrī*, p. 119).

33 There is a question mark to the place, but it is clear that the appointment was not in Baghdad; see Pomerantz, 'Licit Magic', p. 125.

34 I have not been able to identify him. See Muʾayyid al-Dawla al-Juvaynī (fl. 1118–57), *ʿAtabat al-kataba* (Tehran, 1950), pp. 63–4. For a study of the work, see Ann Lambton, 'The Administration of Sanjar's Empire as Illustrated in the "ʿAtabat al-kataba"', *Bulletin of the School of Oriental and African Studies* 20 (1957), pp. 367–88.

35 This is of a generic kind and does not name any particular person; see Aḥmad b. ʿAlī al-Qalqashandī (d. 821/1418), *Ṣubḥ al-aʿshā fī ṣināʿat al-inshāʾ*, 14 vols (Cairo, 1331/1913), vol. X, pp. 405–9. The source for this document is the fifth-/eleventh-century scribe ʿAlī b. Khalaf, who was one of al-Qalqashandī's main sources. He was a secretary for the Fāṭimids and in 437/1045 composed his *Elements of Good Written Style (Māwadd al-bayān)*, which survives and has been published by Fuat Sezgin (Frankfurt, 1986; reproduced from MS 4128, Fatih Collection, Süleymaniye Library, Istanbul). See also S. M. Stern, *Fāṭimid Decrees: Original Documents from the Fāṭimid Chancery* (Oxford, 1965), p. 105; ʿAbd al-Ḥamīd Ṣāliḥ, 'Une source de Qalqašandī, Māwadd al-bayān et son auteur, ʿAlī b. Ḫalaf', *Arabica* 20 (1973), pp. 192–200; and S. A. Bonebakker, 'A Fatimid Manual for Secretaries', *Annali dell'Instituto Orientale di Napoli* 37, n.s. 27 (1977), pp. 295–337. The role of the *naqīb* under the Fāṭimids and the Mamlūks may well have differed somewhat from that in the eastern Islamic world. According to Madelung, 'the *naqīb al-ashrāf* in addition to his official role as syndic of the descendants of the Prophet apparently often acted as the unofficial leader of the Imāmī Shiites, who in the fanatically anti-Shiite Mamlūk society could have no official representation. This unofficial role, however, greatly enhanced their importance for the Mamlūk regime'; see Wilferd Madelung, review of *Muslim Cities in the later Middle Ages*, by Ira Lapidus, *Journal of Near Eastern Studies* 29 (1970), p. 134.

that the *naqīb* was generally appointed by local rulers from the Būyid period onwards;[36] indeed, there are few instances of caliphal appointments in the later period.[37]

The majority of examples dating from the second/tenth to the fourth/twelfth centuries do not say how the *naqīb* was appointed or whether he was appointed at all. In most cases the *niqāba* was held within one family for a number of generations and passed on from father to son, or to a brother or a nephew.[38] Expressions such as '*wa-fīhim al-niqāba*' (and they [a particular family] held the *niqāba*) are ubiquitous. Al-Bukhārī, for example, says about the descendants of Muḥammad b. ʿAlī b. Ḥamza b. Yaḥyā b. al-Ḥusayn b. Zayd al-Shahīd that they were *nuqabāʾ* and *ruʾasāʾ* in Kufa, Basra and Wāsiṭ;[39] and al-Marwazī reports that Abū al-Ḥusayn al-Ṭāhir, a descendant of al-Ḥusayn al-Ṣaghīr, had lots of offspring in Balkh who were in charge of the *niqāba* there (*lahu ʿaqib kathīr bi-Balkh fīhim al-nuqabāʾ bihā*).[40]

Indeed, the pattern of succession was at times explicitly hereditary: In his discussion of the *naqīb* of Iṣfahān in the early sixth/twelfth century, Ibn Funduq even uses the term 'heir apparent' (*walī ʿahd*). The son was to succeed his father as *naqīb* and to continue the administration of the endowments and benefits (*al-awqāf wa-l-maṣāliḥ*).[41] The explicitness of this phrase is perhaps exceptional, and this family in Iṣfahān may have become particularly powerful and influential, especially among other ʿAlids.[42] However, many other examples confirm that within a given locality, the office was frequently passed on within the family. In Nishapur, for example, only two families (the first Ḥusaynid, the second Ḥasanid) were in charge of the *niqāba* from the late third/ninth century until the early sixth/twelfth century, if not later.[43] Another branch of the Ḥasanid family in Nishapur was also head of the *sādāt* in Hamadān. They had been there since the late fourth/tenth century and were in charge of the *riʾāsa* and the *niqāba* well into the sixth/twelfth century.[44]

36 Hossein Modarressi, 'Sukhanī chand dar bārah-yi niqābat-i sādāt va barnāma-yi kār-i naqīb', *Āyanda* 10–12 (1358/[1979]), p. 756.

37 Morimoto records one instance in the late sixth/twelfth century in which the caliph al-Nāṣir is said to have appointed the *naqīb* in Khurāsān. See Morimoto, 'Diffusion', p. 36; see also al-Marwazī, *al-Fakhrī*, p. 19.

38 There are many examples, from a wide range of places and periods. For examples of father to son succession, see al-ʿUmarī, *al-Majdī*, p. 294 (Damascus in 347/958); al-Rāzī, *al-Shajara*, p. 168 (Wāsiṭ) and p. 193 (Iṣfahān); and al-Marwazī, *al-Fakhrī*, p. 119 (Basra; the author met a son there in 598/1201). For uncle to nephew succession, see al-Rāzī, *al-Shajara*, p. 131 (Qum). For brother to brother succession, see Ibn Funduq, *Lubāb*, p. 595 (Ṭūs and Mashhad; one brother died in 522/1128) and p. 609 (Nishapur); al-ʿUmarī, *al-Majdī*, pp. 317–20 (Baghdad); al-Rāzī, *al-Shajara*, p. 166 (Balkh); and al-ʿUbaydalī, *Tahdhīb*, p. 36 (Kufa).

39 Al-Bukhārī, *Sirr al-silsila*, p. 64.

40 Al-Marwazī, *al-Fakhrī*, p. 62.

41 Ibn Funduq, *Lubāb*, p. 562. Zayd al-Shahīd is Zayd b. ʿAlī b. al-Ḥusayn b. ʿAlī.

42 This *naqīb* in Iṣfahān seems to have been very highly regarded among other ʿAlids, and they supported him in the *niqāba*; see Ibn Funduq, *Lubāb*, p. 562.

43 Al-Rāzī, writing in the late sixth/twelfth century, says that the Ḥasanids still held the *niqāba* in his day; see al-Rāzī, *al-Shajara*, p. 58.

44 Ibn Funduq, *Lubāb*, p. 560, where he also gives the genealogies of the Hamdānid *sādāt*; al-Marwazī, *al-Fakhrī*, p. 136.

Who were the *nuqabāʾ*?

If the succession of the *niqāba* was hereditary within the family, the question of who the next *naqīb* would be was of course more or less answered. When the *niqāba* was passed on to a son, it appears that it was generally the eldest son. There are some examples where this was not the case, such as with the Sharīf al-Raḍī and the Sharīf al-Murtaḍā in Baghdad, where the younger son became the *naqīb* first; however, the genealogies explicitly comment on this sequence, thus suggesting that it may be exceptional.[45]

But what if the *niqāba* was not passed on within the family but was rather transferred to someone else? How was the *naqīb* chosen in that case? In very general terms, there were three principal possibilities: the new *naqīb* had the support of local factions, the new *naqīb* had a good standing with the ruler, or the new *naqīb* had family relations to the previous *naqīb* or other influential ʿAlids.

As was the case with the choice of the *qāḍī*, *khaṭīb* (public preacher) or *raʾīs*, the support of local factions was often crucial in deciding who the *naqīb* would be.[46] The case of the two rival families in Nishapur illustrates this clearly. In 395/1004, the *niqāba* was transferred from the long-established Zubāra Ḥusaynids to the more recently arrived Buṭḥānī Ḥasanids, apparently because the Buṭḥānī family was supported locally, having made strategic alliances with both of the dominant Nishapuri legal schools.[47] Indeed, Ibn Funduq, in his local history of Bayhaq, says that it was the Shāfiʿīs who supported the Buṭḥānīs over the Āl Zubāra for the *niqāba*: 'The followers of the imām Muṭṭalibī Shāfiʿī, may God be pleased with him, considered it advisable to help the sons of the Sayyid Abū ʿAbdallāh [the Buṭḥānīs], and the *niqāba* passed from this line to the other one, and the sons of the Sayyid al-Ajall Abū ʿAlī [the Āl Zubāra] became dispersed'.[48] The Buṭḥānīs were Sunni, and Everett Rowson has therefore suggested that the transfer was an anti-Shiʿite move on the part of the Ghaznavid rulers.[49] This may have been the case, but the Shāfiʿī support clearly carried some weight in the selection of the new *naqīb*. As discussed in the previous chapter, there was also a marriage connection between the Buṭḥānīs and the Shāfiʿīs, which was probably another factor: Abū Muḥammad al-Ḥasan (d. 402/1011), the first *naqīb* of the Buṭḥānī family in Nishapur, was married to al-Ḥurra bt. al-Imām al-Muwaffaq Hibat Allāh b. al-Qāḍī ʿUmar b. Muḥammad, the chief of the Shāfiʿīs (*muqaddam aṣḥāb al-Shāfiʿī*) in Nishapur.[50]

45 See, for instance, al-Rāzī, *al-Shajara*, p. 97.

46 Richard Bulliet has suggested that the official appointment of the *qāḍī*, *khaṭīb* or *raʾīs* was similarly determined by local factions; see Bulliet, 'Local Politics in Eastern Iran under the Ghaznavids and Saljuqs', *Iranian Studies* 11 (1978), pp. 47–9.

47 See Chapter 2.

48 Ibn Funduq, *Tārīkh-i Bayhaq*, p. 55, translated in Bosworth, *Ghaznavids*, p. 197.

49 Rowson argues that the transfer of the *niqāba* to the Ḥasanids 'is probably to be seen as an anti-Shīʿite move, under the militant Sunnī regime of Maḥmūd of Ghazna'; see Everett Rowson, 'Religion and Politics in the Career of Badīʿ al-Zamān Hamadhānī', *Journal of the American Oriental Society* 107 (1987), p. 657.

50 Ibn Funduq, *Lubāb*, pp. 608–9.

Moreover, in addition to garnering local support and making strategic marriage alliances with both Nishapuri *madhhab*s, the Buṭḥānīs also took pains to cultivate their relations with the dynastic rulers, the Ghaznavids and the Saljūqs. One member of the family, Abū al-Qāsim Zayd, took part in the Somnath raids into Gujarat in India with Maḥmūd b. Sebuktekīn in 416/1025, and one source says that 'for that reason he was then given the *niqāba* of Nishapur in the 420s'.[51] In fact, this was a most significant appointment, as it was this very same ʿAlid who took a leading role in the first surrender of the city to the Saljūqs in 428/1036.[52] But he maintained his loyalty to the Ghaznavids, so when the Saljūqs established permanent control of the city in 431/1039 after a brief Ghaznavid reconquest, the *niqāba* went to another branch of the family, to a nephew of Abū al-Qāsim called Abū ʿAlī Muḥammad. The latter was entrusted with the *niqāba* (*fuwwiḍat ilayhi al-niqāba fī ʿahd . . .*) by the Saljūq Malikshāh and was even appointed as the *naqīb al-nuqabāʾ al-Hāshimiyya*.[53] Both Ghaznavids and Saljūqs thus integrated this family into their own structures while recognising their power at a local level.

Apart from local factions and rulers, family connections clearly figured in determining who would become the *naqīb*. This is particularly apparent in cases in which a family held the *niqāba* in one place and was then also established (whether or not appointed) in the position elsewhere. One particularly interesting example, involving a female *naqība*, is recorded for Marw in the fourth/tenth and fifth/eleventh centuries. Abū ʿUbaydallāh b. al-Ḥasan, a descendant of Jaʿfar b. al-Ḥasan b. al-Ḥasan b. ʿAlī, had been *naqīb* in Farāgha.[54] His son Abū al-Ḥasan Muḥammad became *naqīb al-nuqabāʾ* in Marw because he married the daughter of the previous *naqīb* there, Abū al-Qāsim al-Mūsawī (lived 440/1048).[55] Abū al-Ḥasan's daughter, who was simply known as *al-sayyida*, then took charge of the *niqāba* in Marw (*tawallat al-niqāba bi-Marw*); as far as I have seen, she is the only female to have been in charge of this office. Her grandfather Abū al-Qāsim al-Mūsawī was clearly an influential man. He reportedly received the *niqāba* as part of his spoils (*min nāfalatihi*),[56] and according to al-Marwazī, Malikshāh had invited him to take the oath of allegiance to the caliphate. He left no male offspring, so after his son-in-law and his granddaughter the *niqāba* in Marw passed over to his brother's sons.[57]

51 Ibn Funduq, *Lubāb*, p. 604.

52 See Bosworth, *Ghaznavids*, pp. 252–7, for the report on the surrender to the Ghaznavid court.

53 Ibn Funduq, *Lubāb*, p. 607.

54 His full name was Abū ʿUbaydallāh b. al-Ḥasan b. Muḥammad b. Aḥmad b. Muḥammad b. Aḥmad b. ʿUbaydallāh *al-amīr* b. ʿAbdallāh b. al-Ḥasan b. Jaʿfar b. al-Ḥasan b. al-Ḥasan b. ʿAlī. ʿUbaydallāh had been *amīr* in Kufa and Mecca and, according to al-Rāzī, in charge of the *ṣadaqāt* of ʿAlī and the *ṣadaqāt* of Fāṭima at Fadak; see al-Rāzī, *al-Shajara*, p. 52. For Farāgha in Khurāsān, see Le Strange, *Lands*, p. 284. For Fadak, see also Ivan Hrbek, 'Muḥammads Nachlass und die ʿAliden', *Archiv Orientalni* 18 (1950), pp. 144–5.

55 His full name was Abū al-Qāsim ʿAlī b. Mūsā b. Isḥāq b. al-Ḥusayn b. al-Ḥusayn b. Isḥāq b. Mūsā al-Kāẓim. The date is given by Ibn Funduq, *Lubāb*, p. 575, who quotes from ʿAlī b. al-Ḥusayn al-Bākharzī's *Dumyat al-Qaṣr*. Al-Bākharzī (d. 467/1075) visited Abū al-Qāsim in 440/1048.

56 Al-Rāzī, *al-Shajara*, p. 54.

57 Al-Marwazī, *al-Fakhrī*, p. 19. I have not found further references to the suggestion that Malikshāh intended

There are a number of other examples of influential families whose offspring held the *niqāba* in different cities. The *nuqabāʾ* and *ruʾasāʾ* of Qum in the late fourth/tenth and early fifth/eleventh centuries, for instance, were descendants of the Ḥusaynid Aḥmad b. Muḥammad b. Ismāʿīl b. ʿAbdallāh al-Arqaṭ. According to al-Rāzī, one member of this family, Abū Jaʿfar Muḥammad b. ʿAlī, was the *naqīb* in Qum and was then given the *niqāba* in Rayy by the Kākwayhid ʿAlāʾ al-Dawla (*walī niqāba bi-l-Rayy fī ʿahd Ibn Kākwayh ʿAlāʾ al-Dawla*). His son was the *naqīb al-Ṭālibiyyīn* of Rayy after him.[58] Similarly, the Buṭḥānī Ḥasanids were in charge of the *niqāba* in Zanjān, Nishapur, Hamadān and Iṣfahān in the fourth/tenth and fifth/eleventh centuries.[59]

Responsibilities of the *naqīb*: genealogy, money and social control

The three duties of the *naqīb* described by al-Māwardī – genealogical, social, and financial – are all confirmed by the evidence of the Ṭālibid genealogies. Some examples of the *naqīb*'s involvement in genealogical control were discussed in Chapter 2; for instance, the registers of the genealogists seem to have been kept by the *naqīb*.[60] In many cases where the sources describe a *naqīb* as doing something (as opposed to mere mentions of a *naqīb*'s name, title and place), the reference relates to a genealogical issue, such as determining the validity of a genealogical claim.[61]

The focus on genealogy may be a consequence of the particular interests of the authors whose works are examined here. However, it appears not only that some of the early *nuqabāʾ* were also genealogists and some of the early genealogists also *nuqabāʾ* – such as the alleged first *naqīb* in Kufa, al-Ḥusayn b. Aḥmad, or the alleged first genealogist in Medina, Yaḥyā b. al-Ḥasan al-ʿAqīqī[62] – but also that the supervision of genealogies remained a major part, if not the main part, of the *naqīb*'s responsibilities. Ibn Funduq, in his brief section on the *niqāba*, refers mainly to the *naqīb*'s role in investigating and protecting Prophetic lineages: He cites *ḥadīth* and poetry to say that the *naqīb* is like an investigator (*al-bāḥith*) of the lineages of the

---

to transfer the caliphate to the ʿAlid. Al-Marwazī goes on to say that Abū al-Qāsim's brother, Abū Muḥammad Isḥāq, was the deputy (*khalīfa*) over the *niqāba* and the Mūsawiyya in Marw. Ibn Funduq, *Lubāb*, pp. 575–6, gives the names of two more *nuqabāʾ* from this branch of the family (*al-rahṭ*), of whom Abū al-Qāsim was the great-uncle (*ʿamm abīhi*). The first of these was *raʾīs* in Marw and *naqīb* of the *sāda*, and his brother was killed by Khwārazm Shāh al-Sirr b. Muḥammad in 536/1141.

58 Al-Rāzī, *al-Shajara*, pp. 130–2. This family also held the *niqāba* in Baghdad later on.

59 Ibn Funduq, *Lubāb*, pp. 561 (Hamadān), 589 (Zanjān) and 602 (Nishapur). For Iṣfahān, see al-Rāzī, *al-Shajara*, p. 61. Another member of this family, Abū ʿAbdallāh Muḥammad al-Aṣghar *al-shāʿir*, is recorded to have been *naqīb al-Ṭālibiyyīn* in Kufa (see al-Rāzī, *al-Shajara*, p. 63), and yet another, the later Zaydī imām al-Nāṭiq bi-l-Ḥaqq (d. 424/1033), is described as *naqīb* in Jurjān; see al-Rāzī, *al-Shajara*, p. 65.

60 For the *jarāʾid al-nuqabāʾ*, see, for instance, al-ʿUbaydalī, *Tahdhīb*, p. 39, and Ibn Funduq, *Lubāb*, p. 696.

61 Ibn Funduq, *Lubāb*, p. 657.

62 Al-Ḥusayn b. ʿUmar in Kufa is discussed in more detail below. For examples where Yaḥyā b. al-Ḥasan al-ʿAqīqī is called a *naqīb*, see al-ʿUbaydalī, *Tahdhīb*, p. 231, and Ibn Ṭabāṭabā, *Muntaqila*, p. 312, cited in Morimoto, 'Diffusion', p. 26. There is also a number of later examples of *nuqabāʾ* who were also genealogists; see, for instance, al-Rāzī, *al-Shajara*, p. 134, for the *nassāba* and *naqīb* Ibn Khadāʿ in Egypt.

*sayyid*s, and he must study them until all of those who belong to the family are included and all of those who do not belong to it are excluded.[63] He also suggests that the *naqīb* should employ two genealogists, one ʿAlid and one non-ʿAlid, so as to fulfil his responsibilities in safeguarding the lineages.[64]

The keeping of genealogical registers was of course important also for financial matters: Only those who were recorded could receive a pension. Regarding one ʿAlid family whose genealogy was disputed, al-ʿUmarī reports that 'they were confirmed in the *jarīda* of Shīrāz and received payment from the endowment of the ʿAlids there, but they were eventually removed' (*wa-thubitū fī jarīdat Shīrāz wa-akhadhū min waqf al-ʿalawiyyīn minhā wa-dufiʿū*),[65] presumably after their false claims had been uncovered.

In Qum, payments were apparently made partly in kind: According to al-Qummī, there were 331 ʿAlids (men and children) in Āva, Qum and Kāshān in 371/981–2, and their monthly allowance or pension (*waẓīfa*) was thirty *mann* of bread and ten silver dirhams. Al-Qummī adds that when one of the ʿAlids died, his name was erased from the book of monthly wages (*kitāb-i mushāhara*).[66] Even though the *naqīb* is not explicitly mentioned as being involved in the distribution of these pensions, it is likely that it was precisely the keeping of these kinds of lists that he was in charge of.

There are a few other references to endowments for and payments to the ʿAlids that were administered by the family: The *walī ʿahd* in Iṣfahān was also in charge of the endowments and benefits (*al-awqāf wa-l-maṣāliḥ*), and al-ʿUmarī mentions an ʿAlid who was in charge (*mutawallī*) of a *waqf* in Aleppo, although he does not explicitly call that person a *naqīb*.[67] Indeed, the administration of endowments does not seem to have been necessarily part of the *naqīb*'s duties; this is also suggested by the investment deeds from the Būyid period, where the certificates for the endowments for Basra, the district of Dijla,[68] Baghdad and the Sawād are given separately from the appointment of the *niqāba*.[69]

In addition to financial matters, the *naqīb*'s duties often included oversight in social terms. A Būyid deed of 354/965 authorises the *naqīb* to judge 'according to the custom'; the Saljūq document in the *ʿAtabat al-kataba* similarly instructs the local officials (*al-nuwwāb*) to hand over all of the affairs of the *sayyid*s to the *naqīb*, including their chastisement (*mālish*) for offences.[70] However, there is little evidence

63 Ibn Funduq, *Lubāb*, pp. 718 and 722.

64 Ibn Funduq, *Lubāb*, p. 722.

65 Al-ʿUmarī, *al-Majdī*, p. 304.

66 Al-Qummī, *Tārīkh-i Qum*, p. 220; Ann Lambton, 'An Account of the *Tārīkhi Qum*', *Bulletin of the School of Oriental and African Studies* 12 (1948), p. 596.

67 Al-ʿUmarī, *al-Majdī*, p. 462. The ʿAlid was a descendant of ʿUmar b. ʿAlī b. Abī Ṭālib.

68 Dijla is a district on the Lower Tigris; see Le Strange, *Lands*, p. 80.

69 Hachmeier, *Briefe*, p. 237 (nos 84 and 87). An investment deed for the *niqāba*, in contrast, includes the supervision of the *maẓālim* courts and the *ḥajj* (no. 86), although there is also another, separate deed for the *maẓālim* courts (no. 85).

70 Al-Juvaynī, *ʿAtabat al-kataba*, p. 64; cited in Ann Lambton, *Continuity and Change in Medieval Persia* (London, 1988).

of a *naqīb* actually applying his jurisdiction over the ʿAlids (except for adjudicating genealogical matters). I have found no reports of a case being handed over to a *naqīb* because of the involvement of an ʿAlid party. Accounts of a *naqīb* acting as a *qāḍī*, as al-Māwardī had suggested, are also noticeably absent from the sources. There are some examples of *nuqabāʾ* who were also *qāḍī*s, so if a non-ʿAlid judging ʿAlids was seen as a problem, this may have been one way of circumventing it.[71]

The purpose of this supervisory role was to ensure that the family's honour be respected. Of this the ʿAlids themselves had to be reminded at times, it seems: Ibn Funduq admionishes that the *naqīb* must keep his flock from the pursuit of illegal gains and ensure that the poor *sādāt* 'find employment and work, so that there is no need for them to go begging in the mosques (*lā yuḥtāj kull wāḥid minhum al-suʾāl fī al-masājid*)'.[72] Clearly, the situation varied considerably from place to place, but it seems fair to suggest that the role of the *naqīb* was generally not so much judicial as punitive, directed either towards those ʿAlids who caused trouble or harmed others or towards non-ʿAlids who falsely claimed an ʿAlid genealogy.[73]

Thus, Madelung's translation of the word *naqīb* as 'registrar' fits its apparent meaning better than the commonly used 'syndic', which implies an authority in legal matters that is not confirmed by the available evidence.[74] But whether or not the *niqāba* gave the ʿAlids real autonomy in every area, its emergence signified the rise of the descendants of the Prophet to the top of the social hierarchy. They received and demanded special treatment on account of their descent, and they had begun to take an interest in preserving and furthering their privileged status.

Origins of the *niqāba*

Although the *nuqabāʾ* became ubiquitous in the medieval period, accounts of the first *naqīb* or the first caliph to introduce the *niqāba* appear surprisingly late in the literature. The fourth-/tenth-century genealogist al-Bukhārī, for example, refers to the *nuqabāʾ* of various places, such as Medina, Fārs, Jurjān and Rayy. He thus clearly knows of the office (unless the terms were inserted by later redactors, which seems unlikely based on a close reading of the text), but he does not mention a first *naqīb* and says nothing about the origins of the *niqāba*.[75]

71 See, for example, al-Rāzī, *al-Shajara*, pp. 183 (Wāsiṭ), 175 (Mecca) and 118 (Damascus).

72 Ibn Funduq, *Lubāb*, p. 722.

73 Professor Modarressi pointed out to me that in the later period the punitive measures were also sometimes directed at prominent non-ʿAlid members of the Shiʿite community. Al-Dhahabī (d. 748/1348) describes how the *naqīb* of al-Shām ordered a prominent Shiʿite, Abū al-Qāsim al-Ḥusayn b. al-ʿŪd (d. 677/1278), to be publicly humiliated for a statement that he allegedly made against the companions of the Prophet; see Muḥammad b. Aḥmad al-Dhahabī, *Taʾrīkh al-Islām wa-ṭabaqāt al-mashāhīr wa-l-aʿlām*, ed. ʿUmar ʿAbd al-Salām Tadmurī, 52 vols (Beirut, 1987–), vol. L (covering the years 671–80/1272–81), p. 337; I am grateful to Professor Modarressi for this reference.

74 Madelung, 'Abū Isḥāq al-Ṣābī', p. 47.

75 See al-Bukhārī, *Sirr al-silsila*, pp. 28 (Rayy) and 74 (Fārs, Jurjān and Medina; for Medina he does not give the genealogy of one particular ʿAlid but says that the descendants of Mūsā b. ʿAlī b. al-Ḥusayn b. ʿAlī b. al-Ḥusayn were *nuqabāʾ sāda* there).

One of the earliest mentions of a first *naqīb* is by Ibn ʿInaba, who calls the Ḥusaynid al-Ḥusayn b. Aḥmad 'the first *naqīb* to govern the Ṭālibids collectively' (*awwal naqīb waliya ʿalā sāʾir al-Ṭālibiyyīn kāffatan*).[76] The text gives no explicit explanation of why al-Ḥusayn was given the title or what it implied. Evidently, a full version of the account is found only in the *Zahrat al-maqūl* by Ibn Shadqam (d. 1033/1623–4), suggesting, as Morimoto says, that 'many elements in the narrative are additions made over time'.[77] According to the account, al-Ḥusayn b. Aḥmad went to the caliph (the name of the caliph is not given) after the killing of his uncle Yaḥyā b. ʿUmar in 250/864–5. He urgently requested that the ruler (*al-ḥākim*) of the Ṭālibids be one of them, someone whose authority they would accept and who would know their numbers, whereabouts and positions, and that the Turkish generals of the ʿAbbāsids would not rule over them (*wa-lā yuḥkam fīhim atrāk banī al-ʿAbbās*). The caliph approved (*istaṣwaba*) his suggestion, and it was the Ṭālibids themselves who selected al-Ḥusayn b. Aḥmad as *naqīb*.[78]

Yaḥyā b. ʿUmar's uprising and killing seems to have been a momentous event for the Ṭālibids, and there are numerous stories about it.[79] According to al-Ṭabarī's version, the reasons for this uprising were basically financial. Yaḥyā b. ʿUmar 'was hard pressed by his creditors' in Medina, and neither ʿUmar b. al-Faraj al-Rukhkhajī, who was entrusted with the affairs of the Ṭālibids (*wa-huwa yatawallā amr al-Ṭālibiyyīn*), nor the Turkish general Waṣīf in Sāmarrāʾ, would give him an allowance (*rizq*); the latter reportedly exclaimed, '[W]hy should anything be given to the likes of you!'[80] Because he was so insulted by these remarks, Yaḥyā b. ʿUmar went to Kufa, gathered followers, among them Bedouins and Zaydīs, and called for a revolt in the name of the most suitable from the family of the Prophet (*al-riḍā min āl Muḥammad*). He was killed in 250/864–5 by the Ṭāhirid Muḥammad b. Ṭāhir.[81]

76 His full genealogy is al-Ḥusayn b. Aḥmad b. ʿUmar b. Yaḥyā b. al-Ḥusayn b. Zayd b. ʿAlī b. al-Ḥusayn b. ʿAlī; Ibn ʿInaba, *ʿUmdat al-ṭālib*, p. 274; new edn (Qum, 2004), p. 337; Morimoto, 'Formation and Development', pp. 558–9; Morimoto, 'Diffusion', p. 23; and Modarressi, 'Sukhanī chand', pp. 756–7. See also the editor's note in Ibn Ṭabāṭabā, *Muntaqila*, pp. 274–5.

77 Morimoro, 'Diffusion', p. 24.

78 Ibn Shadqam, *Zahrat al-maqūl* (Najaf, 1961), p. 76; see Modarressi, 'Sukhanī chand', p. 757; Morimoto, 'Formation and Development', p. 559; and Morimoto, 'Diffusion', p. 8.

79 Such as the account given by the Arab poet and thinker al-Tanūkhī (d. 384/994) according to which this killing sealed the fate of the Ṭāhirids; see al-Tanūkhī, *Nishwār al-muḥāḍara*, ed. ʿAbbūd al- Shāljī, 8 vols (Beirut, 1971–3), vol. II, pp. 240–2.

80 Al-Ṭabarī, *Taʾrīkh*, vol. III, pp. 1516–23, year 250/864; for Waṣīf, see Matthew Gordon, *The Breaking of a Thousand Swords: A History of the Turkish Military of Samarra, A.H. 200–275/815–889 C.E.* (Albany, NY, 2001), p. 43 and index; for ʿUmar b. al-Faraj al-Rukhkhajī, see also al-Iṣfahānī, *Maqātil*, pp. 369, 396, 406 and 420 (Yaḥyā b. ʿUmar), and Ibn ʿInaba, *ʿUmdat al-ṭālib*, p. 316 (on al-Qāsim b. ʿAbdallāh, see below).

81 Al-Ṭabarī, *Taʾrīkh*, vol. III, pp. 1,516–23; see also al-Iṣfahānī, *Maqātil*, pp. 639–64, and Ibn al-Athīr, *al-Kāmil*, vol. VII, p. 126 (year 250). According to al-Ṭabarī, the Ṭāhirid received some land grants in Ṭabaristān as a reward, 'to mark his success in killing Yaḥyā b. ʿUmar and the subsequent entry of his officers and troops into Kufa'; see al-Ṭabarī, *Taʾrīkh*, vol. III, p. 1,524.

The earliest *nuqabāʾ* in Kufa

The historical sources do not mention al-Ḥusayn b. Aḥmad as the first *naqīb*, nor do al-ʿAqīqī or al-Bukhārī, the two genealogists who lived at the time that was closest to the events. Al-Bukhārī briefly mentions the uprising of Yaḥyā b. ʿUmar against the caliph al-Mustaʿīn (r. 248–52/862–6) and notes that the rebel's head was sent to Sāmarrāʾ – but he says nothing of the nephew al-Ḥusayn b. Aḥmad and the *niqāba*.[82] Nevertheless, an investigation into the affairs of this family does shed some light on the early *niqāba*: not only did this family, or the descendants of Yaḥyā b. al-Ḥusayn b. Zayd b. ʿAlī b. al-Ḥusayn b. ʿAlī more broadly, supply a series of *nuqabāʾ* in Kufa in the fourth/tenth century,[83] it is also likely that there was a *naqīb* in late third-/ninth-century Kufa before there was one anywhere else in Iraq.[84]

There are, however, a number of candidates for the early *niqāba* in Kufa other than the alleged first *naqīb*. Al-Masʿūdī, for example, suggests that in the period after the defeat of Yaḥyā b. ʿUmar, the *naqīb* in Kufa was ʿAlī b. Muḥammad b. Jaʿfar al-Ḥimmānī *al-shāʿir*. Al-Ḥimmānī refused to greet the *ṣāḥib jaysh* al-Ḥusayn b. Ismāʿīl when he returned to the city after his victory over Yaḥyā b. ʿUmar; later on he was imprisoned by al-Muwaffaq, the brother of the caliph al-Muʿtamid, because he was accused of planning another uprising.[85] In the genealogies, this ʿAlid is singled out as a famous poet (with the full genealogy ʿAlī b. Muḥammad b. Jaʿfar b. Muḥammad b. Zayd b. ʿAlī b. al-Ḥusayn), who had descendants in Kufa – but he is not said to have been a *naqīb*.[86]

The Ṭālibid genealogists, such as al-ʿUmarī, al-ʿUbaydalī and Ibn Ṭabāṭabā, mention two further *nuqabāʾ* in Kufa, who belong to the same generation as the alleged first *naqīb* al-Ḥusayn b. Aḥmad. Both of them are Ḥasanids, descendants of Muḥammad al-Nafs al-Zakiyya: Abū Jaʿfar Muḥammad b. al-Ḥasan b. Muḥammad al-Kābulī b. ʿAbdallāh al-Ashtar b. Muḥammad al-Nafs al-Zakiyya and his brother al-Ḥusayn b. al-Ḥasan.[87] There was a marriage connection with the Ḥusaynid

82 Al-Bukhārī, *Sirr al-silsila*, p. 62.

83 Ibn Funduq records that the *naqīb* in Kufa in the early sixth/twelfth century still came from this family; see Ibn Funduq, *Lubāb*, pp. 540–1. He also mentions the alleged first *naqīb* al-Ḥusayn b. Aḥmad (here as Abū ʿAlī), calling him '*raʾīs al-Kūfa wa-naqībuhā*'.

84 This is unsurprising given the importance of the ʿAlids in the town as well as its large pro-ʿAlid population. See also Morimoto, 'Diffusion', p. 19. For this section generally see the family tree 'The early *niqāba* in Kufa'.

85 Al-Masʿūdī, *Murūj*, vol. IV, pp. 64–5 (§ 3,029–32). Al-Masʿūdī says that he was the most senior ʿAlid in Kufa at the time and refers the reader to another book on the Ṭālibids, called *Kitāb Mazāhir al-akhbār wa-ṭarāʾif al-āthār*; see Ahmad Shboul, *Al-Masʿūdī and His World* (London, 1979), p. 66. Elsewhere al-Masʿūdī says that the slayings of the ʿAlids are discussed in a third book, the *Kitāb Akhbār al-zamān*; al-Masʿūdī, *Murūj*, vol. IV, p. 153 (§ 2,412); for the *Akhbār al-zamān*, see Shboul, *Al-Masʿūdī*, p. 72. Al-Iṣfahānī, *Maqātil*, p. 662, quotes a poem by ʿAlī b. Muḥammad al-Ḥimmānī about the slaying of Yaḥyā b. ʿUmar.

86 See, for example, Ibn Funduq, *Lubāb*, p. 248, and al-ʿUmarī, *al-Majdī*, p. 386, '*huwa al-Ḥimmānī shāʿir*', where he is also said to have died in 270/883 (or alternatively, according to Ibn Ḥabīb, in 301/913) after he escaped from prison.

87 Al-ʿUbaydalī, *Tahdhīb*, p. 36; Ibn Ṭabāṭabā, *Muntaqila*, p. 264, '*wa-huwa naqīb hunāka*' (in Kufa); al-ʿUmarī, *Majdī*, p. 226.

V	VI	VII	VIII	IX	X
Yaḥyā b. al-Ḥusayn b. Zayd b. ʿAlī b. al-Ḥusayn b. ʿAlī	ʿUmar	Yaḥyā, rebel (d. 250/864-665)			
		Aḥmad	Abū ʿAbdallāh/Abū ʿAlī al-Ḥusayn, the alleged first *naqīb*	Abū al-Ḥusayn Yaḥyā, known as *ʿamm ʿUmar*	Abū ʿAlī ʿUmar
					Abū Muḥammad al-Hasan b. Yaḥyā, *naqīb*
		Muḥammad	Abū ʿAbdallāh al-Ḥusayn al-Faddān	Abū Muḥammad al-Ḥasan	
				Abū ʿAbdallāh Jaʿfar	
				Abū al-Ḥusayn Zayd	
			al-Qāsim (descendents in Ṭabaristān)		
			ʿUmar		
			Jaʿfar		
	Muḥammad	Aḥmad			
		Abū Jaʿfar Muḥammad			
		Abū al-Ḥasan ʿAlī, *naqīb* (*Tahdhīb*, p. 190)	Abū Ṭālib Aḥmad		
			Abū ʿAbdallāh al-Ḥusayn		
			Abū Jaʿfar Muḥammad	Abū al-Qāsim al-Ḥasan, *naqīb*	Abū al-Ḥasan ʿAlī b. Muḥammad, *naqīb* according to al-Masʿūdī
	ʿAlī	Umm Jaʿfar bt. ʿAlī b. Yaḥyā	Abū Jaʿfar Muḥammad b. al-Ḥasan b. Muḥammad al-Kābulī b. ʿAbdallāh al-Ashtar b. Muḥammad al-Nafs al-Zakiyya, *naqīb* (*Muntaqila*, p. 264 ; *Majdī*, p. 226)		
			al-Ḥusayn b. al-Ḥasan, *naqīb* after his brother (*Tahdhīb*, p. 36, *Muntaqila*, p. 264)		

Figure 4.1 The early *niqāba* in Kufa

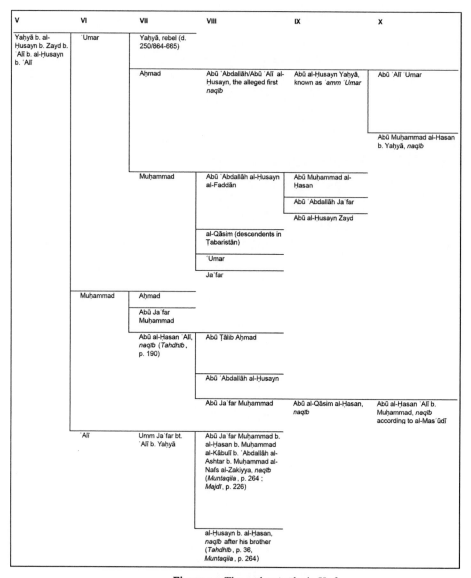

nuqabāʾ (the descendants of Yaḥyā b. al-Ḥusayn b. Zayd b. ʿAlī b. al-Ḥusayn b. ʿAlī), for the mother of Abū Jaʿfar Muḥammad was the daughter of ʿAlī b. Yaḥyā. A few other names are mentioned as well, but who was *naqīb* when is not clear: There are no dates for any of them, and few external pointers.[88]

What mattered to the genealogists, it seems, was whether or not a family generally belonged to the *nuqabāʾ* in the first place, not when it held the *niqāba*. Indeed, as the example of Kufa suggests, there may even have been more than one *naqīb* in a given location at one time. This may be an impression suggested by the scarcity of dates in the sources, but some of the expressions likewise at least leave open the possibility: al-Marwazī, for instance, says that someone was 'today one of the *nuqabāʾ* of Balkh' (*wa-huwa al-yawm min nuqabāʾ Balkh*).[89] In the absence of precise dates it is difficult to say more, but the confusion over who the *naqīb* was at a particular time is more understandable if there was in fact more than one.

The origins of the *niqāba*

Of the Ṭālibid genealogies, only Ibn Funduq's gives a different account of the origins of the *niqāba*. He states that the first to establish (*sanna*) the *niqāba* and to designate (*ʿayyana*) a *naqīb* and a *muqaddam* (administrator or trustee) for the descendants of the Prophet was 'al-Muqtaṣid bi-llāh', who did so on account of a dream. Ibn Funduq says no more about the matter but refers the reader to the discussion in another book of his, the *Kitāb Azāhir al-riyāḍ al-murīʿa*. He adds that the episode is also mentioned in other books, such as the *Taʾrīkh* of Muḥammad b. Jarīr, that is, the historian al-Ṭabarī.[90]

Unfortunately, the *Kitāb Azāhir* seems to be lost, and the edition of the *Lubāb* seems to contain an erroneous form of the dreamer's name – 'al-Muqtaṣid bi-llāh' was not the name of any caliph, Zaydī imām, or any other known figure. One may suggest, as Modarressi and others have done, that the correct reading is the name of the ʿAbbāsid caliph al-Muʿtaḍid bi-llāh (r. 280–90/893–902).[91] Al-Ṭabarī in fact records that al-Muʿtaḍid had a dream in which ʿAlī instructed him about his attitude

88 Other *nuqabāʾ* in Kufa include Abū al-Ḥasan Muḥammad b. al-Ḥusayn b. ʿAlī Katīla b. Yaḥyā b. Yaḥyā b. al-Ḥusayn b. Zayd al-Shahīd, for whom see Ibn Ṭabāṭabā, *Muntaqila*, pp. 275–6, and Ibn Funduq, *Lubāb*, p. 541 (as Abū al-Ḥasan Muḥammad b. al-Ḥasan); ʿAlī b. ʿUbaydallāh (ʿAbdallāh) b. ʿAlī b. ʿUbaydallāh b. al-Aʿraj b. al-Ḥusayn b. ʿAlī b. al-Ḥusayn b. ʿAlī; and his grandson Muḥammad b. ʿUbaydallāh b. ʿAlī *al-amīr al-Ḥaramayn wa-raʾīs al-Ṭālibiyyīn wa-l-naqīb bi-l-Kūfa*; see al-Marwazī, *al-Fakhrī*, p. 67, and also al-Rāzī, *al-Shajara*, pp. 171–2, where the grandson is only called *amīr al-Ḥaramayn wa-raʾīs al-Ṭālibiyyīn bi-l-Kūfa*. The grandfather, ʿAlī b. ʿUbaydallāh, is Morimoto's first *naqīb*; see Morimoto, 'Diffusion', p. 27.

89 See, for example, al-Marwazī, *al-Fakhrī*, p. 63.

90 Ibn Funduq, *Lubāb*, p. 717.

91 See Modarressi, 'Sukhanī chand', p. 757, and al-Ḥusayn al-Zurbātī, who discusses the origins of the *niqāba* in a study entitled *Awlād al-Imām al-Bāqir* (Qum, 1417), p. 186, which is clearly based on Ibn Funduq's *Lubāb*, although he does not quote the work. Al-Zurbātī uses the same terminology ('*awwalun man sanna al-niqāba* . . .'), which does not appear to be used otherwise in the literature. Thanks to Amikam Elad for checking his *ahl al-bayt* database.

towards the ʿAlids.[92] The dream is told in the context of an account of the ʿAlids of Ṭabaristān. Muḥammad b. Zayd (d. 287/900), who succeeded his brother al-Ḥasan (d. 270/883) to the leadership in 270/883, is said to have sent money to one Muḥammad b. Ward al-ʿAṭṭār to distribute to his followers in Kufa and Baghdad. Muḥammad b. Ward was caught, but when al-Muʿtaḍid heard about the incident, he ordered that the money and the man be released. His reason for doing so was that ʿAlī b. Abī Ṭālib had appeared to him in a dream and promised that a number of al-Muʿtaḍid's descendants would become caliph after him, but he had warned him that they were to protect the descendants of ʿAlī.

There are other accounts of al-Muʿtaḍid's lenient policies towards the ʿAlids, and it may have been precisely these kinds of reports that caused the establishment of the *niqāba* to be ascribed to this caliph.[93] Al-Ṭabarī's dream story, moreover, should not be dismissed out of hand as a literary convention. As Rosenthal points out, this was a contemporary report and may have been circulated for political purposes.[94] Beyond bringing under ʿAlid control territory that had previously belonged to the ʿAbbāsids, the establishment of an ʿAlid state in Ṭabaristān also changed the situation of the ʿAlids especially in the Ḥijāz and in Iraq. After the repressive policies of al-Mutawakkil, who according to al-Iṣfahānī caused the Ṭālibids to disperse to all parts of the Islamic lands,[95] his successors were more lenient. Whether or not al-Muʿtaḍid reacted in the way that al-Ṭabarī and al-Masʿūdī report, it is known also from other sources that Muḥammad b. Zayd sent money to members of his family and other Zaydīs in the Ḥijāz, Kufa, Basra, Ṭabaristān and other regions. He was allegedly also the first to rebuild the shrines at the graves of ʿAlī and al-Ḥusayn after they had been destroyed by al-Mutawakkil.[96] No doubt such actions put some pressure on the ʿAbbāsids as well.

Whether there was a closer connection between the ʿAlid rule in Ṭabaristān and the establishment of the *niqāba*, that is, whether the ʿAlids of Ṭabaristān actually founded the *niqāba*, cannot be discerned from the sources, but it is unlikely. Morimoto suggests that the *niqābat al-Ṭālibiyyīn* was established in the second half of the third/ninth century by the ʿAbbāsids, probably in the reign of al-Mustaʿīn, when 'a change in the power balance between the caliphate and Talibids occurred because of the emergence of independent Talibid powers', such as the Zaydīs in Ṭabaristān or the Ukhayḍirids in Yamāma.[97] The evidence examined here confirms

92 Al-Ṭabarī, *Ta'rīkh*, pp. 2,147–8.

93 See also al-Masʿūdī, *Murūj*, vol. V, p. 172; al-Tanūkhī, *Nishwār al-muḥāḍara*, vol II, p. 209 ('he did not harm them and none of them [the ʿAlids] was killed').

94 Franz Rosenthal (trans.), *The History of al-Ṭabarī*, vol. XXXVIII (Albany, NY, 1985), p. 25, note 137.

95 Al-Iṣfahānī, *Maqātil*, p. 615.

96 Ibn al-Jawzī, *Muntaẓam*, vol. XII, p. 344 (the money was sent to the ʿAlids); al-Masʿūdī, *Murūj*, vol. VIII, p. 205; and Ibn Isfandiyār, *Tārīkh-i Ṭabaristān*, ed. ʿAbbās Iqbāl, 2 vols (Tehran 1320/[1940–1]), vol. I, p. 95. See also Madelung, 'Abū Isḥāq al-Ṣābī', p. 29, and Madelung, *Imām al-Qāsim*, p. 187.

97 Morimoto, 'Diffusion', p. 19, and the list of early *naqībs*, pp. 26–42. He thus suggests that the *niqāba* was most likely established by one of the successors of al-Mutawakkil and that the 'Talibid principalities' then also introduced the office. For the Banū al-Ukhayḍir, descendants of Yūsuf al-Ukhayḍir Ibrāhīm

Morimoto's findings, although exact conclusions should probably be treated with some caution. As I have repeatedly noted, the genealogies give very few dates for any of the ʿAlids, and the *nuqabāʾ* are no exception. Because of this lack of dates, it is often unclear which ʿAlid held the *niqāba* in a given town at what precise time – as is evident in the example of the early *niqāba* in Kufa. The Ṭālibid genealogies, moreover, clearly ascribe the term *naqīb* also to famous ʿAlids of earlier periods; one such example is the genealogist Yaḥyā b. al-Ḥasan al-ʿAqīqī.[98] It is therefore necessary to identify clearly which sources frequently use the title and for whom, and when someone is first referred to as a *naqīb* in the sources.[99]

Conclusion

The establishment of an ʿAlid state in Ṭabaristān, the increased dispersal of the ʿAlids, and the many revolts of the mid-third/ninth century may all have contributed to a greater urgency in regulating the affairs of the family of the Prophet, especially in genealogical terms but also in financial and social terms. The revolt of the Zanj, 255–70/868–83, for instance, was a most serious uprising in the ʿAbbāsid heartland.[100] Its leader, ʿAlī b. Muḥammad, claimed ʿAlid descent, first through ʿUmar b. ʿAlī and later through Zayd b. ʿAlī b. al-Ḥusayn b. ʿAlī. The choice of an ʿAlid genealogy clearly sought to legitimise his revolt against the ʿAbbāsids, and its success showed the potency of an ʿAlid association.[101] According to al-Ṭabarī, some ʿAlids were also among his followers, and many members of the family moved further east as well as south after the uprising was finally put down.[102]

---

b. Mūsā b. ʿAbdallāh b. al-Ḥasan b. al-Ḥasan b. ʿAlī who established themselves in Yamāma after the failed revolt of Ibrahīm b. Yūsuf and his brother Muḥammad in Mecca in 251–2/865–6, see al-ʿUmarī, *al-Majdī*, pp. 232–5, and Madelung, 'al-Ukhayḍir', *EI2*.

98 He is given by Morimoto as the possible second *naqīb* in Medina; see Morimoto, 'Diffusion', p. 26.

99 This is what Morimoto does, yet there are two possible problems with his method. First, dates within one generation could vary quite significantly, primarily because of multiple marriages contracted over an extended period of time: Because a man took wives and had children over a considerable time span, there were often significant gaps between siblings in ages. There were, for instance, probably as many as 25 years separating Muḥammad al-Nafs al-Zakiyya from his younger brother Yaḥyā, because they were from different mothers (Muḥammad is usually said to have been born in the year 100/718, and Yaḥyā in about 128/745). This is one entire generation according to Morimoto's calculations. If this age gap is extrapolated to further generations, cousins of the same numerical generation quickly become contemporaries of their uncles. Second, Morimoto makes no distinction between earlier and later sources, with their variations and changes in terminology, for example. He thus lists someone as a *naqīb* even when the term is not used in the earlier source that discusses the person but only in a later one, or even only in the genealogy of a later descendant. All of the surviving Ṭālibid genealogies date from a period when the *niqāba* had been commonplace for some time; because the families of *nuqabāʾ* came to be among the most highly regarded ʿAlid families, it is not surprising that the title would be ascribed to an ʿAlid of a previous generation who was also held in high esteem.

100 For the revolt of the Zanj, see al-Ṭabarī, *Taʾrīkh*, vol. III, pp. 1,742–87; Michael Brett, *The Rise of the Fāṭimids* (Leiden, 2001), p. 58.

101 Al-Ṭabarī, *Taʾrīkh*, vol. III, pp. 1,742–87; Halm, *Traditionen*, pp. 16–20; and Popovic, *Révolte*, pp. 71–73 and 187–90.

102 Al-Ṭabarī, *Taʾrīkh*, vol. III, p. 1,845; see also Ibn Ḥazm, *Jamhara*, p. 51. ʿAlī b. Muḥammad changed his

There were a number of other ʿAlid revolts around the middle of the third/ninth century, some connected to the rebellion of the Zanj, and some independent of it. A close look at ʿAlid rebellions clearly shows that there was a geographic concentration in the Ḥijāz and expecially in Kufa, both places where we find early references to the *niqāba*. Whether or not the establishment of the office was directly connected to these rebellions, the ʿAlids certainly re-emerged at this time with a new forcefulness and greater visibility.

The absence of early accounts on the origins of the *niqāba* may also indicate that its origins were less momentous than one may presume. The *niqāba* may have formalised what had already been in place, namely the headship of the family in various places. It is known that in the early Islamic period there was such a headship of the family; for instance, ʿAbdallāh b. al-Ḥasan b. al-Ḥasan b. ʿAlī, the father of the rebels Muḥammad and Ibrāhīm, is known to have been the head of the family, or at least of part of it, in the late Umayyad period (al-Iṣfahānī calls him the *shaykh Banī Hāshim*).[103] There were also leading members of the family throughout the early ʿAbbāsid period; al-Bukhārī, for example, mentions one al-Qāsim b. ʿAbdallāh b. al-Ḥusayn and says, 'I have not seen the Ṭālibids follow anyone in leadership (*bi-l-riʾāsa*) like they followed al-Qāsim b. ʿAbdallāh.'[104] Al-Qāsim b. ʿAbdallāh was another ʿAlid who was treated badly by ʿUmar b. al-Faraj al-Rukhkhajī. He was sent from Medina to al-ʿAskar in Sāmarrāʾ, apparently to be under closer watch. He refused to wear the black clothes of the ʿAbbāsids, but the authorities continued to pressure him (*fa-jahadū bi-hi fī kull al-jahd*), until he donned the *qalansuwa*, the ʿAbbāsids' distinctive hat.[105] Within the family, the role of these kinds of leaders perhaps consisted of the supervision of other members of the family, not unlike the role performed by the later *nuqabāʾ*.

alleged genealogy once more when some descendants of Zayd b. ʿAlī joined him; they were ʿAlī b. Aḥmad b. ʿĪsā b. Zayd and his son ʿAbdallāh. According to al-Bukhārī, *Sirr al-silsila*, p. 66, ʿAlī b. Aḥmad had three daughters only, so this ʿAlī may have been a false claimant, too.

103 Al-Iṣfahānī, *Maqātil*, p. 180; see also al-Balādhurī, *Ansāb al-ashrāf*, vol. II, p. 183, and Madelung, 'Zayd b. ʿAlī b. al-Ḥusayn', *EI2*.

104 See al-Bukhārī, *Sirr al-silsila*, p. 70; similarly al-Iṣfahānī, *Maqātil*, pp. 617–18.

105 Clearly the aim was to show that this influential ʿAlid supported the ʿAbbāsids, for whom the *qalansuwa* was a mark of their authority. See W. Björkman, '*Ḳalansuwa*', *EI2*: 'High, black *ḳalansuwas* were worn by the ʿAbbāsid caliphs from al-Manṣūr to al-Mustaʿīn and by their viziers.' See also, more generally, Boaz Shoshan, 'On Costume and Social History in Medieval Islam', *Asian and African Studies* 22 (1988), pp. 35–51.

5

The ʿAlids as Local Nobility

Much of the secondary literature on local notables in medieval Islam has focused on the question of the extent of state authority versus local autonomy. The role of local elites has been examined mainly with regard to their relationship to the centre. There has been less discussion of who those elites were and from where their authority derived.[1] There is little doubt that scholarship was an important factor in determining one's social standing in medieval Islamic society: As Richard Bulliet has shown, the local elites in fifth-/eleventh-century Nishapur were almost entirely made up of *qāḍī*s and scholars, and it was not uncommon for a merchant to trade his wealth for scholarship in order to gain respectability.[2] Chase Robinson has similarly suggested that in second-/eighth-century Mosul this idea of status preservation through scholarship had already been applied; Robinson says of one family of politicians and landowners whose sons became scholars that they were 'not the only Mosuli family that understood that scholarship was one of the best ways to retain elite status in an Abbasid commonwealth of learning'.[3] Scholarship, moreover, could be the basis for real power. Some families, such as the Burhān family in fifth-/eleventh-century Bukhārā, initially rose to prominence on account of their learning.[4]

This emphasis on learning and scholarship is not surprising. As Roy Mottahedeh has cautioned, much of our information on local elites comes from biographical

1 See Hugh Kennedy, 'Central Government and Provincial Elites in the Early ʿAbbāsid Caliphate', *Bulletin of the School of Oriental and African Studies* 44 (1981), pp. 26–38; Axel Havemann, *Riyāsa und qaḍāʾ: Institutionen als Ausdruck wechselnder Kräfteverhältnisse in syrischen Städten vom 10. bis zum 12. Jahrhundert* (Freiburg, 1975); Claude Cahen, 'Mouvements populaires et autonomisme urbain dans l'Asie musulmane du moyen age', *Arabica* 5 (1958), pp. 225–50, and *Arabica* 6 (1959), pp. 25–56 and 233–65; Chase Robinson, *Empire and Elites after the Muslim Conquest* (Cambridge, 2000), especially pp. 152–64; Boaz Shoshan, 'The 'Politics of Notables' in Medieval Islam', *Asian and African Studies* 20 (1986), pp. 179–215; Ira Lapidus, *Muslim Cities in the Later Middle Ages* (Cambridge, MA, 1967); and Peter von Sievers, 'Military, Merchants and Nomads: Social Evolution of the Syrian Cities and Countryside During the Classical Period, 780–969/164–358', *Der Islam* 56 (1979). Only very few studies focus on the Islamic East; see, for example, Jürgen Paul, *Herrscher, Gemeinwesen, Vermittler: Ostiran und Transoxanien in vormongolischer Zeit* (Stuttgart, 1996); Richard Bulliet, 'Local Politics', pp. 35–56; and Jean Aubin, 'L'aristocratie urbaine dans l'Iran seljoukide', in Pierre Gallais (ed.), *Melanges offerts à René Crozet* (Poitiers, 1966), pp. 323–32.

2 Bulliet, *Patricians*, p. 23.

3 Robinson, *Empire and Elites*, p. 156.

4 For this family, see Omeljan Pritsak, 'Āl-i Burhān', *Der Islam* 30 (1952), pp. 81–96.

dictionaries, works that were 'written by *ʿulamāʾ* for *ʿulamāʾ*'.[5] However, the local histories that are written in the form of biographical dictionaries – such as the *Histories of Nishapur* – are often not *ṭabaqāt* works in the strict sense. They include information that would be irrelevant for the study of *ḥadīth* and *isnād*s, but they omit information that would be of great importance, such as death dates.[6] The impetus for writing these works can thus not have been primarily to provide handbooks for scholars; surely the incentive for writing such a book was as much local patriotism, so as to shed a positive light on the region or city through its scholarly achievements.[7]

It is in this sense that many ʿAlids appear in the local histories. In contrast to many examples of non-ʿAlid noble families who claimed authority and status over some generations, the ʿAlids did not generally hold an official position. The exception is of course the *niqāba*, the headship of the ʿAlid or Ṭālibid family, but as discussed above, it is questionable to what extent this was an official post.[8] That the ʿAlids were nonetheless part of the local elite is clear from their inclusion in the local histories. Although they were rarely well-known scholars or judges, the presence of members of the Prophet's family became almost part of the *faḍāʾil* (virtues) of a place: It linked the locality genealogically with the earliest period of Islam. In the local histories of Iran, ʿAlids who travelled through or settled in a place are thoroughly discussed; as Ibn Funduq says at the end of his chapter on the *sādāt* in the *Tārīkh-i Bayhaq*, one ought to write about the descendants of the Prophet, because whoever writes about them in a positive manner will find favour with God.[9]

In a recent study, Jürgen Paul identifies social groups in various cities in the Islamic East who, on account of a certain social status, could act as intermediaries (*Vermittler*) and representatives between the changing rulers and the local populations. He distinguishes between three different kinds of intermediaries, whom he classifies according to the extent of their official appointment: first, intermediaries who take on state responsibilities through some kind of contract (for example, tax collectors); second, persons who have an official appointment but also need the approval of the local population; and third, persons who act as intermediaries without any official appointment, with authority based on the loyalty of the local population. Paul identifies the elites from which these intermediaries are drawn as, first, the *dahāqīn*, the landed aristocracy of pre-Islamic Iran, who continued to have some importance as landowners; second, Islamic dignitaries, such as *qāḍī*s and imāms;

5 Roy Mottahedeh, review of *The Patricians of Nishapur*, by Richard Bulliet, *Journal of the American Oriental Society* 95 (1975), p. 495; see also Richard Bulliet, 'City Histories in Medieval Iran', *Iranian Studies* 1 (1968), pp. 104–6.

6 For distinctions between the different kinds of local historiography, see, for instance, R. Stephen Humphreys, *Islamic History: A Framework for Inquiry*, revised edn (London, 1995), pp. 131–2; Bulliet, 'City Histories', p. 104; Wadād al-Qāḍī, 'Biographical Dictionaries: Inner Structure and Cultural Significance', in George N. Atiye (ed.), *The Book in the Islamic World* (Albany, NY, 1995), p. 94; and Charles Melville, 'Persian Local Histories: Views from the Wings', *Iranian Studies* 33 (2000), pp. 10–13.

7 See Jürgen Paul, 'The Histories of Samarqand', *Studia Iranica* 22 (1993), p. 71.

8 See Chapter 4.

9 Ibn Funduq, *Tārīkh-i Bayhaq*, p. 65.

third, the urban nobility, some of whom were also Islamic dignitaries; and fourth, Sufis or other ascetics.[10]

Paul notes that the descendants of the Prophet could be found among the Islamic dignitaries, but this was not a necessary condition for their authority.[11] Indeed, the sources show that until the end of the fifth/eleventh century, there are very few ʿAlid *qāḍī*s and even fewer ʿAlid families who held this office for more than one generation (as came to be fairly common in many medieval Islamic cities for non-ʿAlid families of judges).[12] Moreover, even though many ʿAlids are praised in the genealogies and other sources for their piety and scholarship, only very few actually appear in the biographical dictionaries of the legal schools. This may be taken as an indication that a great number of ʿAlids were neither clearly Sunni nor Imāmī and thus were not claimed by either scholarly community; indeed, as seen below, the ʿAlids associated themselves with scholars from a variety of schools.

This chapter examines how two important ʿAlid families in the Islamic East, the Āl Zubāra and the Āl Buṭḥānī, whom we have encountered throughout this book, combined different kinds of elite status, such as their Prophetic genealogy, wealth and learning, to rise to local prominence. The focus is on Nishapur, one of the most important cities of medieval Islam.[13]

The ʿAlids in Nishapur

There are examples of ʿAlids in the histories of Qum, Iṣfahān, Qazwīn, Samarqand and Jurjān, and much information on the Zubāras and Buṭḥānīs is found in the histories of Nishapur. The originally lengthy work of al-Ḥākim al-Nīsābūrī (d. 405/1014) is extant only in a much abbreviated Persian translation, and its biographical section is condensed to a mere list of names, often incomplete or even faulty – according to Bulliet, it 'amounts to little more than an index to its original multi-volume dictionary'.[14] However, even though little remains of this probably once very rich source, it is clear that various ʿAlids played an important role in the city.

10 Paul, *Herrscher, Gemeinwesen, Vermittler*, pp. 2–7 and 237–51. Paul furthermore found that ʿAlids often took a leading role in the defence of cities and that their importance in military matters increases over the period examined; see p. 123.

11 Paul, *Herrscher, Gemeinwesen, Vermittler*, p. 246.

12 The situation in fourth-/tenth- and fifth-/eleventh-century Syria seems to have been somewhat different. There are examples of ʿAlid *qāḍī*s in fifth-/eleventh-century Damascus; see, for example, Thierry Bianquis, 'Notables ou malandrins d'origine rurale à Damas à l'époque Fatimide', *Bulletin d'Etudes Orientales* 26 (1973), p. 198, and Shoshan, 'Politics', p. 200. There are also some examples from medieval Ramlah; see Wasim Dahmash, '*Sādāt* Role', pp. 441–9. During the fourth/tenth century, the *ashrāf* of Damascus were also involved in politics and actively organised the resistance against the Fāṭimids; see Yaacov Lev, 'Fāṭimid Policy towards Damascus (358/968–386/996): Military, Political and Social Aspects', *Jerusalem Studies in Arabic and Islam* 3 (1981–2), pp. 165–83.

13 For previous studies on ʿAlid families in Nishapur and Bayhaq, see Bulliet, *Patricians*, pp. 234–45 (Buṭḥānīs), and Krawulsky, 'Zur Shīʿitischen Tradition', pp. 293–311 (Zubāras).

14 Richard Bulliet, 'A Quantitative Approach to Medieval Muslim Dictionaries', *Journal of the Economic and Social History of the Orient* 13 (1970), p. 196.

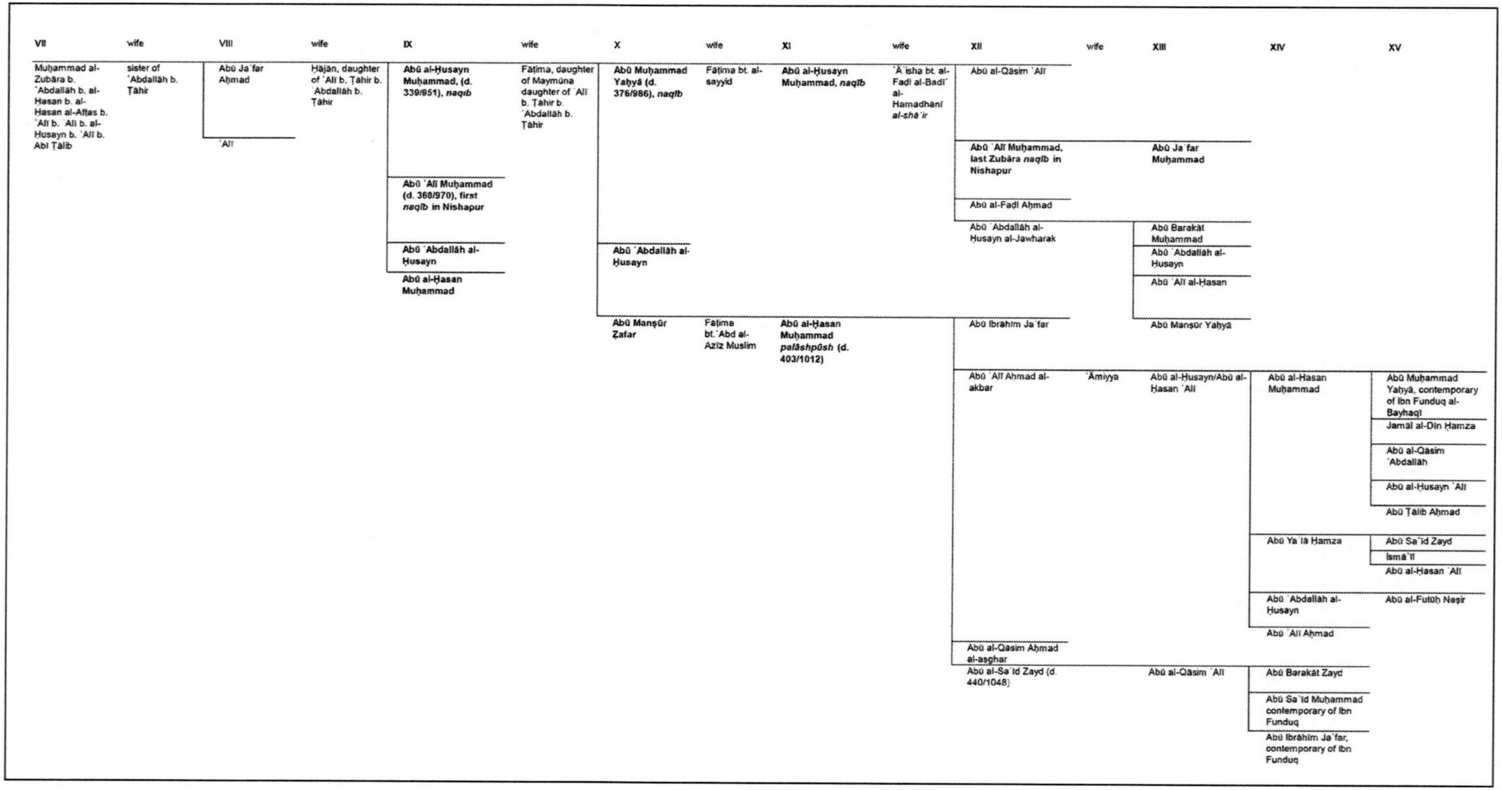

Figure 5.1 Family tree: Āl Zubāra

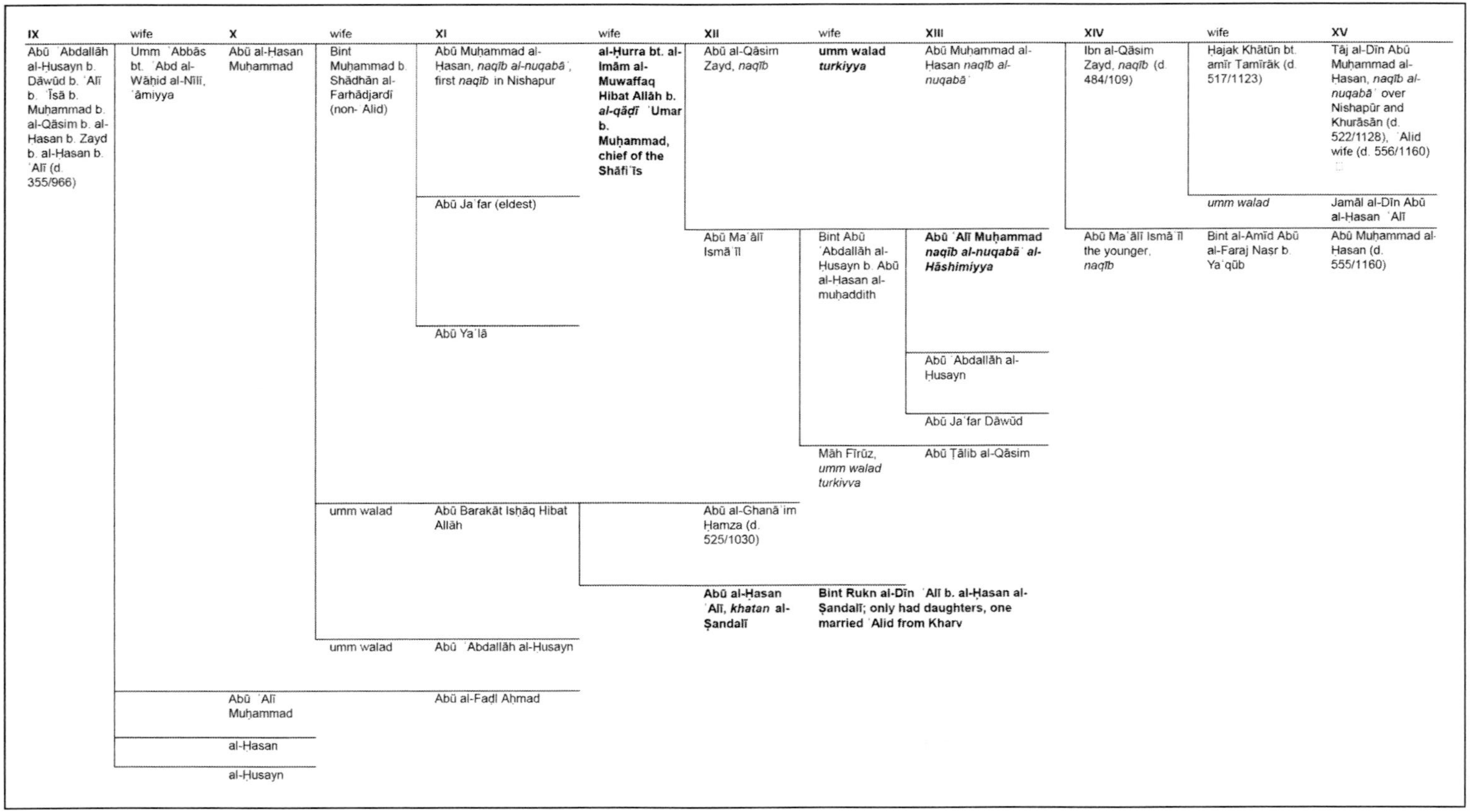

Figure 5.2 Family tree: Āl Buṭḥānī

More than seventy ʿAlids who came through or lived in Nishapur are listed in the *Taʾrīkh Nīsābūr* and its continuations, such as the *Siyāq Taʾrīkh Nīsābūr* of ʿAbd al-Ghāfir al-Fārisī (d. 529/1134).[15] In the *Taʾrīkh Nīsābūr* reports on ʿAlids appear also in the section of brief accounts: on the names of great *sādāt* and their burial places, on ʿAlī b. Mūsā al-Riḍā's (d. 203/818) stay in Nishapur, and on a letter to one Sayyid Ṣadr al-Dīn al-Ḥusaynī.[16]

Detailed information is also found in the *Tārīkh-i Bayhaq* of Ibn Funduq as well as in his genealogy of the descendants of the Prophet, the *Lubāb al-ansāb*. There is even some indication that there may have been more material on the ʿAlids in the area: Ibn Funduq lists fifteen histories of Khurāsān, which he used for his *Tārīkh-i Bayhaq* in the mid-sixth/twelfth century.[17] In the *Lubāb*, Ibn Funduq also refers to now lost works, such as a *Taʾrīkh Nīsābūr* by Abū Aḥmad al-Ghāzī.[18] The importance of local histories as a source for his genealogy is also shown by his extensive citations from al-Ḥākim: He includes one section on the *sādāt* from the *Taʾrīkh Nīsābūr* (*Faṣl fī ansāb al-sādāt al-madhkūrīn fī taʾrīkh Nīsābūr*), where the ʿAlids appear in the same order in which they are mentioned in the surviving Persian abridgement. Ibn Funduq clearly used a more complete version of al-Ḥākim's work than the one extant today, because he gives more extensive information on the ʿAlids than is found in al-Ḥākim's surviving history. He may also have used a different version or edited his source, because not all of the ʿAlids listed in the *Taʾrīkh Nīsābūr* are mentioned.[19]

Be that as it may, the entries reflect the great variety of ʿAlids in Nishapur. For instance, one Ḥusaynid, a descendant of Jaʿfar al-Ṣādiq, was an *ʿālim* of genealogy and history and a follower of the *madhhab* of Mālik b. Anas, and he issued legal opinions.[20] Another Ḥusaynid, Abū ʿAbdallāh al-Ḥusayn b. ʿAlī, is described as a Zaydī who came from Kufa to Nishapur in 373/983 and died there in 397/1006.[21] One Ḥasanid from the Buṭḥānī family, Abū ʿAbdallāh al-Ḥusayn b. Dāwūd al-Ṭabarī, was apparently a Sunni and cried at the mention of ʿUthmān, calling him *amīr al-muʾminīn al-shahīd*, and also at the mention of ʿĀʾisha, calling her *umm al-muʾminīn al-ṣādiqa bt. al-ṣādiq*. Abū ʿAbdāllah al-Ḥusayn died in 355/966, and al-Ḥākim

15 Al-Ḥākim al-Nīsābūrī, *Tārīkh-i Nīsābūr*; ʿAbd al-Ghāfir b. Ismāʿil al-Fārisī, *al-Ḥalqa al-ūla min taʾrīkh Nīsābūr: al-muntakhab min al-Siyāq (Kitāb al-Siyāq)*, ed. Muḥammad Kāẓim al-Maḥmūdī (Qum, 1983). There is another abridgement by al-Sarīfīnī (d. 641/1243), *Muntakhab min kitāb al-Siyāq li-taʾrīkh Nīsābūr*, ed. Khālid Ḥaydar (Beirut, 1993). For the works in facsimile edition, see R. N. Frye, *The Histories of Nishapur* (The Hague, 1965). See also the discussion of the texts in Wilfred Madelung, review of *The Histories of Nishapur*, by R. N. Frye, *Journal of Near Eastern Studies* 27 (1968), pp. 155–7.

16 See al-Ḥākim, *Tārīkh-i Nīsābūr*, p. 223 (no. 2789) for names; p. 211 (no. 2,731) for burial places; p. 208 (no. 2,833) for ʿAlī b. Mūsā al-Riḍā; and p. 221 (no. 2,783) for a letter to Sayyid Ṣadr al-Dīn al-Ḥusaynī.

17 Ibn Funduq, *Tārīkh-i Bayhaq*, p. 21.

18 Ibn Funduq, *Lubāb*, p. 492; see also pp. 492, 496 and 510 for other histories of Khurāsān. He explicitly names al-Ḥākim among his sources; see Ibn Funduq, *Lubāb*, pp. 476, 495 and throughout the work.

19 Ibn Funduq, *Lubāb*, pp. 712–6.

20 His full name is Abū Jaʿfar Muḥammad b. Hārūn b. Mūsā b. Jaʿfar al-Ṣādiq; see Ibn Funduq, *Lubāb*, p. 715.

21 His full name is Abū ʿAbdallāh al-Ḥusayn b. ʿAlī b. Muḥammad b. Zayd b. Aḥmad b. ʿĪsā b. Yaḥyā b. al-Ḥusayn b. Zayd b. ʿAlī b. al-Ḥusayn b. ʿAlī; see Ibn Funduq, *Lubāb*, p. 716.

knows three of his sons.[22] The list also contains an ʿAlid claimant whose genealogy was proven to be false after a register (*kashf*) was checked.[23]

When the first ʿAlids settled in Nishapur is not entirely clear. Yaḥyā b. Zayd (d. 125/743) is reported to have passed through on his flight eastwards after the defeat of his father's revolt in Kufa in 122/739,[24] and ʿAlī al-Riḍā stayed in the city for some time; but whether either one was accompanied by ʿAlids who settled in the city is not known.[25] ʿAlids are attested from the mid-third/ninth century onwards, and Abū Jaʿfar Aḥmad b. Muḥammad al-Zubāra may well have been among the first to actually settle down in Nishapur. There were most probably others as well, particularly at the Ṭāhirid court: al-Ṭabarī, for example, says that there were 'Hāshimites and Ṭālibids' present at the assembly of Muḥammad b. Ṭāhir.[26]

Not all of the ʿAlids in the area, however, were on good terms with the Ṭāhirids. There were a number of ʿAlids in Ṭāhirid prisons, having generally been put there after uprisings connected to the Zaydī *daʿwa* in Ṭabaristān. The Ḥasanid al-Ḥusayn b. Ibrāhīm b. ʿAlī, for instance, died in prison in Nishapur in 270/883,[27] as did Muḥammad b. Jaʿfar b. al-Ḥasan b. ʿUmar b. ʿAlī b. al-Ḥusayn, who had called for allegiance to the *dāʿī* al-Ḥasan b. Zayd in Rayy.[28] There were some earlier encounters with the Ṭāhirids as well: The first ʿAlid uprising dealt with by a Ṭāhirid was led by the *ṣāḥib al-Ṭāliqān* Muḥammad b. al-Qāsim b. ʿAlī b. ʿUmar, who was defeated by ʿAbdāllah b. Ṭāhir in 219/834. The ʿAlid fled but was eventually captured and sent to the caliph al-Muʿtaṣim in Sāmarrāʾ, from where he escaped; nothing more is known of him.[29] Another ʿAlid from this branch of the family, Muḥammad b. Jaʿfar b. al-Ḥasan b. ʿAlī b. ʿUmar [b. ʿAlī b. al-Ḥusayn b. ʿAlī] died in the prison of Muḥammad b. Ṭāhir,[30] which was also the fate of a Ḥasanid, al-Ḥusayn b. Ibrāhīm b. ʿAlī b. ʿAbd al-Rahmān b. al-Qāsim b. al-Ḥasan b. Zayd b. al-Ḥasan.[31]

22 Ibn Funduq, *Lubāb*, p. 713. In al-Ḥākim's work, they are often called 'al-Ḥusaynī', which may be a mistake of the copyist; see al-Hakīm, *Tārīkh-i Nīsābūr*, nos. 1943 (Dāwūd b. Muḥammad b. al-Ḥusayn, Bulliet, *Patricians*, no. 6) and 2,339 (Muḥammad b. al-Ḥusayn b. Dāwūd al-Ḥusaynī, Bulliet, *Patricians*, no. 4; Frye, *The Histories of Nishapur*, fol. 50a). All later members of this family appear in al-Fārisī's continuation.

23 Ibn Funduq, *Lubāb*, p. 714.

24 See, for example, al-Isfahānī, *Maqātil*, pp. 152–8, and Wilferd Madelung, 'Yaḥyā b. Zayd', *EI2*.

25 Al-Ḥākim, *Tārīkh-i Nīsābūr*, p. 208 (no. 2,833).

26 Al-Ṭabarī, *Taʾrīkh*, vol. III, p. 1,523. See also Ibn Funduq, *Lubāb*, p. 716, for Ibrāhīm b. Muḥammad b. Mūsā b. Jaʿfar al-Ṣādiq, who came to Nishapur in 285/898 and transmitted *ḥadīth* there.

27 His full name is al-Ḥusayn b. Ibrāhīm b. ʿAlī b. ʿAbd al-Rahmān b. al-Qāsim b. al-Ḥasan b. Zayd b. al-Ḥasan b. ʿAlī; see al-Bukhārī, *Sirr al-Silsila*, p. 23 (he is not mentioned in al-Isfahānī's *Maqātil*). Another example is Muḥammad b. Jaʿfar b. al-Ḥasan b. ʿAlī b. ʿUmar b. ʿAlī, known as *dībāja*, who came from Rayy and died in Nishapur in a Ṭāhirid prison; see al-Bukhārī, *Sirr al-silsila*, p. 55.

28 Al-Isfahānī, *Maqātil*, p. 615; al-Bukhārī, *Sirr al-silsila*, p. 55.

29 Al-Bukhārī calls him *al-ṣūfī*; see al-Bukhārī, *Sirr al-silsila*, pp. 55–6. See also al-Isfahānī, *Maqātil*, pp. 578–88, and al-Yaʿqūbī, *Taʾrīkh (Historiae)*, ed. M. Th. Houtsma, 2 vols (Leiden, 1883), vol. II, p. 576. According to al-Ṭabarī, *Taʾrīkh*, vol. III, pp. 1,165–7, he called to *al-riḍā min āl Muḥammad*; according to al-Isfahānī, *Maqātil*, p. 578, he belonged to the Jārūdiyya, and his call was for 'justice and oneness' (*al-ʿadl wa-l-tawḥīd*). See Madelung, *Imam al-Qāsim*, p. 79.

30 Al-Bukhārī, *Sirr al-silsila*, p. 55. He is also called a Sufi; see Ibn Funduq, *Lubāb*, vol. II, p. 510.

31 He died in 260/873; see al-Bukhārī, *Sirr al-silsila*, pp. 22–3.

Despite the many imprisonments, by the early fourth/tenth century Nishapur seems to have had a substantial ʿAlid population. According to the genealogist al-Bukhārī, the majority of the descendants of al-Ḥusayn were in Baghdad, Dīnawar, Ābā, Jurjān and Nishapur,[32] and many of the descendants of ʿUbaydallāh b. ʿAbdāllah b. al-Ḥasan b. Jaʿfar b. al-Ḥasan b. al-Ḥasan b. ʿAlī lived in Kāshān and Nishapur.[33] Some of the ʿAlids came via Ṭabaristān and Jurjān, including both the Zubāra Ḥusaynids and the Buṭḥānī Ḥasanids, the two most prominent families in early medieval Nishapur.[34] This route was clearly popular because of Zaydī–ʿAlid presence in Ṭabaristān. Al-Sarīfīnī lists some ʿAlids with the *nisba* 'al-Jurjānī' or 'al-Astarābādī', which also implies that they had come from that region.[35]

Ibn Funduq adds to and continues the information cited from al-Ḥākim. He begins the genealogical part of his *Lubāb* with a section on the Āl Zubāra ('Bāb al-ansāb banī Zubāra'). His information on this family is so rich because he knew many family members personally,[36] especially members of one branch of the family that had moved to Bayhaq in the late fourth/tenth century. Abū al-Ḥasan Muḥammad b. Ẓafar b. Muḥammad b. Aḥmad b. Muḥammad al-Zubāra (d. 403/1012) is said to have been the first ʿAlid in Bayhaq; he was called *palāspūsh*, because of the *palās*, a woolen cloth, that he used to wear. Al-Thaʿālibī describes him as a Sufi, saying that he was '*sharīf, fāḍil, ʿālim, zāhid yalbasu al-ṣūf*'.[37] Ibn Funduq met four generations of this branch of the family in Bayhaq in the sixth/twelfth century: Abū ʿAlī, two of his sons, Muḥammad and Ḥamza, Abū ʿAlī's father, Abū al-Ḥasan, and his grandfather Abū Manṣūr Ẓafar b. Muḥammad. He lists their genealogies until the year 559/1163–4 and says that he read the information he collected back to them for verification.[38]

Until the move to Bayhaq, the Āl Zubāra were based mainly in Nishapur. They had settled there after two sons of Muḥammad al-Zubāra, Abū Jaʿfar Aḥmad and ʿAlī b. Muḥammad, left Medina for Ṭabaristān in the mid-third/ninth century following a call by a group of local Zaydīs. According to Ibn Funduq, the Zaydīs had written to Abū Jaʿfar Aḥmad and invited him to take on their leadership on the grounds that he was more worthy of the imāmate than the *dāʿī* (*awlā bi-l-imāma minhu*); the

32 Al-Bukhārī, *Sirr al-silsila*, p. 80.

33 Al-Bukhārī, *Sirr al-silsila*, p. 20.

34 Ibn Ṭābāṭabā, for instance, lists the Ḥasanids under Nishapur but notes that they came from Ṭabaristān (*min nāqalat Ṭabaristān*); see Ibn Ṭābāṭabā, *Muntaqila*, p. 335.

35 See al-Sarīfīnī, *Muntakhab min kitāb al-Siyāq*, nos 883, 685 and 671; see also Bosworth, *Ghaznavids*, p. 197.

36 Ibn Funduq, *Lubāb*, p. 473. He goes on to discuss the genealogies of the Zubāra ancestors, beginning with the descendants of ʿAlī Zayn al-ʿĀbidīn, p. 477. Among the Zubāras he knows, he mentions, for example, one Abū al-Ḥasan ʿAlī b. Ḥamza, with whom he was in al-ʿAskar (or the military?) for a number of years (*kāna maʿiyya fī al-ʿaskar sinīn kathīr*); see Ibn Funduq, *Lubāb*, p. 515.

37 Abū al-Ḥasan *palāspūsh* was born in 351/962; see Ibn Funduq, *Lubāb*, p. 511, and Ibn Funduq, *Tārīkh-i Bayhaq*, pp. 54–5. Elsewhere Ibn Funduq says that he was born and that he lived in the village of Sevīz, which would suggest that his father, Abū Manṣūr Ẓafar b. Muḥammad, had already moved to Bayhaq; see Ibn Funduq, *Tārīkh-i Bayhaq*, p. 169. For the Sufi description, see al-Thaʿālibī, *Yatīmat al-dahr fī maḥāsin ahl al-aṣr*, 4 vols in 2 (Cairo, 1955), vol. IV, pp. 421–2; Krawulsky, 'Zur Shīʿitischen Tradition', p. 305.

38 Ibn Funduq, *Lubāb*, pp. 697–703. He does not give any dates for the ʿAlids he lists here.

dāʿī al-Ḥasan b. Zayd had established rule in Ṭabaristān in 250/864.[39] When Abū Jaʿfar Aḥmad and his brother answered the call of the Zaydīs and went out to Ṭabaristān, however, they did not take control from the *dāʿī*. Abū Jaʿfar Aḥmad is said to have been betrayed (*ghudira*); al-Ḥasan b. Zayd stayed in power, and the two Ḥusaynids left Ṭabaristān for Ābā. From there, ʿAlī went to Jurjān and Aḥmad to Nishapur.[40]

Perhaps it was the family connections of his mother, a sister of ʿAbdāllah b. Ṭāhir, that caused Abū Jaʿfar Aḥmad to settle in Nishapur. Aḥmad and his son Muḥammad in any case continued this connection by marrying daughters of ʿAlī b. Ṭāhir b. ʿAbdāllah b. Ṭāhir.[41] According to al-Ḥākim, Abū ʿAlī Muḥammad b. Aḥmad and his grandson Abū Muḥammad Yaḥyā were both buried in the burial place of the descendants of the Prophet (*guristan-i sādāt*), next to ʿAbdāllah b. Ṭāhir.[42]

Of Abū Jaʿfar Aḥmad's four sons, one was a *ra'īs* and a *naqīb*, the first *naqīb* in Nishapur as far as we know; another is called a *qāḍī* and a poet,[43] and a third proclaimed himself caliph.[44] The family's prominence in Nishapur thus continued

39 His full name was al-Ḥasan b. Zayd b. Muḥammad b. Ismāʿīl b. al-Ḥasan b. Zayd b. al-Ḥasan b. ʿAlī b. Abī Ṭālib. He was expelled from Ṭabaristān three times (in 251/865 by the Ṭāhirids, in 255/869 by the ʿAbbāsids and in 260/974 by the Ṣaffārids), but he managed to add Jurjān to his territories. When he died in 270/884, his brother Muḥammad succeeded him in Ṭabaristān as well as Jurjān. See al-Ṭabarī, *Ta'rīkh*, vol. III, pp. 1,523–33; Ibn Isfandiyār, *An Abridged Translation of the History of Ṭabaristān*, trans. E. G. Brown (Leiden and London, 1905), pp. 161–87; Wilferd Madelung, 'ʿAlids of Ṭabarestān, Daylamān, and Gīlān', *Encyclopaedia Iranica*; Madelung, 'Abū Isḥāq al-Ṣābi', pp. 17–57; F. Buhl, 'al-Ḥasan b. Zayd', *EI2*; M. S. Khan, 'The Early History of Zaydī Shīʿism in Daylamān and Gīlān', *Zeitschrift der Deutschen Morgenländischen Gesellschaft* 125 (1975), pp. 301–14; and S. M. Stern, 'The Coins of Āmul', *Numismatic Chronicle*, 7th ser., 6 (1967), especially pp. 210–12.

40 Ibn Funduq, *Lubāb*, p. 492; Ibn Funduq, *Tārīkh-i Bayhaq*, p. 254; Ibn Ṭabāṭabā, *Muntaqila*, pp. 338 (Nishapur) and 112 (Jurjān).

41 Ibn Funduq, *Tārīkh-i Bayhaq*, p. 55.

42 Al-Ḥākim, *Tārīkh-i Nīsābūr*, p. 223 (no. 2,789). ʿAlī b. Ṭāhir b. ʿAbdallāh b. Ṭāhir does not seem to have played any particular role; see Mongi Kaabi, *Les Tāhirides: Étude historico-littéraire de la dynastie des Banū Ṭahir b. al-Ḥusayn au Ḫurāsān et en Iraq au IIIème s. de l'Hégire/IXème s. J.-C* (Paris, 1983). According to Ibn Funduq, *Lubāb*, p. 494, Abū ʿAlī Muḥammad was buried in the cemetery of the ʿAlids, next to the cemetery of ʿAbdallāh b. Ṭāhir.

43 He is one of the very few ʿAlid *qāḍīs*. I have not been able to find him in the biographical dictionaries, and he is also not included in Bulliet's list of the *qāḍīs* of Nishapur; see Bulliet, *Patricians*, pp. 256–9. This does not mean that Abū al-Ḥasan Muḥammad was not a *qāḍī*; as Bulliet also says, particularly for the period before 300/913 the available information is not complete.

44 In the *Tārīkh-i Bayhaq*, Ibn Funduq twice mentions this uprising, on pp. 55 and 254, and he seems to have confused some reports in the second passage. He says there that there were two calls to the caliphate by the Āl Zubāra, the first by Abū al-Ḥusayn Muḥammad b. Aḥmad during the reign of the Ṭāhirid ʿAbdallāh b. Ṭāhir, and the second by Abū al-Ḥusayn Muḥammad b. Yaḥyā b. Muḥammad b. Aḥmad during the reign of the Sāmānid al-Naṣr b. Aḥmad. The first uprising is not otherwise mentioned in the sources (not in al-Samʿānī's *Ansāb*, not in Ibn Funduq's other work, the *Lubāb*, and not in any of the other genealogies), and it appears that Ibn Funduq simply confused the two Abū al-Ḥusayn Muḥammads. He goes on to give details on the second Abū al-Ḥusayn Muḥammad (such as that he was the first to receive an allowance in Khurāsān; see below) that are otherwise known to refer to the first Abū al-Ḥusayn Muḥammad. I am grateful to Luke Treadwell for sharing his notes on the Āl Zubāra. Treadwell also notes this confusion and says that the first uprising probably never took place; see also Luke Treadwell, 'The Political History of the Sāmānid State' (DPhil dissertation, University of Oxford, 1991), p. 152, n. 28.

after the Ṭāhirids were defeated by the Ṣaffārids from 259/873 to 261/875, although nothing is known of the Zubāras' encounters with the new rulers.[45]

The first *naqīb* Abū ʿAlī Muḥammad b. Aḥmad (d. 360/970) was a *muḥaddith* and a scholar who is called the *shaykh al-Ṭālibiyya bi-Nīsābūr bal bi-Khurāsān fī ʿaṣrihi* (*shaykh* of the Ṭālibids in Nishapur and even Khurāsān in his time). He reportedly lived for 100 years.[46] His brother Abū al-Ḥusayn Muḥammad is also called *al-naqīb wa-l-raʾīs*, and he reportedly made a bid for power in Nishapur in the 320s/930s: He proclaimed himself caliph, and a great number of people – from the *amīrs*, the generals and the common people (according to al-Samʿānī) – joined him. According to Ibn Funduq, his rule lasted for four months, during which time he took the *laqab* 'al-ʿĀḍid bi-llāh' and the *khuṭba* was given in his name. He was eventually arrested and brought to Bukhārā by the Sāmānid Naṣr b. Aḥmad (r. 301–31/914–43), who first imprisoned him but soon let him go free and even gave him a monthly allowance of 200 dirhams, according to Ibn ʿInaba.[47] This made Abū al-Ḥusayn Muḥammad the first ʿAlid in Khurāsān to receive a state pension, and he was thus called the *ṣāḥib al-arzāq*.[48] Ibn ʿInaba also says that it was his brother (perhaps in his function as the *naqīb*) who turned Abū al-Ḥusayn to the Sāmānid authorities, namely to Ḥamūya b. ʿAlī, the *ṣāḥib jaysh* of Naṣr b. Aḥmad.[49]

From the few mentions in the local history of Bukhārā, it appears that ʿAlid–Sāmānid relations were generally good: According to al-Narshakhī (fl. 332/943), the ʿAlids received part of the income from a village called Barkad, and taxes were remitted to them from some land in Bukhārā that was owned by ʿAlids.[50] As for the

45 C. E. Bosworth, *The History of the Saffarids of Sistan and the Maliks of Nimruz* (247/861 to 949/1542–3) (Costa Mesa, CA, 1994), pp. 116–35. Some ʿAlids are known to have been killed by the Ṣaffārids. For example, al-Ḥusayn b. Ibrāhīm b. ʿAlī b. ʿAbd al-Raḥmān b. al-Qāsim b. al-Ḥasan b. Zayd b. al-Ḥasan b. ʿAlī was imprisoned by Yaʿqūb al-Layth when the latter conquered Nishapur; Yaʿqūb took al-Ḥusayn with him to Ṭabaristān, and according to al-Isfahānī, *Maqātil*, p. 689, the ʿAlid died on the way there. Another Ḥasanid died in a Ṣaffārid prison after having been caught in Ṭabaristān. This was Muḥammad b. ʿAbdallāh b. Zayd b. ʿUbaydallāh b. Zayd b. ʿAbdallāh b. al-Ḥasan b. Zayd b. al-Ḥasan b. ʿAlī; see al-Isfahānī, *Maqātil*, p. 690.

46 Ibn Funduq, *Lubāb*, p. 493; see also al-Samʿānī, *al-Ansāb*, vol. VI, p. 246.

47 Ibn ʿInaba, *ʿUmdat al-ṭālib*, p. 347.

48 Ibn Funduq, *Lubāb*, p. 495; al-Samʿānī, *al-Ansāb*, vol. VI, pp. 246 and 249. On allowances (*arzāq*) in the *dīwān* of Khurāsān, see C. E. Bosworth, 'Abū ʿAbdallāh al-Khwārazmī on the Technical Terms of the Secretary's Art', *Journal of the Economic and Social History of the Orient* 12 (1969), p. 144.

49 Ibn ʿInaba, *ʿUmdat al-ṭālib*, p. 347. Al-Rāzī, *al-Shajara*, p. 187, adds that ten thousand men joined him and also says that his brother, Abū ʿAlī Muḥammad, called him to his home and put him in chains when he heard about the uprising. For Ḥamūya b. ʿAlī, see Treadwell, 'Sāmānid State', p. 316.

50 Abū Bakr Muḥammad b. Jaʿfar al-Narshakhī (wrote 332/943), *Tārīkh-i Bukhārā*, ed. Mudarris Razavi (Tehran, 1351/1972–3), pp. 22 ('Barkad ʿAlawiyān') and 47. Richard N. Frye (trans.), *The History of Bukhārā* (Cambridge, MA, 1954), p. 16: 'The village is called Barkad of the ʿAlīds because the amīr Ismāʿīl Sāmānī bought this village and gave it as an endowment, one-third to the descendants of ʿAlī and Jaʿfar, a third to the poor, and a third to his own heirs'; see also p. 33 for the land in Bukhārā from which taxes were remitted. Regarding the work, Jürgen Paul says that 'it is astounding that this very early text should differ from most of what followed in being so close to what we would term a "local history": local perspective, local events and developments, traditions and so forth'; see Paul, 'Histories of Herat', p. 95, n. 4. The original version of the work was written in Arabic and dedicated to the Sāmānid Naṣr b. Nūḥ in 322/934.

Āl Zubāra, the family does not seem to have suffered any further disadvantage from the caliphal episode of Abū al-Ḥusayn, for the *niqāba* passed on to the rebel's son, Abū Muḥammad Yaḥyā, who took the title *naqīb al-nuqabāʾ*. He is described as a very pious and learned man. According to Ibn Funduq, he died while staying with the Būyid vizier al-Ṣāḥib b. ʿAbbād in Jurjān in the year 376/986, at the age of fifty-eight.[51] A letter of condolence (*kitāb al-taʿāzī*) by Ibn ʿAbbād to Abū al-Ḥusayn Muḥammad b. Yaḥyā on the death of his father survives, and it is reproduced in an abridged form in the *Lubāb*.[52]

Abū Muḥammad Yaḥyā was most probably a Shiʿite. He is one of the very few ʿAlids included in the Imāmī *rijāl* works and is said to have theologised (*takallama*) and debated on questions of *tawḥīd*, *qiyās* and *ijtihād*. He is said to have written a number of books on the imāmate as well as a book on the validity of *qiyās* entitled *Ibṭāl al-qiyās*.[53] Ibn Funduq relates a number of stories about him to emphasise his piety and generosity, some of which are of interest in this context as well; regardless of their historicity, they convey a sense of the importance, wealth and authority of this particular ʿAlid and his family.

One story emphasises Abū Muḥammad's piety as well as his standing in Nishapur. An Ismāʿīlī *dāʿī* (*rajul min dāʿāt al-miṣriyyīn*) had gone to Bukhārā, apparently in order to convert the Sāmānid Nūḥ b. Manṣūr.[54] After the Sāmānid showed some interest, the *dāʿī* went to Nishapur and gained a following among the people (*al-ashrāf wa-l-awbāsh*). When he wanted to proclaim his mission openly, however, he was told that he could do so only with the consent of Abū Muḥammad Yaḥyā. The ʿAlid agreed to come to the *dāʿī*'s house, listen to his secret mission (*asrār*) and debate whatever he wished. The *dāʿī* consulted with his followers, and – perhaps sensing a threat – they decided to take the opportunity to kill the ʿAlid. But when the latter arrived with his entourage (*mawākib al-haybat al-nabawiyya*) for the debate, he answered the *dāʿī* with 'brilliant proofs' and won the dispute. Abū Muḥammad Yaḥyā returned to his house and sent out his servants to catch the *dāʿī*; this they did, dragging him out and executing him. The story continues that the Sāmānid *amīr* was not pleased by this news; he ordered Abū Muḥammad Yaḥyā to

51 Ibn Funduq, *Lubāb*, p. 498.

52 Al-Ṣāḥib Ismāʿīl Ibn ʿAbbād, *Rasāʾil al-Ṣāḥib b. ʿAbbād*, ed. ʿAbd al-Wahhāb ʿAzzām and Shawqī Dayf (Cairo, 1947), p. 136, and Ibn Funduq, *Lubāb*, p. 497.

53 Ibn Funduq, *Lubāb*, p. 498; al-Najāshī (d. 450/1058), *Rijāl al-Najāshī*, ed. Muḥammad Jawād al-Nāʾīnī, 2 vols (Beirut, 1988), vol. II, pp. 413 and 414; al-Ṭūsī, *Fihrist kutub al-Shīʿa* (Beirut, 1983), p. 264 (no. 706); Ibn Shahrāshūb, *Maʿālim al-ʿulamāʾ*, p. 118 (no. 858); Āghā Buzurg al-Ṭihrānī, *Ṭabaqāt aʿlām al-Shīʿa*, 6 vols (Beirut, 1971–), vol. I, pp. 332–4. For the Shiʿite position on *qiyās*, see Hossein Modarressi, *An Introduction to Shīʿite Law* (London, 1986), p. 29.

54 The specific description seems to suggest a connection to the Fāṭimids and thus a later stage in the Ismāʿīlī mission in Khurāsān; see Patricia Crone and Luke Treadwell, 'A New Text on Ismailism at the Samanid Court', in Chase Robinson (ed.), *Texts, Documents and Artefacts: Islamic Studies in Honour of Donald Richards* (Leiden, 2003), p. 66, and pp. 37–67 for earlier Ismāʿīlī activity at the Sāmānid court. See also S. M. Stern, 'The Early Ismāʿīlī Missionaries in North-West Persia and in Khurāsān and Transoxania', *Bulletin of the School of Oriental and African Studies* 23 (1960), pp. 56–90.

come to Bukhārā and planned to get rid of him. The plan failed and, according to Ibn Funduq, the ruin and demise of Nūḥ b. Manṣūr was sealed by his treatment of the ʿAlid.[55] The message of the story is similar to that of the account about the demise of the Ṭāhirids after their killing of Yaḥyā b. ʿUmar in Kufa[56] and of numerous other stories in the historical tradition; namely, that to conspire against an ʿAlid was not a good idea.

Abū Muḥammad Yaḥyā died in 376/986. The *niqāba* passed on to his son, Abū al-Ḥusayn Muḥammad,[57] and after him to one of his four sons, Abū ʿAlī Muḥammad. The latter was the last *naqīb* from the Zubāra family in Nishapur.[58] By his generation, the Āl Zubāra had become well established among the cultural, political and religious elites of the city. Rowson has written about a contest between the famous poet Badīʿ al-Zamān al-Hamadhānī (d. 398/1008) and Abū Bakr al-Khwārazmī (d. 383/993), which took place in the house of the *naqīb* Abū ʿAlī Muḥammad.[59]

As has been discussed above, in 395/1004 the *niqāba* was transferred to the Buṭḥānī family, following a quarrel that involved the *naqīb*'s brother, Abū ʿAbdallāh al-Ḥusayn Jawharak. Ibn Funduq does not explain what the quarrel concerned beyond noting that Jawharak was 'an impetuous youth'. However, he says that the Shāfiʿīs played a key role in the transfer of the *niqāba* to the Buṭḥānīs, and he reports that the Zubāra family subsequently dispersed.[60] Indeed, from the account in the *Lubāb* it is clear that the Āl Zubāra no longer played a major role in Nishapur after the *niqāba* had passed to the Buṭḥānīs, who were prominent in the city's public life for some generations.[61] Nonetheless, some Zubāras remained in the city, but many moved away to Ṭūs or Iṣfahān or joined their cousins in Bayhaq.[62] Ibn ʿInaba, in the early ninth/fifteenth century, described the Zubāras as the most important family among the descendants of al-Ḥasan al-Afṭas – probably not because of their time in Nishapur, but because in the eighth/fourteenth century they had again risen to prominence. They had obtained governorships in Basra and Irbīl and were part of the Ilkhānid court at Tabrīz.[63]

Scholarship

Both Buṭḥānīs and Zubāras also equipped themselves with a key tool of power and prestige in medieval Muslim society, that is, with learning. They studied with some

55 Ibn Funduq, *Lubāb*, pp. 505–6.
56 Al-Tanūkhī, *Nishwār al-muḥāḍara*, vol. II, pp. 240–2.
57 There is little information about him in the *Lubāb*, as there seems to be a lacuna in the text; see Ibn Funduq, *Lubāb*, p. 502.
58 The four sons are Abū al-Qāsim ʿAlī, Abū ʿAlī Muḥammad, Abū al-Faḍl Aḥmad and Abū ʿAbdallāh al-Ḥusayn Jawharak; see Ibn Funduq, *Lubāb*, p. 502.
59 Rowson, 'Religion and Politics', p. 660.
60 Ibn Funduq, *Tārīkh-i Bayhaq*, p. 55, translated in Bosworth, *Ghaznavids*, p. 197.
61 See Chapter 2 and Bulliet, *Patricians*, pp. 234–45.
62 Ibn Funduq, *Lubāb*, pp. 508–9.
63 Ibn ʿInaba, *ʿUmdat al-ṭālib*, p. 346; see also Krawulsky, 'Zur Shīʿitischen Tradition', p. 303.

of the main *ḥadīth* scholars of their time, who were often Shāfiʿīs but also Ḥanafīs and even Ḥanbalīs; many of their teachers, therefore, were authorities who are not regarded as Shiʿites.[64] Some of the ʿAlids were known as *muḥaddithūn*, and some are known to have been teachers themselves. Al-Ḥākim al-Nīsābūrī, for instance, heard *ḥadīth* from Abū Manṣūr Ẓafar, a son of the short-lived caliph Abū al-Ḥusayn Muḥammad.[65]

Like many other ʿAlid scholars, members of both families are rarely found in the biographical dictionaries: They do not appear in the Sunni dictionaries, as students of their teachers or otherwise, and the Shiʿite *rijāl* works record only Abū Muḥammad Yaḥyā.[66] Perhaps the reason for this absence is that although they transmitted *ḥadīth*, they were not really Sunni or Shiʿite scholars. Nevertheless, the ʿAlids clearly enjoyed great freedom in choosing their teachers in fourth-/tenth- and fifth/eleventh-century Nishapur, perhaps especially because they were descendants of the Prophet.

One of the outstanding scholars of Nishapur in the late fourth/tenth century was Abū Bakr Muḥammad b. Isḥāq b. Khuzayma (d. 311/923), a Shāfiʿī and a teacher to many ʿAlids.[67] Both Abū ʿAlī Muḥammad (the first *naqīb*) and Abū al-Ḥusayn Muḥammad (the caliph) heard *ḥadīth* from him, as did two Ḥasanids, al-Ḥasan b. Dāwūd b. ʿĪsā and Abū ʿAbdāllah al-Ḥusayn al-Ṭabarī, whose sons took over the *niqāba* from the Āl Zubāra in 395/1004.[68] Christopher Melchert has questioned the assertion of Heinz Halm that Ibn Khuzayma was instrumental in the spread of the Shāfiʿī *madhhab* in Khurāsān. He suggests instead that the Shāfiʿism of the Khurāsānian *ahl al-ḥadīth*, to whom Ibn Khuzayma adhered, was only loosely Shafiʿī; he describes it as 'a matter more of theology than jurisprudence'.[69] Whether the ʿAlids studied Shāfiʿī jurisprudence with Ibn Khuzayma is not known; the sources certainly never say so explicitly. As Ibn Khuzayma was also, and perhaps primarily, known as a *ḥadīth* scholar, they may simply have heard *ḥadīth* from him.

Another Shāfiʿī who appears in the ʿAlids' lists of teachers is Abū Bakr Muḥammad b. ʿAbdāllah al-Shāfiʿī (d. 354/956). He is known to have held pro-ʿAlid views, as he is the author of a *Kitāb Faḍāʾil amīr al-muʾminīn ʿAlī b. Abī Ṭālib* and

64 For a list of the Āl Zubāra and their teachers, see Teresa Bernheimer, 'A Social History of the ʿAlid Family from the Eighth to the Eleventh Century' (DPhil thesis, Oxford, 2006), Appendix II.

65 Ibn Funduq, *Lubāb*, p. 509.

66 Even Abū Muḥammad Yaḥyā did not, as far as we know, study with Shiʿite authorities.

67 Abū Bakr Muḥammad b. Isḥāq b. Khuzayma al-Sulamī al-Nīsābūrī heard *ḥadīth* from Isḥāq b. Rāhūya, and al-Bukhārī and Muslim related *ḥadīth* from him; see Tāj al-Dīn al-Subkī (d. 771/1370), *Ṭabaqāt al-shāfiʿiyya al-kubrā*, ed. Muṣṭafa ʿAbd al-Qādir ʿAṭā (Beirut, 1999), vol. II, pp. 84–91; Fuat Sezgin, *Geschichte des Arabischen Schrifttums*, 15 vols (Leiden, 1967–), vol. I, p. 601; al-Dhahabī (d. 748/1348), *Siyār aʿlām al-nubalāʾ*, ed. Shuʿayb al-Arnaʾūṭ *et al.*, 25 vols (Beirut, 1981–8), vol. XIV, p. 365; and Abū Isḥāq Fīrūzābādī al-Shīrāzī (d. ca 476/1083), *Ṭabaqāt al-fuqahāʾ*, ed. Iḥsān ʿAbbās (Beirut, 1981), p. 105. He is also mentioned in Ibn Shahrāshūb, *Maʿālim al-ʿulamāʾ*, p. 103 (no. 744).

68 For Abū ʿAbdallāh al-Ḥusayn, see Hamza b. Yūsuf al-Sahmī (d. 427/1035), *Taʾrīkh Jurjān*, ed. Yaḥyā Murād (Beirut, 2004), p. 200 (no. 290); for his brother al-Ḥasan, see al-Dhahabī, *Taʾrīkh al-Islām*, vol. XXVI, p. 122; al-Khaṭīb al-Baghdādī, *Taʾrīkh Baghdād*, vol. VII, p. 306 (no. 3,822).

69 Christopher Melchert, *The Formation of the Sunnī Schools of Law, 9th–10th Centuries C.E.* (Leiden, 1997), p. 98.

a *Musnad Mūsā al-Kāẓim b. Jaʿfar b. Muḥammad.* However, according to Etan Kohlberg, he cannot be suspected of anti-Sunni tendencies, because when the Būyids prohibited the transmission of traditions on the virtues of the Prophet's companions (*faḍāʾil al-ṣaḥāba*), Abū Bakr defied them and openly transmitted these kinds of traditions in the mosque.[70] He may not be a good example of an 'Imāmī Shāfiʿī', apparently not an uncommon phenomenon; but clearly his defence of the companions did not prevent him from also writing about the descendants of the Prophet, in this case even a Twelver imām.[71]

Devin Stewart has recently discussed the connection between Twelver Shiʿites and the Shāfiʿī *madhhab*. He suggests that the development of the Twelver Shiʿite legal system must be understood in relation to the Sunni legal system, to which the Shiʿites reacted and responded in various ways: They conformed to it, adopted important concepts from it or rejected it. Being eager to escape their position as a marginalised minority, they mostly took steps to be included; they thus chose to conform to the Sunni legal system or to adopt Sunni legal concepts. One way of conforming was to join a Sunni *madhhab* while 'inwardly still holding to Shiite beliefs'.[72] A number of Shiʿite scholars did so and chose the Shāfiʿī *madhhab*, perhaps because of a shared aversion to *qiyās*.[73] Shiʿite scholars have often pointed out that in terms of jurisprudence they are closest to the Shāfiʿīs; Stewart suggests that beyond this, there was 'a long and self-conscious tradition' of Twelver Shiʿites studying with Shāfiʿī teachers.[74]

To show the extent of this tradition, Stewart provides a list of scholars, starting with al-Faḍl b. Shādhān, an important Shiʿite jurist and theologian who wrote a *Kitāb al-Dībāj fī masāʾil al-Shāfiʿī wa-Abī Thawr wa-l-Iṣfahānī*. According to Stewart, this work

> presents the opinions of al-Shāfiʿī, Abū Thawr (d. 240/854) and Dāwūd b. Khalaf al-Iṣfahānī (d. 269/882) but is not designed as a refutation (*radd*), like so many of al-Faḍl's other works, which suggests that he had some important connections to the currents of legal thought that constituted the nascent Shāfiʿī *madhhab*.[75]

70 Kohlberg, *Ibn Ṭāwūs*, p. 156 (no. 131); see al-Khaṭīb al-Baghdādī, *Taʾrīkh Baghdād*, vol. V, pp. 456–7, and Sezgin, *Geschichte des Arabischen Schrifttums*, vol. I, p. 191.

71 See, for example, Christopher Melchert, 'The Imāmīs between Rationalism and Traditionalism', in L. Clarke (ed.), *The Shīʿite Heritage: Essays on Classical and Modern Traditions* (New York, 2001), pp. 280–2.

72 Devin Stewart, *Islamic Legal Orthodoxy: Twelver Shiite Responses to the Sunni Legal System* (Salt Lake City, 1998), p. 61; see also the critical reviews of Stewart's work by Wilferd Madelung, *Journal of the American Oriental Society* 120 (2000), pp. 111–14, and by Robert Gleave, *Islamic Law and Society* 7 (2000), pp. 102–4. Melchert, *Formation*, pp. 83–4, suggests that semi-rationalists of all backgrounds may have found a convenient cover in the Shāfiʿī school: 'Adherence to the Shāfiʿī schools fit well with a widespread disposition among the proto-Imāmīyah toward semi-rationalism. Additionally, these Shīʿah may have been repelled by the association of Ḥanafism with *irjāʾ*, a largely anti-Shīʿi movement.'

73 Stewart, *Islamic Legal Orthodoxy*, p. 106.

74 Stewart, *Islamic Legal Orthodoxy*, p. 63.

75 Stewart, *Islamic Legal Orthodoxy*, p. 65. For al-Faḍl b. Shādhān, see, for example, Sezgin, *Geschichte des Arabischen Schrifttums*, vol. I, p. 537; al-Ṭūsī, *Fihrist kutub al-Shīʿa* (Najaf, n.d.), pp. 150–1; Ibn

Whether it was these currents of legal thought that attracted both Abū ʿAlī Muḥammad and Abū al-Ḥusayn Muḥammad to al-Faḍl b. Shādhān is not known. Both related *ḥadīth* from him: Abū ʿAlī Muḥammad knew his books, having heard them from ʿAlī b. Qutayba (*qaraʾa kutub al-Faḍl b. Shādhān samāʿan min ʿAlī b. Qutayba*),[76] and Abū al-Ḥusayn Muḥammad related *ḥadīth* from ʿAlī b. Qutayba, 'who related from al-Faḍl b. Shādhān, who related from ʿAlī b. Mūsā al-Riḍā'.[77] Aside from the Shāfiʿīs, the ʿAlids had connections with well-known scholars of other *madhhab*s as well. For instance, one of the Bayhaqī Zubāras, Abū Yaʿlā Zayd b. ʿAlī b. Muḥammad (d. 447/1055), had settled in the town of Fariyūmad, where he owned much property (*amlāk*).[78] Al-Ḥākim Abū al-Qāsim al-Ḥaskānī (d. after 470/1077–8), one of the great Ḥanafī scholars of fifth-/eleventh-century Nishapur, is said to have gone out to Fariyūmad to study with him.[79] According to Bulliet, al-Ḥaskānī was probably the most important member of any generation of the Ḥanafī branch of the Ḥaskānīs, and his distinction was in learning, in particular *ḥadīth*.[80] Al-Ḥaskānī also related from other ʿAlids, such as one Ḥasanid who was also from the Buṭḥānī family.[81] According to his entry in al-Fārisī's biographical dictionary, al-Ḥaskānī heard *ḥadīth* from his father and his grandfather, al-Sayyid Abū al-Ḥasan, as well as other members of his family (*wa-ahl baytihi*).[82]

Shahrāshūb, *Maʿālim al-ʿulamāʾ*, pp. 80–1 (no. 606); and al-Najāshī, *Rijāl*, vol. II, pp. 168–9. See also Tamima Bayhom-Daou, 'The Imam's Knowledge and the Quran According to al-Faḍl b. Shadhān al-Nīsābūrī (d. 260 A.H. /874 A.D.)', *Bulletin of the School of Oriental and African Studies* 64 (2001), pp. 188–207.

76 Ibn Funduq, *Lubāb*, p. 494. ʿAlī b. Qutayba should probably be ʿAlī b. Muḥammad b. Qutayba; see al-Kashshī/al-Kishshī, *Kitāb Maʿrifāt al-rijāl*, ed. Ḥasan al-Mustafawī (Mashhad, 1348/1969), pp. 451–6 (no. 415). Al-Samʿānī makes the same mistake, but his source is also al-Ḥākim; al-Samʿānī, *al-Ansāb*, vol. VI, p. 249. There is generally some confusion about his name: al-Najāshī calls him ʿAlī Aḥmad b. Qutayba; see al-Najāshī, *Rijāl*, vol. II, pp. 168–9.

77 Ibn Funduq, *Lubāb*, p. 496.

78 Ibn Funduq, *Tārīkh-i Bayhaq*, p. 186. For the village, see Le Strange, *Lands*, p. 392.

79 Ibn Funduq, *Lubāb*, p. 502. He is al-Ḥākim Abū al-Qāsim ʿUbaydallāh b. ʿAbdallāh al-Ḥaskānī al-Hadhdhāʾ. Ibn Ṭāwūs describes him as a Sunni, but there is some discussion about this; see Kohlberg, *Ibn Ṭāwūs*, p. 151: '[T]he usual biographical notices about him, which portray him as a Ḥanafī, should therefore probably be taken as reflecting his true belief, and not merely his outward position.' There were two books by al-Ḥākim al-Ḥaskānī in the library of Ibn Ṭāwūs, the *Kitāb Shawāhid al-tanzīl* and the *Kitāb Duʿāʾ al-hudāt ilā adāʾ ḥaqq al-muwālāt* (Kohlberg, *Ibn Ṭāwūs*, nos 542 and 120). See also Muḥammad b. Aḥmad al-Dhahabī, *Tadhkirat al-ḥuffāẓ*, 4 vols (Hyderabad, 1955–8), vol. III, pp. 120–1 (no. 1,032), and al-Qurashī, *Jawāhir al-muḍiyya*, vol. II, pp. 496–7.

80 For the Ḥaskānī family, see Bulliet, *Patricians*, pp. 227–33.

81 See al-Ḥaskānī, *Shawāhid al-tanzīl*, ed. Muḥammad Bāqir al-Maḥmūdī (Beirut, 1393/1974), pp. 80 and 82, where he relates from a Ḥasanid called Abū al-Ḥasan Muḥammad b. al-Ḥusayn b. al-Ḥasanī (d. 401/1010). There are also other ʿAlids from whom he relates; see, for example, pp. 284–5 and 302, and for a Jaʿfarī, p. 289.

82 Al-Fārisī, *Kitāb al-Siyāq*, nos. 706 and 707: *qaraʾa ʾalayhī al-Ḥaskānī*. His own entry is no. 982, on pp. 463–4.

Conclusion

The disintegration of the ʿAbbāsid state, Patricia Crone notes, paved the way for the emergence of local notables, 'the distinctive figure of the medieval polity'. The local notable was the product of the fusion of landed and commercial wealth and scholarship, and he was

> epitomized by the appearance of the *sharīf* in the medieval sense of *sayyid*, descendant of the Prophet. The medieval *sharīf* was an ʿAlid who is *not* a political pretender, usually not even a Shiʿite, and who instead encashes his Prophetic genealogy as a title to local status . . . Wherever they appear, they are a sure sign that morally states have ceased to matter.[83]

Both the Buṭḥānīs and the Zubāras were just this kind of medieval *sharīf*. Some of them rebelled against the authorities, some of them were Shiʿites, and a few of them made it into the *rijāl* books, yet their sacred descent, combined with wealth, shrewd marriage relations and scholarly connections ensured their place among the Eastern Islamic elites.

83 Patricia Crone, *Slaves on Horses: The Evolution of the Islamic Polity* (Cambridge, 1980), pp. 85–6.

6

Conclusion

It is difficult to estimate how many ʿAlids there were by the late fifth/eleventh century. Al-Ṭabarī reports that al-Maʾmūn had the ʿAbbāsids counted in 200/815–6 and that this count yielded 33,000 men and women. If we assume that there were as many ʿAlids around that time, there must have been thousands more some 200 years later.[1] This is a vast number of people, some of whom significantly shaped the history of Islam. Yet whether or not they became well known as rebels or rulers or eponymous founders of Islamic sects or were recorded in the history books, the ʿAlids were able to carry out a variety of roles in Muslim societies that few others were able to fill: as living links to the Prophet, as negotiators on behalf of a town or a people, as intermediaries between humans and the Divine.

From our current perspective, most significant was perhaps the ʿAlids' ability to bridge differences between Sunnis and Shiʿites. As the examples in this book have shown, not only were there Sunni and Shiʿite members of the Prophet's family, the ʿAlids were also able to move between the different communities, studying with eminent Sunni and Shiʿite scholars and inter-marrying with prominent Sunni and Shiʿite families. Throughout the centuries, ʿAlid shrines were visited and received patronage from Muslims of all denominations.[2] A similar role transcending and bridging community divisions was in later centuries played by also Sufi *shaykh*s, who quite explicitly called themselves 'the true *ahl al-bayt*'.[3] Yet the advantage of an actual genealogical link to the Prophet was not lost on these later Sufis either, many of whom came to claim ʿAlid descent.[4]

Virtually all Muslim communities agreed on the special position of the descendants of the Prophet Muḥammad. As a consequence, there is no other family in the history of Islam, perhaps in the history of any civilisation that has left more traces for historians to uncover. This book has examined how the ʿAlids attained and

1 Al-Ṭabarī, *Taʾrīkh*, vol. III, p. 1,001; see also Hans Ferdinand Uhrig, *Das Kalifat von al-Maʾmūn* (Frankfurt, 1988), p. 55, n. 281, for further references to this 'census'. For some estimates on the Mūsawī *sayyid*s in present-day Iran, see Amir Taheri, *The Spirit of Allah*, pp. 26–7.

2 See Bernheimer, 'Shared Sanctity', and references there.

3 See for instance the discussion by al-Tirmidhī (d. 318–20/936/938), cited in Bernd Radtke, *Al-Ḥakīm al-Tirmiḏī, ein islamischer Theosoph des 3./9. Jahrhunderts* (Freiburg, 1980), p. 91.

4 The literature on the link between *sayyid*s and Sufis is vast; see, for instance, Esther Peskes, *Al-ʿAidarūs und seine Erben. Eine Untersuchung zu Geschichte und Sufismus einer ḥaḍramitischen Sāda-Gruppe vom Fünfzehnten bis zum Achtzehnten Jahrhundert* (Stuttgart, 2005).

extended their special status from the ʿAbbāsid Revolution of 132/750 to the end of the fifth/eleventh century, the crucial period in the formation of ʿAlidism. With the rise of their ʿAbbāsid cousins to the caliphate, the ʿAlids began to delineate ever more clearly what it meant to be part of the kinsfolk of the Prophet. Genealogies were written to record the branches of the family and to clarify and verify who belonged to it and could thus claim a share in the social, religious and economic privileges of membership.

The pre-eminence of a Prophetic genealogy was emphasised also through marriage. While in the first 200 years of Islam the ʿAlids inter-married with other, mostly Arab, families, after the early third/ninth century their social circles were progressively narrowed. ʿAlid daughters especially were no longer married to other families, Arab or non-Arab; despite the explicit sanction of exogamous marriage by the early scholars as well as by prominent contemporary *sayyid*s, ʿAlid women were married only to ʿAlid men. Of course, there must have been exceptions, but the sources do not record them. The men also married increasingly within the family (as Ibn Funduq says, 'so that no daughters of the Prophet remain unmarried');[5] if they married out, their brides came from other elite families, whose backgrounds reflected the changing makeup of the Islamic empire.

In terms of their outward appearance, it seems that the family of the Prophet came to distinguish themselves rather late, if at all: according to al-Suyūṭī, it was not until 773/1371–2 that the Mamlūk sultan al-Ashraf Shaʿbān (r. 765–78/1363–76) ordered all the *ashrāf* (which, he explains, in Egypt referred to the descendants of al-Ḥasan and al-Ḥusayn only since Fāṭimid times) to attach a green cloth to their turbans.[6] Nonetheless, their differentiation from the rest of society had been made official much earlier, certainly with the establishment of the *niqāba* in the late third/ninth century. This office clearly indicated that the Prophet's kin were considered to be distinct from the rest of society and that the ʿAlids themselves had developed self-consciousness as a group, even though by no means a homogeneous one. Indeed, their heterogeneity is brought out in the *naqīb*'s remit, which included not only genealogical control but also provision for the poor and supervision of the unruly members of the family.

Not least through the ʿAlids' own efforts, the concept of nobility in Islam came to centre decidedly on Prophetic descent. How potent this idea was is evidenced also by its effect on the Jews living in Muslim lands. In a recent study of the Jewish descendants of King David in the fourth-/tenth- and fifth-/eleventh-century Middle

5 Ibn Funduq, *Lubāb*, p. 722.

6 Al-Maʾmūn's change of colour from the ʿAbbāsid black to green when he appointed ʿAlī al-Riḍā his heir apparent in 201/817 perhaps suggests that green was already associated with the ʿAlids; see al-Ṭabarī, *Taʾrīkh*, vol. III, pp. 1,013 and 1,037. For the changes introduced under the Mamlūks, see al-Suyūṭī, *al-Ḥāwī li-l-fatāwī* (Cairo, 1378/1959), vol. II, pp. 84–5; he says explicitly that this was not the custom in old times (*lā kāna fī al-zaman al-qadīm*). The most detailed account of the order by al-Ashraf Shaʿbān is found in Ibn Taghrībirdī (d. 875/1470), *al-Nujūm al-zāhira fī mulūk Miṣr wa-l-Qāhira*, 16 vols (Cairo, 1929–72), vol. XI, pp. 56–7.

East, Arnold Franklin explores the community's profound concern with lineage, arguing that the Arab-Islamic regard for tracing the lineage of Muḥammad provided the impetus for deploying traditions about descent from David in new and unprecedented ways.[7] Franklin examines the proliferation of the title *nasi* (prince, pl. *nesi'im*), which was at first used only for the serving exilarch, the leader of the Jewish community in the Babylonian exile, but subsequently came to refer to a broader circle of individuals who claimed descent from David even though they were only distantly related to the exilarchs. He argues that even though an established belief in the Davidic descent of the exilarchs is attested in older Rabbinic texts, it was not until the fourth/tenth century that numerous genealogies began to appear; this he sees as evidence for 'an intensification and broadening of that ancestral claim as well as a new and profound concern with its demonstrability'.[8]

As regards claims to Davidic and Prophetic lineage, there are a number of noteworthy parallels in genealogical record keeping, in the entitlement to privileges and in the appearance of false claimants. Even the titles *sayyid* and *sharīf* were shared: In one letter from the Cairo *genīza* a thirteenth-century *nasi* calls the addressee 'the *sharīf* of the Jewish nation, and the *sayyid* of the Davidic faction' (*sharīf al-milla al-yahūdiyya wa-sayyid al-ṭā'ifa al-dā'ūdiyya*).[9] Although a network of genealogical control comparable to the ʿAlid one never emerged, and Davidic genealogy never developed into a distinct genre as Ṭālibid genealogy can be said to have done, the rise of the Prophet's family among Muslims was clearly mirrored by developments among David's descendants in the Jewish community.[10]

An ʿAlid lineage, like descent from King David, did not automatically entitle one to a position of authority; but it could help to support claims to political and religious power. Many famous early rebels, the founders or eponyms of the major Islamic sects, and numerous Islamic rulers such as the Idrīsids in ninth-century Morocco, the Fāṭimids in tenth-century Egypt, the current-day kings of Morocco and Jordan, the Ayatollah Khomeini and the Aga Khan all claimed descent from the Prophet Muḥammad. As this book has shown, to the many who did not rebel or rule, those thousands of ʿAlids, rich and poor, Sunni or Shiʿite, who settled throughout the Middle East and beyond, their lineage brought social distinction. It made them part of the First Family of Islam.

7 Arnold Franklin, *This Noble House: Jewish Descendants of King David in the Islamic East* (Philadelphia, 2012)

8 Arnold Franklin, 'Cultivating Roots: The Promotion of Exilarchal Ties to David in the Middle Ages', *Association for Jewish Studies Review* 29 (2005), p. 93.

9 Franklin, *Noble House*, p. 60.

10 Interactions and mutual influence between Jews and Muslims is a well-known phenomenon, particularly in the fourth/tenth to sixth/twelfth centuries. See Abraham Ibn Daud, *Sefer Ha-Qabbalah: The Book of Tradition*, ed. Gerson D. Cohen (Philadelphia, 1967; reprinted Oxford, 2005), pp. L–LVII, where the influence of Islamic historiography on Rabbinic writing is emphasised, or the recent discussion in Moshe Gil, *Jews in Islamic Countries in the Middle Ages*, trans. David Strassler (Leiden, 2004), especially pp. 272–431, and the many references in Marina Rustow, *Heresy and the Politics of Community: The Jews of the Fatimid Caliphate* (Ithaca, NY, 2008).

Bibliography

Primary sources

Anonymous, *Akhbār al-dawla al-ʿAbbāsiyya*, eds ʿA. ʿA. al-Dūrī and ʿA.-J. al-Muṭṭalibī (Beirut, 1971).

Anonymous, *Kitāb al-ʿUyūn wa-l-ḥadāʾiq fī akhbār al-ḥaqāʾiq*, eds M. J. de Goeje and E. de Jong, *Fragmenta Historicorum Arabicorum*, (Leiden, 1869–71), vols I and II; (Damascus, 1973), vol. III.

Anonymous, *Taʾrīkh al-khulafāʾ* (Moscow, 1967).

Anonymous, *Tārīkh-i Sistān*, ed. M. S. Bahār (Tehran, 1314/1935); trans. M. Gold (Rome, 1976).

Abū al-Shaykh, ʿAbdallāh b. Muḥammad b. Jaʿfar (d. 269/979), *Kitāb Ṭabaqāt al-muḥaddithīn bi-Iṣbahān*, ed. ʿA. ʿA. al-Balūshī (Beirut 1407/1987).

Abū Yaʿlā ibn al-Farrāʾ (d. 458/1066), *al-Aḥkām al-sulṭāniyya*, ed. M. H. al-Fiqī (Cairo, 1966).

Al-ʿAbbādī (d. 458/1065), *Ṭabaqāt al-fuqahāʾ al-Shāfiʿiyya*, ed. Gösta Vitestam (Leiden, 1964).

Al-ʿAlawī, ʿAlī b. Muḥammad (fl. late 3rd/9th century), *Sīrat al-Hādī ilā al-Ḥaqq Yaḥyā b. al-Ḥusayn*, ed. S. al-Zakkār (Beirut, 1972).

Al-ʿAqīqī, Yaḥyā b. al-Ḥasan b. Jaʿfar (d. 277/891), *Kitāb al-Muʿaqqibīn min wuld al-imām amīr al-muʾminīn*, ed. Muḥammad Kāẓim al-Maḥmūdī (Qum, 2001).

Al-ʿAskarī, Abū Hilāl (d. 395/1005), *Kitāb al-Awāʾil*, eds M. al-Miṣrī and W. Qaṣṣāb, 2 vols (Damascus, 1975).

Al-Balādhurī, Aḥmad b. Yaḥyā (d. 279/892), *Futūḥ al-buldān*, ed. M. J. de Goeje (Leiden, 1866).

Al-Balādhurī, Aḥmad b. Yaḥyā (d. 279/892), *Kitāb Ansāb al-ashrāf*, ed. Wilferd Madelung (Beirut, 2003), vol. II; ed. Muḥammad Bāqir al-Maḥmūdī (Beirut, 1974), vol. II (Wiesbaden and Beirut, 1978), vol. III; ed. M. J. Kister (Jerusalem, 1971), vol. IV, part 1; ed. Max Schloessinger (Jerusalem, 1973), vol. IV, part 2; ed. S. D. F. Goitein (Jerusalem, 1996), vol. V; ed. Khalil Athamina (Jerusalem, 1993), vol. VI, part 2; ed. Maḥmūd Firdaws al-ʿAẓm, 20 vols (Damascus, 1996); ed. Suhayl Zakkār, 13 vols (Beirut, 1996).

Al-Balkhī, Abū Bakr b. ʿAbdallāh (wrote in 610/1214), *Faḍāʾil Balkh*; Persian trans. ʿAbdallāh b. Muḥammad b. Muḥammad Ḥusaynī al-Balkhī (wrote 676/1278), *Faḍāʾil-i Balkh*; ed. Bernd Radtke, 'Theologen und Mystiker in Ḫurasan und Transoxanien', *Zeitschrift der Deutschen Morgenländischen Gesellschaft* 136 (1986), pp. 536–69.

Al-Barqī, Aḥmad b. Muḥammad b. Khālid (d. 274–280/887–94), *Rijāl al-Barqī*, ed. Jawwād al-Qayyūm al-Iṣfahānī (Tehran, 1999).
Al-Bukhārī, Abū Naṣr (d. mid-fourth/tenth century), *Sirr al-silsila al-ʿAlawiyya*, ed. Muḥammad Ṣādiq Baḥr al-ʿUlūm (Najaf, 1962).
Al-Dhahabī, Muḥammad b. Aḥmad (d. 748/1348), *Taʾrīkh al-Islām wa-ṭabaqāt al-mashāhīr wa-l-aʿlām*, ed. ʿUmar ʿAbd al-Salām Tadmurī, 52 vols (Beirut, 1987).
Al-Dhahabī, Muḥammad b. Aḥmad (d. 748/1348), *Siyar aʿlām al-nubalāʾ*, ed. Shuʿayb al-Arnaʾūṭ *et al.*, 25 vols (Beirut, 1981–8).
Al-Dhahabī, Muḥammad b. Aḥmad (d. 748/1348), *Tadhkirat al-ḥuffāẓ*, 4 vols (Hyderabad, 1955–8).
Al-Dīnawarī, Abū Ḥanīfah Aḥmad ibn Dāwūd (d. 282/895) *al-Akhbār al-ṭiwāl*, eds ʿA. ʿĀmir and J. Shayyāl (Cairo, 1960).
Al-Fārisī, ʿAbd al-Ghāfir b. Ismāʿil (d. 529/1134), *al-Ḥalqa al-ūla min taʾrīkh Nīsābūr: al-muntakhab min al-Siyāq*, ed. Muḥammad Kāẓim al-Maḥmūdī (Qum, 1983).
Al-Ḥākim al-Nīsābūrī, Abū ʿAbdallāh (d. 405/1014), *Tārīkh-i Nīsābūr* (Tehran, 1996).
Al-Ḥaskānī, ʿUbayd Allāh ibn ʿAbd Allāh ibn Aḥmad (d. after 470/1077–8), *Shawāhid al-tanzīl*, ed. Muḥammad Bāqir al-Maḥmūdī (Beirut, 1393/1974).
Al-Idrīsī (d. 405/1005), *Taʾrīkh Astarābād*, published as appendix to al-Sahmī, *Taʾrikh Jurjān* (Beirut, 1981).
Al-Iṣfahānī, Abū al-Faraj (d. 356/967), *Kitāb al-Aghānī* (Cairo, 1984).
Al-Iṣfahānī, Abū al-Faraj (d. 356/967), *Kitāb Maqātil al-Ṭālibiyyīn*, ed. Aḥmad Ṣaqr, 2 vols (Beirut, 1949).
Al-Iṣṭakhrī (wrote c. 340/951), *Masālik al-mamālik*, ed. M. J. de Goeje (Leiden, 1870).
Al-Jāḥiẓ (d. 255/869), 'Maqālat al-zaydiyya wa-l-rāfiḍa', in al-Jāḥiẓ, *Rasāʾil*, ed. ʿAbd al-Salām Muḥammad Hārūn, 4 vols (Cairo, 1965–79).
Al-Jahshiyārī (d. 331/942), *Kitāb al-Wuzarāʾ wa-l-kuttāb*, ed. M. al-Saqqā (Cairo, 1938).
Al-Juvaynī, Muʾayyid al-Dawla (fl. 1118–57), *ʿAtabat al-kataba* (Tehran, 1950).
Al-Kāsānī, Abū Bakr b. Masʿūd (d. 587/1189), *Bidāyat al-ṣanāʾiʿfī tartīb al-sharāʾiʿ*, 7 vols (Cairo, 1327–8).
Al-Kashshī/Al-Kishshī (d. 340/951), *Kitāb Maʿrifāt al-rijāl*, ed. Ḥasan al-Mustafawī (Mashhad, 1348/1969).
Al-Khaṭīb al-Baghdādī (d. 463/1071), *Taʾrīkh Baghdād*, 14 vols (Cairo, 1931).
Al-Kulīnī (d. 329/941), *Uṣūl min al-Kāfī*, ed. ʿAlī Akbar Ghaffārī, 8 vols (1375–81/1955–61).
Al-Kumayt b. Zayd (d. 126/743), *Die Hāsimijjāt des Kumeit*, ed. and trans. J. Horovitz (Leiden, 1904).
Al-Madāʾinī (d. 225/839 or 840), 'Kitāb al-Murdifāt', in ʿAbd al-Salām Muḥammad Hārūn (ed.), *Nawādir al-makhṭūṭāt*, 2 vols (Beirut, 1991), vol. I.

Al-Marwazī al-Azwarqānī, Isma'īl b. al- Ḥusayn (d. after 614/1217), *al-Fakhrī fī ansāb al-Ṭālibiyyīn*, ed. Mahdī al-Rajā'ī (Qum, 1409/1988/9).

Al-Mas'ūdī (d. 345/956 or 357), *Murūj al-dhahab*, ed. C. Barbier de Meynard, 5 vols (Paris, 1861–77); ed. C. Pellat, 7 vols (Beirut, 1966–79).

Al-Māwardī (d. 450/1058), *al-Ḥāwī al-kabīr*, 24 vols (Beirut, 1414/1994).

Al-Māwardī (d. 450/1058), *Kitāb al-Aḥkām al-sulṭāniyya*, ed. M. Enger (Bonn, 1853); French trans. E. Fagnan, *Les statuts gouvernementaux* (Algiers, 1915); English trans. W. H. Wahba, *The Ordinances of Government* (Reading, 1996).

Al-Miskawayh (d. 421/1030), 'Tajārib al-umam', in H. F. Amedroz and D. S. Margoliouth (eds and trans), *The Eclipse of the 'Abbāsid Caliphate*, 7 vols (Oxford, 1920).

Al-Mufīd (d. 413/1022), *al-Muqnī'a* (Beirut, 1994).

Al-Mufīd (d. 413/1022), *Kitāb al-Irshād* (Najaf, 1382/1962); trans. I. K. A. Howard (London, 1981).

Al-Muqaddasī (wrote c. 375/985), *Aḥsān al-taqāsīm fī ma'rifat al-aqālīm*, ed. M. J. de Goeje (Leiden, 1906).

Al-Murtaḍā, al-Sharīf (d. 436/1044), *al-Nihāya fī mujarrad al-fiqh wa-l-fatāwā* (Tehran, 1954).

Al-Murtaḍā, al-Sharīf (d. 436/1044), *Rasā'il al-Sharīf al-Murtaḍā*, ed. Mahdī al-Rajā'ī, 3 vols (Qum, 1405/1984–85).

Al-Najāshī (d. 450/1058), *Rijāl al-Najāshī*, ed. Muḥammad Jawād al-Nā'īnī, 2 vols (Beirut, 1988); also as *Asmā' al-Rijāl*, ed. H. Muṣṭafawī (Tehran, n.d.).

Al-Narshakhī, Abū Bakr Muḥammad b. Ja'far (wrote 332/943), *Tārīkh-i Bukhārā*, ed. Mudarris Razavi (Tehran, 1351/1972–3); trans. Richard N. Frye, *The History of Bukhārā* (Cambridge, MA, 1954).

Al-Nasafī, Najm al-Dīn 'Umar b. Muḥammad (d. 537/1142), *al-Qand fī dhikr 'ulamā' Samarqand*, ed. Yūsuf al-Hādī (Tehran, 1999).

Al-Nāṭiq bi-l-Ḥaqq, Yaḥyā b. al-Ḥusayn b. Hārūn (d. 424/1032–3), *al-Ifāda fī ta'rīkh a'immat al-Zaydiyya*, ed. Muḥammad Yaḥyā Sālim (Ṣan'ā', 1996).

Al-Nāṭiq bi-l-Ḥaqq, Yaḥyā b. al-Ḥusayn b. Hārūn (d. 424/1032–3), *Kitāb al-Taḥrīr*, ed. Muḥammad Yaḥyā Sālim, 2 vols (Ṣan'ā', 1418/1997).

Al-Qalqashandī, Aḥmad b. (d. 821/1418), *Ṣubḥ al-a'shā fī ṣinā'at al-inshā'*, 14 vols (Cairo, 1331/1913).

Al-Qazwīnī, al-Ḥamd Allāh Mustawfī (fl. 730–40/1330–40), *Tārīkh-i guzīda*, ed. Ḥusayn Navā'ī (Tehran, 1983); abridged English trans. E. G. Brown and R. A. Nicholson, *Tārīkh-i Guzīda by Ḥamdu'llāh Mustawfī l-Qazwīnī* (Leiden, 1913), vol. II.

Al-Qummī, al-Ḥasan b. Muḥammad b. al-Ḥasan (d. 406/1015), *Kitāb Ta'rīkh Qum*, trans. al-Ḥasan b. 'Alī b. al-Ḥasan b. 'Abd al-Malik al-Qummī (fl. 805–6/1403), *Tārīkh-i Qum*, ed. Sayyid Jalāl al-Dīn al-Ṭīhrānī (Tehran, 1982).

Al-Qurashī, 'Abd al-Qādir b. Muḥammad (d. 776/1374 or 5), *Jawāhir al-muḍiyya fī ṭabaqāt al-Ḥanafiyya*, ed. 'Abd al-Fattāḥ al-Ḥulw, 3 vols (Cairo, 1978).

Al-Rāfiʿī (d. 623/1226), *Kitāb al-Tadwīn fī dhikr akhbār Qazwīn*, ed. ʿAzīz ʿAllāh al-Uṭāridī (Beirut, 1987).
Al-Rāzī, Aḥmad b. Sahl (fl. late 9th century), *Kitāb Akhbār Fakhkh wa-khabar Yaḥyā b. ʿAbdallāh*, ed. M. Jarrar (Beirut, 1995).
Al-Rāzī, Fakhr al-Dīn (d. 606/1209), *al-Shajara al-mubāraka fī ansāb al-Ṭālibiyya*, ed. Maḥmūd al-Marʿashī (Qum, 1410).
Al-Ṣābiʾ, Abū Isḥāq (d. 384/994), *al-Muntazaʿ min kitāb al-tājī*, ed. Muḥammad Ḥusayn al-Zubaydī (Baghdad, 1977).
Al-Ṣābiʾ, Abū Isḥāq (d. 384/994), *Rasāʾil*, part I, ed. Shakīb Arslān (Baʿabdā, 1898).
Al-Ṣābiʾ, Abū Isḥāq (d. 384/994), *Rasāʾil al-Ṣābiʾ wa-l-Sharīf al-Raḍī*, ed. Yūsuf Najm (Kuwait, 1961).
Al-Ṣābiʾ Hilāl (d. 448/1056–7), *The Historical Remains of Hilāl al-Sābiʾ: First Part of His Kitāb al-wuzarāʾ (Gotha Ms. 1756)*, ed. H. F. Amedroz (Leiden, 1904).
Al-Sadūsī, Muʾarrij (d. 195/810, or 174, or 200), *Kitāb Ḥadhf min nasab Quraysh*, ed. Ṣalāḥ al-Dīn al-Munajjid (Cairo, 1960).
Al-Sahmī, Hamza b. Yūsuf (d. 427/1035), *Taʾrīkh Jurjān* (Beirut, 1981).
Al-Samʿānī (d. 562/1166), *Kitāb al-Ansāb*, 13 vols (Hyderabad, 1962–82).
Al-Sarakhsī (d. 483/1091), *Kitāb al-Mabsūṭ*, ed. Muḥammad Rādī al-Ḥanafī, 13 vols (Cairo, 1324–31).
Al-Sarīfīnī (d. 641/1243), *Muntakhab min kitāb al-Siyāq li-taʾrīkh Nīsābūr*, ed. Khālid Ḥaydar (Beirut, 1993).
Al-Shīrāzī, Abū Isḥāq Fīrūzābādī (d. ca 476/1083), *al-Muhadhdhab*, ed. Muḥammad al-Zuḥaylī, 5 vols (Damascus, 1412–17/1992–6).
Al-Shīrāzī, Abū Isḥāq Fīrūzābādī (d. 476/1083), *Ṭabaqāt al-fuqahāʾ*, ed. Iḥsān ʿAbbās (Beirut, 1981).
Al-Shuhārī, Ibrāhīm b. al-Qāsim (d. c. 1730), *Ṭabaqāt al-Zaydiyya al-kubrā*, 3 vols (Amman, 2001).
Al-Subkī, Tāj al-Dīn (d. 771/1370), *Ṭabaqāt al-Shāfiʿiyya al-kubrā*, eds Maḥmūd Muḥammad al-Ṭanāḥī and ʿAbd al-Fattāḥ Ḥilw (Cairo, 1964–76); also ed. Muṣṭafa ʿAbd al-Qādir ʿAṭā (Beirut, 1999).
Al-Sulamī (d. 412/1021), *Ṭabaqāt al-ṣūfiyya*, ed. J. Pedersen (Leiden, 1960).
Al-Ṣūlī (d. 335/957), *Kitāb al-Awrāq* (Petersburg, 1998).
Al-Suyūṭī, Jalāl al-Dīn (d. 911/1505), 'al-ʿAjāja al-zarnabiyya fī al-sulāla al-Zaynabiyya', in al-Suyūṭī, *al-Ḥāwī li-l-fatāwī*, 2 vols (Cairo, 1352/1933), vol. II, pp. 31–4.
Al-Suyūṭī, Jalāl al-Dīn (d. 911/1505), *al-Ḥāwī li-l-fatāwī*, 2 vols (Cairo, 1378/1959).
Al-Suyūṭī, Jalāl al-Dīn (d. 911/1505), *Taʾrīkh al-khulafāʾ*, ed. Ibrāhīm Ṣāliḥ (Beirut, 1997).
Al-Ṭabarī (d. 310/923), *Taʾrīkh al-rusul wa-l-mulūk*, ed. M. J. de Goeje *et al.* (Leiden, 1879–1901); English trans. *The History of al-Ṭabarī*, ed. E. Yarshater, 39 vols (Albany, NY, 1989–98).
Al-Tanūkhī (d. 384/994), *al-Faraj baʿd al-shidda*, ed. ʿAbbūd al-Shāljī, 5 vols

(Beirut, 1971–3); partial German trans. A. Hottinger, *Ende Gut, Alles Gut: Das Buch der Erleichterung nach der Bedrängnis* (Zürich, 1979).

Al-Tanūkhī (d. 384/994), *Nishwār al-muḥāḍara*, ed. ʿAbbūd al-Shāljī, 8 vols (Beirut, 1971–2); partial English trans. D. S. Margoliouth, *The Table-Talk of a Mesopotamian Judge* (Hyderabad, n.d.).

Al-Thaʿālibī (d. 429/1038), *Tatimmat yatīmat al-dahr* (Beirut, 1983).

Al-Thaʿālibī (d. 429/1038), *Laṭāʾif al-maʿārif*, ed. P. de Jong (Leiden, 1867); English translation C. E. Bosworth, *The Book of Curious and Entertaining Information* (Edinburgh, 1968).

Al-Thaʿālibī (d. 429/1038), *Yatīmat al-dahr fī maḥāsin ahl al-aṣr*, 4 vols in 2 (Cairo, 1955),

Al-Ṭūsī, Abū Jaʿfar (d. 460/1067), *Kitāb al-Khilāf*, 4 vols (Qum, 1413).

Al-Ṭūsī, Abū Jaʿfar (d. 460/1067), *Taṣḥīḥ al-iʿtiqād bi-ṣawāb al-intiqād* (Beirut, 1983).

Al-Ṭūsī, Abū Jaʿfar (d. 460/1067), *Tahdhīb al-aḥkām*, 10 vols (Tehran, 1390/1970), or as *Tahdhīb al-aḥkām fī sharḥ al-Muqniʿa*, 10 vols (Tehran, 1997).

Al-Ṭūsī, Abū Jaʿfar (d. 460/1067), *Fihrist kutub al-Shīʿa* (Beirut, 1983); also (Najaf, n.d.)

Al-Ṭūsī, Abū Jaʿfar (d. 460/1067), *al-Mabsūṭ*, 8 vols in 7 (Tehran, 1352/1968).

Al-Ṭūsī, Abū Jaʿfar (d. 460/1067), *al-Nihāya fī mujarrad al-fiqh wa-l-fatāwā* (Tehran, 1954).

Al-Ṭūsī, Abū Jaʿfar (d. 460/1067), *Tusy's list of Shiʿa Books* (Calcutta, 1853).

Al-ʿUbaydalī, Shaykh al-Sharaf (d. 435/1043), *Tahdhīb al-ansāb wa-nihāyat al-aʿqāb*, ed. Muḥammad Kāẓim al-Maḥmūdī (Qum, 1413/1992–3).

Al-ʿUmarī al-Nassāba, Abū al-Ḥasan (d. 450/1058), *al-Majdī fī ansāb al-Ṭālibiyyīn*, ed. Aḥmad al-Mahdāwī al-Dāmghānī (Qum, 1409/1988/9).

Al-Yaʿqūbī (d. after 292/905), *Taʾrīkh (Historiae)*, ed. M. Th. Houtsma, 2 vols (Leiden, 1883).

Al-Zubayr b. Bakkār (d. 256/870), *Jamharat nasab Quraysh wa-akhbārihā*, ed. Maḥmūd Muḥammad Shākir (Cairo, 1381/1961), vol. I.

Al-Zubayrī, Muṣʿab (d. 236/851), *Kitāb Nasab Quraysh*, ed. É. Lévi-Provençal (Cairo, 1953).

ʿAlī b. Khalaf (fl. 437/1045), *Māwadd al-bayān* (Frankfurt, 1986; reproduced from MS 4128, Fatih Collection, Süleymaniye Library, Istanbul).

Awliyāʾ Allāh al-Āmulī (fl. 763/1362), *Tārīkh-ī Rūyān*, ed. M. Sotūdeh (Tehran, 1348/1969).

Benjamin of Tudela (fl. 12th century), *The World of Benjamin of Tudela: A Medieval Mediterranean Travelogue*, ed. and trans. Sandra Benjamin (London, 1995).

Ibn ʿAbbād, al-Ṣāḥib Ismāʿīl (d. 385/995), *Rasāʾil al-Ṣāḥib b. ʿAbbād*, eds ʿAbd al-Wahhāb ʿAzzām and Shawqī Dayf (Cairo, 1947).

Ibn Abī al-Ḥadīd (d. 655/1257), *Sharḥ nahj al-balāgha*, ed. M. A.-F. Ibrāhīm (Cairo, 1965–7); or (Beirut, 1998).

Ibn al-Athīr (d. 630/1233), *al-Kāmil fī al-taʾrīkh*, ed. C. J. Tornberg (Leiden, 1851–76); reprinted 13 vols (Beirut, 1965–7).
Ibn al-Jawzī (d. 597/1200), *al-Muntaẓam fī tārīkh al-mulūk wa al-umam*, eds Muḥammad and Muṣṭafā ʿAbd al-Qādir ʿAṭā, 18 vols (Beirut, 1992–3); or (Hyderabad, 1357–9/1938–40).
Ibn al-Kalbī (d. 204/819), *Ǧamharat al-nasab: Das genealogische Werk des Hisām ibn Muḥammad al-Kalbī*, ed. Werner Caskel, 2 vols (Leiden, 1966); also published as *Jamharat al-nasab*, ed. Maḥmūd Firdaws al-ʿAẓm, 3 vols (Damascus, 1982–6), and *Jamharat al-nasab*, ed. Nājī Ḥasan, 2 vols (Beirut, 1986).
Ibn al-Nadīm (d. 380/990), *Kitāb al-Fihrist*, ed. Gustav Flügel, 2 vols (Leipzig, 1871); new edn Riḍā Tajaddud (Tehran, 1971); trans. B. Dodge, *The Fihrist of al-Nadīm*, 2 vols (New York, 1970).
Ibn Asākir (d. 517/1176), *Taʾrīkh madīnat Dimashq*, ed. ʿA Shīrī (Beirut, 1995–8).
Ibn Bābūya al-Qummī (d. 381/991), *al-Iʿtiqadāt fī dīn al-Imāmiyya* (Qum, 1412).
Ibn Bābūya al-Qummī (d. 381/991), *al-Muqniʿ wa-l-hidāya*, ed. Muḥammad b. Mahdī al-Wāʿiẓ (Tehran, 1377q/1957).
Ibn Bābūya al-Qummī (d. 381/991), *ʿIlal al-sharāʾiʿ* (Najaf, 1383/1963).
Ibn Bābūya al-Qummī (d. 381/991), *Man lā yaḥḍuruhu al-faqīh* (Najaf, 1376/1954); new edn, 4 vols (Beirut, 1981).
Ibn Bābūya al-Qummī (d. 381/991), *Risālat al-iʿtiqād* (Najaf, 1343); trans. Asaf A. A. Fyzee, *A Shiʿite Creed* (Oxford, 1942).
Ibn Daud, Abraham, *Sefer Ha-Qabbalah: The Book of Tradition*, ed. Gerson D. Cohen (Philadelphia, 1967); reprinted (Oxford, 2005).
Ibn Funduq al-Bayhaqī (d. 565/1169), *Lubāb al-ansāb*, ed. Mahdī al-Rajāʾī (Qum, 1410/1989/90).
Ibn Funduq al-Bayhaqī (d. 565/1169), *Tārīkh-i Bayhaq*, ed. Aḥmad Bahmanyār (Tehran, 1938).
Ibn Ḥabīb, Muḥammad (d. 245/860), 'Asmāʾ al-mughtalīn min al-ashrāf fī al-jāhiliyya wa-l-Islām', in ʿAbd al-Salām Muḥammad Hārūn (ed.), *Nawādir al-makhṭūṭāt*, 2 vols (Beirut, 1991), vol. II.
Ibn Ḥabīb, Muḥammad (d. 245/860), *Kitāb al-Muḥabbar*, ed. Ilse Lichtenstädter (Hyderabad, 1942).
Ibn Ḥabīb, Muḥammad (d. 245/860), *Kitāb al-Munammaq fī akhbār Quraysh*, ed. Khurshīd Aḥmad Fāriq (Hyderabad, 1964).
Ibn Ḥajar al-ʿAsqalānī (d. 852/1449), *Tahdhīb al-Tahdhīb*, 12 vols (Hyderabad, 1325–7).
Ibn Ḥawqal (d. after 362/973), *Kitāb Ṣūrat al-arḍ*, ed. J. H. Kramers (Leiden, 1967).
Ibn Ḥazm (d. 456/1064), *Jamharat ansāb al-ʿarab*, ed. É. Lévi-Provençal (Cairo, 1948); ed. ʿAbd al-Salām Muḥammad Hārūn (Cairo, 1962).
Ibn ʿInaba (d. 828/1424–5), *ʿUmdat al-ṭālib fī ansāb āl Abī Ṭālib* (Najaf, 1961); ed. Nizār Riḍā (Beirut, 1963?); new edn Mahdī al-Rajāʾī (Qum, 1425q/2004).
Ibn Isfandiyār (fl. 1210–16), *Tārīkh-i Ṭabaristān*, ed. ʿAbbās Iqbāl, 2 vols (Tehran

1320/1940–1); English trans. E. G. Brown, *An Abridged Translation of the History of Ṭabaristān* (Leiden and London, 1905).
Ibn Manẓūr (d. 711/1311 or 1312), *Lisān al-ʿArab*, 20 vols in 10 (Cairo, 1880–9); new edn (Beirut, 1968).
Ibn Qayyim al-Jawziyya (d. 751/1350), *Aḥkām ahl al-dhimma*, ed. Yūsuf ibn Aḥmad al-Bakrī and Shākir ibn Tawfīq al-ʿĀrūrī, 3 vols (Beirut, 1997).
Ibn Qutayba (d. 276/889), *Kitāb al-Maʿārif*, ed. T. ʿUkāsha (Cairo, 1981).
Ibn Saʿd (d. 230/845), *al-Ṭabaqāt al-kabīr*, ed. E. Sachau, 9 vols (Leiden, 1904–40).
Ibn Saʿd (d. 230/845), *al-Ṭabaqāt al-kubrā*, ed. Muḥammad ʿAbd al-Qādir ʿAṭā, 9 vols (Beirut, 1990–1).
Ibn Shahrāshūb (d. 588/1192), *Maʿālim al-ʿulamāʾ*, ed. ʿAbbās Iqbāl (Tehran, 1934).
Ibn Shahrāshūb (d. 588/1192), *Manāqib Āl Abī Ṭālib*, ed. Yūsuf al-Biqāʿī, third printing, 5 vols (Beirut, 1991).
Ibn Shadqam, (d. 1033/1623–4), *Zahrat al-maqūl* (Najaf, 1961).
Ibn Ṭabāṭabā, Abū Ismāʿīl Ibrāhīm (d. second half of the 5th/11th century), *Muntaqilat al-Ṭālibiyya*, ed. Muḥammad Mahdī al-Sayyid Ḥasan al-Kharsān (Najaf, 1388/1968).
Ibn Taghrībirdī (d. 875/1470), *al-Nujūm al-zāhira fī mulūk Miṣr wa-l-Qāhira*, 16 vols (Cairo, 1929–71).
Ibn Taymiyya, *Minhāj al-sunna al-nabawiyya*, cited in Kazuo Morimoto, 'Introduction', in Kazuo Morimoto (ed.), *Sayyids and Sharifs in Muslim Societies: The Living Links to the Prophet* (London and New York, 2012).
Ibn al-Ṭiqṭaqā, Muḥammad b. ʿAlī (d. 708/1308), *al-Aṣīlī fī ansāb al-Ṭālibiyyīn*, ed. Mahdī al-Rajāʾī (Qum, 1418/1997).
Khalīfa b. Khayyāṭ, *Kitāb al-Ṭabaqāt* (Damascus, 1966).
Khalīfa b. Khayyāṭ (d. 240/854), *Taʾrīkh*, ed. al-ʿUmarī (Beirut, 1995).
Saḥnūn (d. 240/854), *al-Mudawwana al-kubrā*, 16 vols in 4 (Cairo, 1323/1905).
ʿUmar b. Shabba (d. 262/875), *Kitāb Taʾrīkh al-Madīna al-munawwara*, 2 vols (Beirut, 1996).
Yāqūt al-Ḥamawī (d. 626/1229), *Muʿjam al-buldān*, 20 vols in 5 (Beirut, 1955–7).
[Pseudo] Zayd b. ʿAlī (d. 122/740), *Musnad al-Imām Zayd* (Beirut, 1991).
[Pseudo] Zayd b. ʿAlī (d. 122/740), *Corpus iuris di Zaid b. ʿAlī*, ed. E. Griffini (Milan, 1919).

Secondary sources

Afsaruddin, Asma, *Excellence and Precedence: Medieval Islamic Discourse on Legitimate Leadership* (Leiden, 2002).
Āghā Buzurg al-Ṭīhrānī (d. 1970), *Al-Dharīʿa ilā taṣānīf al-shīʿa* (Najaf, 1936–78).
Āghā Buzurg al-Ṭīhrānī (d. 1970), *Ṭabaqāt aʿlām al-Shīʿa*, 6 vols (Beirut, 1971–).
Ahmed, Asad, 'Prosopography and the Reconstruction of Ḥijāzī History for the Early Islamic Period: The Case of the ʿAwfī Family', in Katharine Keats-Rohan (ed.),

Prosopography Approaches and Applications: A Handbook (Oxford, 2007), pp. 415–58.

Ahmed, Asad, *The Religious Elite of the Early Islamic Ḥijāz: Five Prosopographical Case Studies* (Oxford, 2011).

Al-ʿĀmilī, Muḥsin al-Amīn (d. 1952), *Aʿyān al-Shīʿa* (Damascus, 1367/1947).

Al-ʿĀmilī, Muḥsin al-Amīn (d. 1952), *Aʿyān al-Shīʿa*, ed. al-Ḥasan al-Amīn (Beirut, 1960).

Al-Dūrī, ʿAbd al-ʿAzīz, *The Rise of Historical Writing Among the Arabs*, ed. and trans. Lawrence I. Conrad (Princeton, 1983).

Al-Qāḍī, Wadād, 'Biographical Dictionaries: Inner Structure and Cultural Significance', in George N. Atiye (ed.), *The Book in the Islamic World* (Albany, NY, 1995), pp. 93–122.

Al-Zuḥaylī, Wahba, *al-Fiqh al-islāmī*, 4th edn, 10 vols (Beirut, 1425/2004).

Al-Zurbātī, *Awlād al-Imām al-Bāqir* (Qum, 1417).

Amedroz, H. F., 'The Office of the Kadi in the Ahkam al-Sultaniyya of Mawardi', *Journal of the Royal Asiatic Society*, n.s., 42 (1910), pp. 761–96.

Arendonk, C. van, *Les debuts de l'Imamat Zaidite au Yemen*, trans. R. Ryckmans (Leiden, 1960).

Arendonk, C. van and W. A. Graham, 'Sharīf', in B. Lewis *et al.* (eds), *Encyclopaedia of Islam, Second Edition* (*EI2*) (Leiden, 1954–2005).

Aubin, Jean, 'L'aristocratie urbaine dans l'Iran seljoukide', in Pierre Gallais (ed.), *Melanges offerts à René Crozet* (Poitiers, 1966), pp. 323–32.

Bayhom-Daou, Tamima, 'ʿAlī al-Riḍā', in *Encyclopaedia of Islam*, 3rd edn (henceforth *EI3*).

Bayhom-Daou, Tamima, *Shaykh al-Mufid* (Oxford, 2005).

Bayhom-Daou, Tamima, 'The Imam's Knowledge and the Quran according to al-Faḍl b. Shadhān al-Nīsābūrī (d. 260 A.H./874 A.D.)', *Bulletin of the School of Oriental and African Studies* 64 (2001), pp. 188–207.

Beck, Herman, *L'Image d'Idrīs II, ses descendants de Fās et la politique sharīfienne des sultans Marīnides (656–869/1258–1465)* (Leiden, 1989).

Beeston, A. F. L., 'Epigraphic South Arabian Nomenclature', *Raydan* 1 (1978), pp. 13–21.

Bernheimer, Teresa, 'A Social History of the ʿAlid Family from the Eighth to the Eleventh Century' (DPhil thesis, University of Oxford, 2006).

Bernheimer, Teresa, 'Genealogy, Marriage, and the Drawing of Boundaries among the ʿAlids (Eigth–twelfth Centuries)', in Kazuo Morimoto (ed.), *Sayyids and Sharifs in Muslim Societies: The Living Link to the Prophet* (London/New York, 2012), pp. 75–91.

Bernheimer, Teresa, 'Shared Sanctity: Some Notes on *Ahl al-Bayt* Shrines in the Early Ṭālibid Genealogies', *Studia Islamica* (forthcoming).

Bernheimer, Teresa, 'The Rise of *Sayyid*s and *Sādāt*: The Case of the Al Zubāra in 9th–11th Century Nishapur', *Studia Islamica* 100/1 (2005), pp. 43–69.

Bernheimer, Teresa and Stephennie Mulder (eds), 'Sharing Sanctity: Veneration of the Family of the Prophet as Non-Sectarian Social Praxis', special issue, *Studia Islamica* (forthcoming).

Bianquis, Thierry, 'Notables ou malandrins d'origine rurale à Damas à l'époque Fatimide', *Bulletin d'Etudes Orientales* 26 (1973), pp. 185–207.

Björkman, W., '*Ḳalansuwa*', *EI2*.

Bodman, H. L., *Political Factions in Aleppo, 1760–1826* (Chapel Hill, NC, 1963).

Bonebakker, S. A., 'A Fatimid Manual for Secretaries', *Annali dell'Instituto Orientale di Napoli* 37, n.s., 27 (1977), pp. 295–337.

Bosworth, C. E., 'Abū ʿAbdallāh al-Khwārazmī on the Technical Terms of the Secretary's Art', *Journal of the Economic and Social History of the Orient* 12 (1969), pp. 113–64.

Bosworth, C. E., 'al-Sahmī', *EI2*.

Bosworth, C. E., 'Raʾīs, 2. In the Sense of "Mayor" in the Eastern Islamic Lands', *EI2*.

Bosworth, C. E., 'Saʿīd b. al-ʿĀṣ', *EI2*.

Bosworth, C. E., *The Ghaznavids: Their Empire in Afghanistan and Eastern Iran, 994–1040* (Edinburgh, 1963).

Bosworth, C. E., *The History of the Saffarids of Sistan and the Maliks of Nimruz (247/861 to 949/1542–3)* (Costa Mesa, CA, 1994).

Bosworth, C. E., 'The Persian Contribution to Islamic historiography in the pre-Mongol Period', in R. Hovannisian and G. Sabagh (eds), *The Persian Presence in the Islamic World* (Cambridge, 1998), pp. 218–36.

Brett, Michael, *The Rise of the Fāṭimids* (Leiden, 2001).

Buhl, F., 'al-Ḥasan b. Zayd', *EI2*.

Bujra, Abdalla S., 'Political Conflict and Stratification in Ḥaḍramaut – I', *Middle Eastern Studies* 3 (1967), pp. 355–75.

Bulliet, Richard, 'A Quantitative Approach to Medieval Muslim Dictionaries', *Journal of the Economic and Social History of the Orient* 13 (1970), pp. 195–211.

Bulliet, Richard, 'City Histories in Medieval Iran', *Iranian Studies* 1 (1968), pp. 104–9.

Bulliet, Richard, 'Local Politics in Eastern Iran under the Ghaznavids and Seljuqs', *Iranian Studies* 11 (1978), pp. 35–56.

Bulliet, Richard, 'Medieval Nishapur: A Topographic and Demographic Reconstruction', *Studia Iranica* 5 (1976), pp. 67–89.

Bulliet, Richard, *The Patricians of Nishapur: A Study in Medieval Islamic Social History* (Cambridge, MA, 1972).

Bulliet, Richard, 'The Political–Religious History of Nishapur in the Eleventh Century', in D. S. Richards (ed.), *Islamic Civilisation 950–1150* (Oxford, 1983), pp. 71–91.

Busse, Heribert, *Chalif und Großkönig: Die Buyiden im Iraq (945–1055)* (Beirut, 1969).

Busse, Heribert, 'Das Hofbudget des Chalifen al-Muʿtaḍid billāh (279/892–289/902)', *Der Islam* 43 (1967), pp. 11–36.

Cahen, Claude, "ʿAṭā", *EI2*.
Cahen, Claude, 'Ḥasanwayh', *EI2*.
Cahen, Claude, 'Mouvements populaires et autonomisme urbain dans l'Asie musulmane du moyen age', *Arabica* 5 (1958), pp. 225–50, and *Arabica* 6 (1959), pp. 25–56 and 233–65.
Calder, Norman, 'Friday Prayer and the Juristic Theory of Government: Sarakhsī, Shīrāzī, Māwardī', *Bulletin of the School of Oriental and African Studies* 49 (1986), pp. 35–47.
Calder, Norman, 'Khums in Imāmī Shīʿī Jurispridence, from the Tenth to the Sixteenth Century A.D.', *Bulletin of the School of Oriental and African Studies* 45 (1982), pp. 39–47.
Calder, Norman, 'Zakāt in Imāmī Shīʿī Jurispridence, from the Tenth to the Sixteenth Century A.D.', *Bulletin of the School of Oriental and African Studies* 44 (1981), pp. 468–80.
Caskel, Werner (ed.), *Ǧamharāt an-nasab: Das genealogische Werk des His̆ām ibn Muḥammad al-Kalbī*, 2 vols (Leiden, 1966).
Caskel, Werner (ed.), 'Nasab', *EI2*.
Cobb, Paul, *White Banners: Contention in ʿAbbāsid Syria, 750–880* (Albany, NY, 2001).
Crone, Patricia, *God's Rule: Government and Islam* (New York, 2004).
Crone, Patricia, 'Mawālī and the Prophet's Family: An Early Shīʿite View', in M. Bernards and J. Nawas (eds), *Patronate and Patronage in Early and Classical Islam* (Leiden, 2005), pp. 167–94.
Crone, Patricia, 'On the Meaning of the ʿAbbāsid call to *al-riḍā*', in C. E. Bosworth (ed.), *The Islamic World: Essays in Honor of Bernard Lewis* (Princeton, 1989), pp. 95–111.
Crone, Patricia, *Slaves on Horses: The Evolution of the Islamic Polity* (Cambridge, 1980).
Crone, Patricia and Luke Treadwell, 'A New Text on Ismailism at the Samanid Court', in Chase Robinson (ed.), *Texts, Documents and Artefacts: Islamic Studies in Honour of Donald Richards* (Leiden, 2003), pp. 37–67.
Dahmash, Wasim, 'On Sādāt in Medieval Ramlah', *Oriente Moderno*, n.s., 18 (1999), pp. 441–9.
Daniel, Elton, *The Political and Social History of Khurāsān under ʿAbbāsid Rule* (Minneapolis, 1979).
DeWeese, Devin, 'The Descendants of *Sayyid* Ata and the Rank of *Naqīb* in Central Asia', *Journal of the American Oriental Society* 115 (1995), pp. 612–34.
Djebeli, Moktar, 'al-Sharīf al-Raḍī, Abū 'l-Ḥasan Muḥammad b. Abī Aḥmad al-Ḥusayn b. Mūsā', *EI2*.
Djebeli, Moktar, 'al-Ṭhaqafī, Ibrāhīm b. Muḥammad, Abū Isḥāq', *EI2*.
Donohue, John, *The Buwayhid Dynasty in Iraq, 334 H./945 to 403 H./1012: Shaping Institutions for the Future* (Leiden, 2003).
Doumani, Beshara (ed.), *Family History in the Middle East: Household, Property and Gender* (Albany, NY, 2003).

Drechler, Andreas, *Die Geschichte der Stadt Qom im Mittelalter (605–1350)* (Berlin, 1999).
Eickelman, Dale, *The Middle East and Central Asia: An Anthropological Approach*, 4th edn (Upper Saddle River, NJ, 2002).
El-Leithy, Tamer, 'Public Punishment in Mamluk Society' (MPhil thesis, Cambridge University, 1997).
Elad, Amikam, 'The Correspondence Between al-Manṣūr and Muḥammad b. ʿAbdallāh', in *The Rebellion of Muḥammad al-Nafs al-Zakiyya in 145/762. A Study of the Relations Between the Early ʿAbbāsīs and the Ṭālibī Factions* [Tentative Title] (Leiden, forthcoming).
Elad, Amikam, 'The Rebellion of Muḥammad b. ʿAbd Allāh b. al-Ḥasan (Known as al-Nafs al-Zakīya) in 145/762', in James E. Montgomery (ed.), *ʿAbbasid Studies: Occasional Papers of the School of ʿAbbasid Studies, Cambridge, 6–10 July 2002* (Leuven, 2004), pp. 145–98.
Elad, Amikam, *The Rebellion of Muḥammad al-Nafs al-Zakiyya in 145/762: A Study of the Relations between the Early ʿAbbāsīs and the Ṭālibī Factions* (Leiden, forthcoming).
Elad, Amikam, 'The Siege of al-Wāsiṭ (132/749): Some Aspects of ʿAbbāsid and ʿAlīd Relations at the Beginning of ʿAbbāsid Rule', in M. Sharon (ed.), *Studies in Islamic History and Civilisation in Honour of Professor Ayalon* (Jerusalem and Leiden, 1986), pp. 59–90.
Ess, Josef van, *Theologie und Gesellschaft im 2. und 3. Jahrhundert Hidschra: Eine Geschichte des religiösen Denkens im frühen Islam*, 6 vols (Berlin and New York, 1991–7).
Ettinghausen, Richard, 'The Man-Made Setting', in Bernard Lewis (ed.), *The World of Islam* (London, 1992), pp. 57–88.
Eustache, Daniel, *Corpus des monnaies ʿAlawites: Collection de la Bank du Maroc et autres collections mondiales* (Rabat, 1984).
Eustache, Daniel, 'Idrīs b. ʿAbdallāh', *EI2*.
Eustache, Daniel, 'Idrīsids', *EI2*.
Fairbanks, Stephen Charles, 'The Tārīkh al-Vuzarāʾ: A History of the Saljuq Bureaucracy' (PhD dissertation, University of Michigan, 1977).
Farhat, May, 'Islamic Piety and Dynastic Legitimacy: The Case of the Shrine of ʿAlī b. Mūsā al-Riḍā in Mashhad (10th – 17th century)' (PhD dissertation, Harvard University, 2002).
Fisher, Michael H., 'Political Marriage Alliances at the Shiʿi Court of Awadh', *Comparative Studies in Society and History* 24 (1983), pp. 593–616.
Fragner, Bert, *Geschichte der Stadt Hamadān und ihrer Umgebung in den ersten sechs Jahrhunderten nach der Hiğra* (Vienna, 1972).
Franklin, Arnold, 'Cultivating Roots: The Promotion of Exilarchal Ties to David in the Middle Ages', *Association for Jewish Studies Review* 29 (2005), pp. 91–110.
Franklin, Arnold, 'Shoots of David: Members of the Exilarchal Dynasty in the Middle Ages' (PhD dissertation, Princeton University, 2001).

Franklin, Arnold, *This Noble House: Jewish Descendants of King David in the Islamic East* (Philadelphia, 2012).
Freitag, Ulrike (ed.), 'Gelehrtenbeziehungen im Spannungsfeld von Tradition und Moderne: Der hadhramische ʿĀlim Aḥmad b. Ḥasan al-ʿAṭṭās (1841–1915)', in Rainer Brunner *et al.* (eds), *Islamstudien Ohne Ende: Festschrift für Werner Ende zum 65. Geburtstag* (Würzburg, 2002), pp. 87–96.
Freitag, Ulrike (ed.), *Indian Ocean Migrants and State Formation in Hadramaut: Reforming the Homeland* (Leiden, 2003).
Frye, R. N., *The Histories of Nishapur* (The Hague, 1965).
Fyzee, Asaf A. A., *A Shiʿite Creed* (Calcutta, 1942); reprinted (Tehran, 1982).
Gabrieli, F., *Al-Maʾmūn e gli ʿAlidi* (Leipzig, 1929).
Gibb, H. A. R., 'Abū 'l-Sarāyā', *EI2*.
Gibb, H. A. R., 'Al-Mawardi's Theory of the Khalifa', *Islamic Culture* 11 (1937), pp. 291–302.
Gil, Moshe, *Jews in Islamic Countries in the Middle Ages*, trans. David Strassler (Leiden, 2004).
Gleave, Robert, 'Between *Ḥādīth* and *Fiqh*: The 'Canonical' Imāmī collections of *Akhbār*', *Islamic Law and Society* 8 (2001), pp. 350–82.
Gleave, Robert, *Inevitable Doubt: Two Theories of Shīʿī Jurisprudence* (Leiden, 2000).
Gleave, Robert, 'Marrying Fāṭimid Women: Legal Theory and Substantive Law in Shīʿī Jurisprudence', *Islamic Law and Society* 6 (1999), pp. 38–68.
Gleave, Robert, review of *Islamic Legal Orthodoxy: Twelver Shiite Responses to the Sunni Legal System*, by Devin Stewart, *Islamic Law and Society* 7 (2000), pp. 102–4.
Gochenour, D. T., 'A Revised Bibliography of Medieval Yemeni History in the Light of Recent Publications and Discoveries', *Der Islam* 63 (1986), pp. 315–17.
Goitein, S. D. F., *A Mediterranean Society: The Jewish Community of the Arab World as Portrayed by the Documents of the Cairo Geniza* (Berkeley, CA, 1967–93).
Goitein, S. D. F., 'Introduction', in al-Balādhurī, *Ansāb al-ashrāf*, vol. V (Jerusalem, 1936).
Goldstein, Sidney, and Calvin Goldschneider, 'Social and Demographic Aspects of Jewish Intermarriages', *Social Problems* 13 (1966), pp. 386–99.
Goldziher, Ignaz, *Mohammedanische Studien*, 2 vols (Halle, 1889–90); English trans C. R. Barber and S. M. Stern, *Muslim Studies*, ed. S. M. Stern, 2 vols (London, 1967–71).
Gordon, Matthew, *The Breaking of a Thousand Swords: A History of the Turkish Military of Samarra, A.H. 200–275/815–889 C.E.* (Albany, NY, 2001).
Grabar, Oleg, 'The Earliest Islamic Commemorative Structures, Notes and Documents', *Ars Orientalis* 6 (1966), pp. 1–46.
Günther, Sebastian, 'Abū l-Faraj al-Iṣfahānī: A Medieval Arabic Author at Work', in Rainer Brunner *et al.* (eds), *Islamstudien Ohne Ende: Festschrift für Werner Ende zum 65. Geburtstag* (Würzburg, 2002), pp. 139–53.

Günther, Sebastian, '*Maqātil* Literature in Medieval Islam', *Journal of Arabic Literature* 25 (1994), pp. 192–212.

Günther, Sebastian, *Quellenuntersuchungen zu den 'Maqātil aṭ-Ṭālibiyyīn' des Abū 'l-Farağ al-Iṣfahānī (gest. 356/967): Ein Beitrag zur Problematik der mündlichen und schriftlichen Überlieferung in der mittelalterlichen arabischen Literatur* (Hildesheim, 1991).

Hachmeier, Klaus, *Die Briefe Abū Isḥāq Ibrāhīm al-Ṣābi'ʾs (st. 384/994 A.H./A.D.)* (Hildesheim, 2002).

Haider, Najam, 'The Contested Life of ʿĪsā b. Zayd (d. 166/783): Notes on the Construction of Zaydī Historical Narratives', *JNES* (forthcoming).

Haider, Najam, *The Origins of the Shīʿa: Identity, Ritual, and Sacred Space in Eighth-Century Kūfa* (Cambridge, 2011).

Haider, Najam, 'Yaḥyā b. ʿAbdāh b. al-Ḥasan b. al-Ḥasan b. ʿAlī', in M. Haleem and M. A. Shah (eds), *IB Tauris Biographical Dictionary of Islamic Civilisation* (London, forthcoming).

Halm, Heinz, 'Der Wesir al-Kundurī und die *fitna* von Nishapur', *Welt des Orients* 6 (1970–1), pp. 205–33.

Halm, Heinz, *Die Ausbreitung der šāfiʿitischen Rechtschule von den Anfängen bis zum 8./14. Jahrhundert* (Wiesbaden, 1974).

Halm, Heinz, *Die Schia* (Darmstadt, 1988).

Halm, Heinz, *Die Traditionen über den Aufstand ʿAlī b. Muhammads, des 'Herren der Zanğ': Eine quellenkritische Untersuchung* (Bonn, 1967).

Havemann, Axel, 'Naḳīb al-Ashrāf', *EI2*.

Havemann, Axel, 'Raʾīs, 1. In the Sense of "Mayor" in the Central Arab Lands', *EI2*.

Havemann, Axel, *Riʾāsa und qaḍāʾ: Institutionen als Ausdruck wechselnder Kräfteverhältnisse in syrischen Städten vom 10. bis zum 12. Jahrhundert* (Freiburg, 1975).

Hinds, Martin, *An Early Islamic Family from Omān: Al-ʿAwtabī's Account of the Muhallabids* (Manchester, 1991).

Hinds, Martin, 'Makhzūm', *EI2*.

Hinds, Martin, 'The Early ʿAbbāsid Caliphs and Sunna', paper presented at the Colloquium on the Study of Hadith (Oxford, 1982).

Ho, Engseng, *The Graves of Tarim: Genealogy and Mobility across the Indian Ocean* (Berkeley and Los Angeles, 2006).

Hodgson, M. G. S., 'How Did the Early Shīʿa Become Sectarian?', *Journal of the American Oriental Society* 75 (1955), pp. 1–13.

Horovitz, Joseph (ed. and trans.), *Die Hasīmijjāt des Kumeit* (Leiden, 1904).

Hoyland, Robert G., *Arabia and the Arabs: From the Bronze Age to the Coming of Islam* (London, 2001).

Hrbek, Ivan, 'Muḥammads Nachlass und die ʿAliden', *Archiv Orientalni* 18 (1950), pp. 143–9.

Humphreys, Stephen, *Islamic History: A Framework for Inquiry*, revised edn (London, 1995).

Humphreys, Stephen, 'Taʾrīkh', *EI2*.
Husaini, Q. S. Kalimulla, 'Life and Works of Zāhir al-Dīn al-Bayhaqī, the Author of the Tarikh-i Bayhaq', *Islamic Culture* 28 (1954), pp. 297–318; *Islamic Culture* 33 (1958), pp. 188–202; *Islamic Culture* 34 (1960), pp. 40–89.
Jafri, M., *Origins and Early Development of Shia Islam* (London, 1979).
Jafri, M., 'The Early Development of Legitimist Shiʿism with Special Reference to the Role of Imām Jaʿfar al-Ṣādiq' (PhD thesis, School of Oriental and African Studies, 1966); published as *Origins and Early Development of Shia Islam* [London, 1979]).
Jarrar, Maher, 'Introduction', in Aḥmad b. Sahl al-Rāzī, *Akhbār Fakhkh*, ed. Maher Jarrar (Tunis, 2011), pp. 9–129.
Johns, Jeremy and Alex Metcalfe, 'The Mystery at Churchuro: Conspiracy or Incompetence in Twelfth-Century Sicily', *Bulletin of the School of Oriental and African Studies* 62 (1999), pp. 226–59.
Kaabi, Mongi, *Les Ṭāhirides au Ḫurāsān et en Iraq* (Paris, 1983).
Kabir, M., *The Buwayhid Dynasty of Baghdad, 334/946–447/1055* (Calcutta, 1964).
Kammūna al-Ḥusaynī, ʿAbd al-Razzāq, *Mawārid al-itḥāf fī nuqabāʾ al-ashrāf*, 2 vols (Najaf, 1968).
Kennedy, Hugh, 'Central Government and Provincial Elites in the Early ʿAbbāsid Caliphate', *Bulletin of the School of Oriental and African Studies* 44 (1981), pp. 26–38.
Kennedy, Hugh, 'From Oral Tradition to Written Record in Arabic Genealogy', *Arabica* 44 (1997), pp. 531–44.
Kennedy, Hugh, *The Early Abbasid Caliphate* (London, 1981).
Khalidi, Tarif, *Arabic Historical Thought in the Classical Period* (Cambridge, 1994).
Khan, M. S., 'A Manuscript of an Epitome of al-Ṣābī's *Kitāb al-Tāǧī*', *Arabica* 12 (1965), pp. 27–44.
Khan, M. S., 'The Early History of Zaydī Shīʿism in Daylamān and Gīlān', *Zeitschrift der Deutschen Morgenländischen Gesellschaft* 125 (1975), pp. 301–14.
Kılıç, Rüya, 'The Reflection of Islamic Tradition on Ottoman Social Structure: The *sayyids* and *sharīfs*', in Kazuo Morimoto (ed.), *Sayyids and Sharifs in Muslim Societies: The Living Links to the Prophet* (London and New York, 2012), pp. 123–38.
Kister, M. J., and M. Plessner, 'Notes on Caskel's Ǧamharat an-nasab', *Oriens* 25–26 (1976), pp. 50–4.
Kohlberg, Etan, *A Medieval Muslim Scholar at Work: Ibn Ṭāwūs and His Library* (Leiden, 1992).
Kohlberg, Etan, 'Mūsā al-Kāẓim', *EI2*.
Krawulsky, Dorothea, 'Untersuchungen zur Shīʿitischen Tradition von Bayhaq: Ein Beitrag zur Frage der Verbreitung der Shīʿa in Persien', in Wadād al-Qāḍī (ed.), *Studia Arabica et Islamica: Festschrift für Iḥsān ʿAbbās* (Beirut, 1981), pp. 293–311.
Kressel, Gideon, *Descent through Males: An Anthropological Investigation into the*

Patterns Underlying Social Hierarchy, Kinship, and Marriage among Former Bedouin in the Ramla-Lod Area (Israel) (Wiesbaden, 1992).
Lalani, Arzina, *Early Shīʿī Thought: The Teachings of Imām Muḥammad al-Bāqir* (London, 2004).
Lambton, Ann, 'An Account of the *Tārīkhi Qumm*', *Bulletin of the School of Oriental and African Studies* 12 (1948), pp 586–96.
Lambton, Ann, *Continuity and Change in Medieval Persia* (London, 1988).
Lambton, Ann, 'Persian Local Histories: The Traditions behind Them and the Assumptions of Their Authors', in B. Scarcia Amoretti and L. Rostagno (eds), *Yād-nāma in Memoria di Alessandro Bausani*, 2 vols (Rome, 1991), vol. I, pp. 227–38.
Lambton, Ann, 'The Administration of Sanjar's Empire as Illustrated in the "ʿAtabat al-kataba"', *Bulletin of the School of Oriental and African Studies* 20 (1957), pp. 367–88.
Lambton, Ann, 'Qazwīn', *EI2*.
Lapidus, Ira, *Muslim Cities in the Later Middle Ages* (Cambridge, MA, 1967).
Lavoix, Henri Michel, *Catalogue des monnaies musulmanes de la Bibliothèque Nationale*, vol. II (Paris, 1891).
Lecker, Michael, 'Thaqīf', *EI2*.
Leder, Stefan, 'al-Zubayr b. Bakkār', *EI2*.
Leisten, Thomas, *Architektur für Tote: Bestattung in architektonischem Kontext in den Kernländern der islamischen Welt zwischen 3./9. und 6./12. Jahrhundert* (Berlin, 1998).
Le Strange, G., *The Lands of the Eastern Caliphate* (Cambridge, 1905).
Lev, Yaacov, 'Fāṭimid Policy towards Damascus (358/968–386/996): Military, Political and Social Aspects', *Jerusalem Studies in Arabic and Islam* 3 (1981–2), pp. 165–83.
Lewis, Bernard, 'ʿAlids', *EI2*.
Linant de Bellefonds, Y., 'Kafāʾa', *EI2*.
Linant de Bellefonds, Y., *Traité de droit musulman comparé*, 3 vols (Paris and La Haya, 1965).
Little, D., 'A New Look at *al-Aḥkām al-Sulṭāniyya*', *Muslim World* 64 (1974), pp. 1–18.
Lowick, Nicholas, 'Une Monnaie ʿAlide d'al-Baṣrah datée de 145 H. (762–3 après J.-C.)', *Revue Numismatique*, 6th ser., 21 (1979), pp. 218–24.
Madelung, Wilferd, 'Abū Isḥāq al-Ṣābī on the ʿAlids of Ṭabaristān and Gīlān', *Journal of Near Eastern Studies* 26 (1967), pp. 17–57.
Madelung, Wilferd, 'al-Ukhayḍir', *EI2*.
Madelung, Wilferd, 'ʿAlī b. al-Ḥosayn', *EIran*.
Madelung, Wilferd, *Arabic Texts Concerning the History of the Zaydī Imāms* (Beirut, 1987).
Madelung, Wilferd, *Der Imam al-Qāsim ibn Ibrāhīm und die Glaubenslehre der Zayditen* (Berlin, 1965).
Madelung, Wilferd, 'Land Ownership and Land Tax in Northern Yemen and Najrān:

3rd–4th/9th–10th Century', in T. Khalidi (ed.), *Land Tenure and Social Transformation in the Middle East* (Beirut, 1984), pp. 189–207.
Madelung, Wilferd, 'Muḥammad b. ʿAlī al-Riḍā', *EI2*.
Madelung, Wilferd, *Religious Trends in Early Islamic Iran* (Albany, NY, 1989).
Madelung, Wilferd, review of *Islamic Legal Orthodoxy: Twelver Shiite Responses to the Sunni Legal System*, by Devin Stewart, *Journal of the American Oriental Society* 120 (2000), pp. 111–14.
Madelung, Wilferd, review of *Muslim Cities in the Later Middle Ages*, by Ira Lapidus, *Journal of Near Eastern Studies* 29 (1970), pp. 133–5.
Madelung, Wilferd, review of *The Histories of Nishapur*, by R. N. Frye, *Journal of Near Eastern Studies* 27 (1968), pp. 155–7.
Madelung, Wilferd, 'Shiʿi Attitudes toward Women as Reflected in Fiqh', in Afaf Lutfi al-Sayyid-Marsot (ed.), *Society and the Sexes in Medieval Islam, Sixth Giorgio Levi Della Vida Conference* (Malibu, CA, 1979), pp. 69–79.
Madelung, Wilferd, 'The Hāshimiyyāt of al-Kumayt and Hāshimī Shiʿism', *Studia Islamica* 70 (1989), pp. 5–26.
Madelung, Wilferd, 'The Minor Dynasties of Northern Iran', in *The Cambridge History of Iran*, vol. IV (Cambridge, 1975), pp. 198–246.
Madelung, Wilferd, 'The Sources of Ismāʿīlī Law', *Journal of Near Eastern Studies* 35 (1976), pp. 29–40.
Madelung, Wilferd, *The Succession to Muḥammad: A Study of the Early Caliphate* (Cambridge, 1997).
Madelung, Wilferd, 'Yaḥyā b. ʿAbd Allāh', *EI2*.
Madelung, Wilferd, 'Yaḥyā b. Zayd', *EI2*.
Madelung, Wilferd, 'Zayd b. ʿAlī b. al-Ḥusayn', *EI2*.
Madelung, Wilferd, 'Zaydiyya', *EI2*.
Makdisi, George, 'Autograph Diary of an Eleventh-Century Historian of Baghdad II–IV', *Bulletin of the School of Oriental and African Studies* 18 (1956), pp. 239–60, and *Bulletin of the School of Oriental and African Studies* 19 (1957), pp. 13–48 and pp. 281–303.
Marin, E., 'Dulafids', *EI2*.
Marlow, Louise, *Hierarchy and Egalitarianism in Islamic Thought* (Cambridge, 1997).
Massignon, Louis, 'Cadis et *naqībs* baghdadiens', *Wiener Zeitschrift für die Kunde des Morgenlandes* 51 (1948), pp. 106–15.
Mauriello, Raffaele, *Descendants of the Family of the Prophet in Contemporary History: A Case Study, the Shīʿī Religious Establishment of al-Najaf (Iraq)* (Pisa and Rome, 2011).
Mauriello, Raffaele, 'Genealogical Prestige and Marriage Strategy among the *Ahl al-Bayt*: The Case of the al-Sadr Family in Recent Times', in Sarah Savant and Helena de Felipe (eds), *Genealogy and Knowledge in Muslim Societies: Understanding the Past* (Edinburgh, forthcoming).
Meisami, Julie, *Persian Historiography to the End of the Twelfth Century* (Edinburgh, 1995).

Melchert, Christopher, 'The Imāmīs between Rationalism and Traditionalism', in L. Clarke (ed.), *The Shīʿite Heritage: Essays on Classical and Modern Traditions* (New York, 2001), pp. 273–83.
Melchert, Christopher, *The Formation of the Sunnī Schools of Law, 9th–10th Centuries C.E.* (Leiden, 1997).
Melville, Charles, 'Persian Local Histories: Views from the Wings', *Iranian Studies* 33 (2000), pp. 7–14.
Melville, Charles,'The Caspian Provinces: A World Apart. Three Local Histories of Mazandaran', *Iranian Studies* 33 (2000), pp. 45–91.
Mez, Adam, *Die Renaissance des Islāms* (Heidelberg, 1922).
Mikhail, Hanna, *Politics and Revelation: Māwardī and After* (Edinburgh, 1995).
Mobini-Kesheh, Natalie, *The Hadrami Awakening: Community and Identity in the Netherlands East Indies, 1900–1942* (Ithaca, NY, 1999).
Modarressi, Hossein, *An Introduction to Shīʿite Law* (London, 1986).
Modarressi, Hossein, *Crisis and Consolidation in the Formative Period of Shīʿite Islam* (Princeton, NJ, 1993).
Modarressi, Hossein, 'Sukhanī chand dar bārah-yi niqābat-i sādāt va barnāma-yi kār-i naqīb', *Āyanda* 10–12 (1358/1979), pp. 754–65.
Modarressi, Hossein, *Tradition and Survival: A Bibliographical Survey of Early Shīʿite Literature* (Oxford, 2003).
Morimoto, Kazuo, 'A Preliminary Study on the Diffusion of the *Niqāba al-Ṭālibīyīn*: Towards an Understanding of the Early Dispersal of *Sayyids*', in Hidemitsu Kuroki (ed.), *The Influence of Human Mobility in Muslim Societies* (London 2003), pp. 3–42.
Morimoto, Kazuo, 'How to Behave toward *Sayyids* and *Sharīfs*: A Trans-sectarian Tradition of Dream Accounts', in Kazuo Morimoto (ed.), *Sayyids and Sharifs in Muslim Societies: The Living Links to the Prophet* (London and New York, 2012), pp. 15–36.
Morimoto, Kazuo, 'Introduction', in Kazuo Morimoto (ed.), *Sayyids and Sharifs in Muslim Societies: The Living Links to the Prophet* (London and New York, 2012), pp. 1–14.
Morimoto, Kazuo, 'Putting the *Lubāb al-ansāb* in Context: *Sayyids* and *Naqībs* in Late Saljuq Khurasan', *Studia Iranica* 36 (2007), pp. 163–83.
Morimoto, Kazuo (ed.), *Sayyids and Sharifs in Muslim Societies: The Living Links to the Prophet* (London and New York, 2012), pp. 1–14.
Morimoto, Kazuo, 'The Formation and Development of the Science of Ṭālibid Genealogies in the 10th and 11th Century Middle East', *Oriente Moderno*, n.s., 18 (1999), pp. 541–70.
Morimoto, Kazuo, *The Guardian of Authenticity: Genealogy of the Prophet's Family in Medieval Islam* (forthcoming).
Morimoto, Kazuo, 'Toward the Formation of Sayyido–Sharifology: Questioning Accepted Fact', *Journal of Sophia Asian Studies* 22 (2004), pp. 87–103.
Mortel, Richard T., 'The Genealogy of the Ḥasanid Sharīfs of Mecca', *Journal of the*

College of Arts, King Saud University 2 (1985), pp. 221–50.
Mortel, Richard T., 'Zaydī Shīʿism and the Ḥasanid Sharīfs of Mecca', *International Journal of Middle Eastern Studies* 19 (1987), pp. 455–75.
Motoki, Yamaguchi, 'Debate on the Status of *sayyid/sharīfs* in the Modern Era: The ʿAlawī-Irshādī Dispute and Islamic Reformists in the Middle East', in Kazuo Morimoto (ed.), *Sayyids and Sharifs in Muslim Societies: The Living Links to the Prophet* (London and New York, 2012), pp. 49–71.
Mottahedeh, Roy Parviz, 'Administration in Būyid Qazwīn', in D. S. Richards (ed.), *Islamic Civilisation 950–1150* (Oxford, 1983), pp. 33–45.
Mottahedeh, Roy Parviz, 'Azod al-Dawla', *EIran*.
Mottahedeh, Roy Parviz, 'Consultation and the Political Process', in C. Mallat (ed.), *Islam and Public Law* (London, 1993), pp. 19–27.
Mottahedeh, Roy Parviz, *Loyalty and Leadership in an Early Islamic Society* (Princeton, NJ, 1980).
Mottahedeh, Roy Parviz, 'Qur'ānic Commentary on the Verse of *khums* (al-Anfāl VIII:41)', in Kazuo Morimoto (ed.), *Sayyids and Sharifs in Muslim Societies: The Living Links to the Prophet* (London and New York, 2012), pp. 37–48.
Mottahedeh, Roy Parviz, review of *The Patricians of Nishapur*, by Richard Bulliet, *Journal of the American Oriental Society* 95 (1975), pp. 491–5.
Mulder, Stephennie, *The Shrines of the ʿAlids in Medieval Syria: Sunnis, Shiʿis, and the Architecture of Coexistence* (Edinburgh, forthcoming).
Murphy, Robert F., and Leonard Kasdan, 'The Structure of Parallel Cousin Marriage', *American Anthropologist* 61 (1959), pp. 17–29.
Nagel, Tilman, 'Ein früher Bericht über den Aufstand von Muḥammad b. ʿAbdallāh im Jahre 145 H.', *Der Islam* 46 (1970), pp. 227–62.
Nagel, Tilman, *Untersuchungen zur Entstehung des abbasidischen Kalifats* (Bonn, 1972).
Newman, Andrew, *The Formative Period of Twelver Shīʿism: Ḥadīth as Discourse between Qum and Baghdad* (London, 2000).
Öhrnberg, Kai, *The Offspring of Fāṭima: Dispersal and Ramification* (Helsinki, 1983).
Orthmann, Eva, *Stamm und Macht: Die arabischen Stämme im 2. und 3. Jahrhundert der Hiğra* (Wiesbaden, 2002).
Ottenheimer, Martin, 'Complementarity and the Structure of Parallel Cousin Marriage', *American Anthropologist* 88 (1986), pp. 934–9.
Pasternak, Burton, *Introduction to Kinship and Social Organisation* (Englewood Cliffs, NJ, 1976).
Paul, Jürgen, *Herrscher, Gemeinwesen, Vermittler: Ostiran und Transoxanien in vormongolischer Zeit* (Stuttgart, 1996).
Paul, Jürgen, 'The Histories of Herat', *Iranian Studies* 33 (2000), pp. 93–115.
Paul, Jürgen, 'The Histories of Samarqand', *Studia Iranica* 22 (1993), pp. 69–92.
Pedersen, J. and Makdisi, G., 'Madrasa', *EI2*.
Pellat, Charles, 'Muṣʿab', *EI2*.

Peskes, Esther, *Al-ʿAidarūs und seine Erben: Eine Untersuchung zu Geschichte und Sufismus einer ḥaḍramitischen Sāda-Gruppe vom Fünfzehnten bis zum Achtzehnten Jahrhundert* (Stuttgart, 2005).
Peters, Emrys, *The Bedouin of Cyrenaica* (Cambridge, 1990).
Pfeiffer, Judith, review of *A Monumental Manifestation of the Shīʿite Faith in the Late Twelfth Century Iran: The Case of the Gunbad-i ʿAlawiyān, Hamādan*, by Raya Shani, *Journal of the American Oriental Society* 121 (2001), pp. 720–3.
Pingree, David and Wilferd Madelung, 'Political Horoscopes Relating to Ninth Century ʿAlids', *Journal of Near Eastern Studies* 36 (1977), pp. 247–75.
Pomerantz, Maurice, 'Al-Ṣāḥib Ismāʿīl b. ʿAbbād (d. 385/995): A Political Biography', *Journal of the American Oriental Society* (forthcoming).
Pomerantz, Maurice, 'Licit Magic and Divine Grace: The Life and Letters of al-Ṣāḥib ibn ʿAbbād (d. 385/995)' (PhD dissertation, University of Chicago, 2010).
Popovijc, A., *La révolte des esclaves en Iraq au III/IX siècle* (Paris, 1976).
Popovijc, A., 'al-Mukhtāra', *EI2*.
Popovijc, A., 'Zandj', *EI2*.
Pourshariati, Parvaneh, 'Local Histories of Khurāsān and the Pattern of Arab Settlement', *Studia Iranica* 27 (1988), pp. 41–81.
Powers, David, *Law, Society and Culture in the Maghrib, 1300–1500* (Cambridge, 2002).
Pritsak, Omeljan, 'Āl-i Burhān', *Der Islam* 30 (1952), pp. 81–96.
Pritsak, Omeljan, 'Die Karachaniden', *Der Islam* 31 (1954), pp. 17–68.
Radtke, Bernd, 'Theologen und Mystiker in Ḫurasan und Transoxanien', *Zeitschrift der Deutschen Morgenländischen Gesellschaft* 136 (1986), pp. 536–69.
Richards, D. S., 'A Mamlūk Petition and a Report from the *Dīwān al-Jaysh*', *Bulletin of the School of Oriental and African Studies* 40 (1977), pp. 1–14.
Robertson-Smith, W., *Kinship and Marriage in Early Arabia* (London, 1903).
Robinson, Chase F., *Empire and Elites after the Muslim Conquest* (Cambridge, 2000).
Robinson, Chase F., *Islamic Historiography* (Cambridge, 2003).
Robinson, Chase F., 'Neck Sealing in Early Islam', *Journal of the Economic and Social History of the Orient* 48 (2005), pp. 401–41.
Rosenthal, Franz, *A History of Muslim Historiography*, 2nd revised edn (Leiden, 1968).
Rosenthal, Franz, 'Nasab', *EI2*.
Rosenthal, Franz, *Political Thought in Medieval Islam* (Cambridge, 1958).
Rowson, Everett, 'Religion and Politics in the Career of Badīʿ al-Zamān al-Hamadhānī', *Journal of the American Oriental Society* 107 (1987), pp. 653–73.
Rustow, Marina, *Heresy and the Politics of Community: The Jews of the Fatimid Caliphate* (Ithaca, NY, 2008).
Sadeghi, Zohreh, *Fāṭima von Qum, Ein Beispiel für die Verehrung heiliger Frauen im Volksglauben der Zwölfer-Shia* (Berlin, 1996).
Ṣāliḥ, ʿAbd al-Ḥamīd, 'Une source de Qalqašandī, Māwadd al-bayān et son auteur, ʿAlī b. Ḫalaf', *Arabica* 20 (1973), pp. 192–200.

Scarcia Amoretti, Biancamaria, 'A Historical Atlas on the ʿAlids: A Proposal and a Few Samples', in Kazuo Morimoto (ed.), *Sayyids and Sharifs in Muslim Societies: The Living Links to the Prophet* (London and New York, 2012), p. 92–122.
Scarcia Amoretti, Biancamaria, 'Foreword', in Hanna Mikhail, *Politics and Revelation: Māwardī and After* (Edinburgh, 1995).
Scarcia Amoretti, Biancamaria, 'Genealogical Prestige and Matrimonial Politics among the Ahl al-Bayt: Status Quaestionis', in Sarah Savant and Helena de Felipe (eds), *Genealogy and Knowledge in Muslim Societies: Understanding the Past* (Edinburgh, forthcoming).
Scarcia Amoretti, Biancamaria, 'Ibn ʿInaba', *EI2*.
Scarcia Amoretti, Biancamaria, 'Ibn Ṭabāṭabā', *EI2*.
Scarcia Amoretti, Biancamaria, 'ʿIlm al-Rijāl', *EI2*.
Scarcia Amoretti, Biancamaria, 'Sulla *ʿUmdat al-Ṭālib fī ansāb āl Abī Ṭālib*, e sul suo autore Ğamāl al-Dīn Aḥmad ibn ʿInaba', *Annali dell'Instituto Orientale di Napoli*, n.s., 13 (1963), pp. 287–294.
Scarcia Amoretti, Biancamaria, and L. Bottini (eds), 'The Role of the *Sādāt/Ashrāf* in Muslim History and Civilisation: Proceedings of the International Conference (Rome, 2–4 March 1998)', *Oriente Moderno*, n.s., 18 (1999).
Schacht, Joseph, 'Nikāḥ', *EI2*.
Schacht, Joseph, *The Origins of Muhammadan Jurisprudence* (Oxford, 1950).
Sezgin, Fuat, *Geschichte des Arabischen Schrifttums*, 15 vols (Leiden, 1967–).
Shamma, Samīr, 'Arbaʿa darāhim lihā Taʾrīkh', *Yarmouk Numismatics*, Yarmouk University Publication 4 (Irbid, 1992), pp. 13–25.
Shani, Raya, *A Monumental Manifestation of the Shīʿite Faith in the Late Twelfth Century Iran: The Case of the Gunbad-i ʿAlawiyān, Hamādan* (Oxford, 1996).
Sharon, Moshe, 'Ahl al-bayt, People of the House: A Study of the Transformation of a Term from Jāhiliyya to Islam', *Jerusalem Studies in Arabic and Islam* 8 (1986), pp. 169–84.
Sharon, Moshe, *Black Banners from the East: The Establishment of the ʿAbbāsid State; Incubation of the Revolt* (Jerusalem and Leiden, 1983).
Sharon, Moshe, *Revolt: The Social and Military Aspects of the ʿAbbāsid Revolution* (Jerusalem, 1990).
Sharon, Moshe, 'The ʿAbbāsid Daʿwa Re-examined', *Arabic and Islamic Studies* 1 (1973), pp. 10–14.
Sharon, Moshe, 'The Development of the Debate around the Legitimacy of Authority in Early Islam', *Jerusalem Studies in Arabic and Islam* 5 (1984), pp. 121–42.
Sharon, Moshe, 'The Umayyads as *Ahl al-Bayt*', *Jerusalem Studies in Arabic and Islam* 14 (1991), pp. 115–52.
Shboul, Ahmad, *Al-Masʿūdī and His World* (London, 1979).
Shimamoto, Takamitsu, 'Some Reflections on the Origin of Qum: Myth and History', *Orient* 27 (1991), pp. 95–113.
Shoshan, Boaz, 'On Costume and Social History in Medieval Islam', *Asian and African Studies* 22 (1988), pp. 35–51.

Shoshan, Boaz, 'The "Politics of Notables" in Medieval Islam', *Asian and African Studies* 20 (1986), pp. 179–215.
Siddiqui, Mona, 'Law and the Desire for Social Control: An Insight into the Hanafi Concept of Kafa'a with Reference to the Fatawa ʿAlamgiri (1664–1672)', in Mai Yamani (ed.), *Feminism and Islam: Legal and Literary Perspectives* (Reading, 1996), pp. 49–85.
Sievers, Peter von, 'Military, Merchants and Nomads: Social Evolution of the Syrian Cities and Countryside During the Classical Period, 780–969/164–358', *Der Islam* 56 (1979), pp. 212–44.
Spectorsky, Susan A., *Chapters on Marriage and Divorce: Responses of Ibn Ḥanbal and Ibn Rāhwayh* (Austin, TX, 1993).
Stern, Gertrude, *Marriage in Early Islam* (London, 1939).
Stern, S. M., 'The Coins of Āmul', *Numismatic Chronicle*, 7th ser., 6 (1967), pp. 205–78.
Stern, S. M., *Fāṭimid Decrees: Original Documents from the Fāṭimid Chancery* (Oxford, 1965).
Stern, S. M., 'The Early Ismāʿīlī Missionaries in North-West Persia and in Khurāsān and Transoxania', *Bulletin of the School of Oriental and African Studies* 23 (1960), pp. 56–90.
Stewart, Devin, *Islamic Legal Orthodoxy: Twelver Shiite Responses to the Sunni Legal System* (Salt Lake City, 1998).
Strothmann, Rudolf, 'Das Problem der literarischen Persönlichkeit Zaid b. ʿAlī', *Der Islam* 8 (1923), pp. 1–52.
Strothmann, Rudolf, 'al-Ḥasan al-Uṭrūsh', *EI2*.
Strothmann, Rudolf, *Das Staatsrecht der Zaiditen* (Strasbourg, 1912).
Strothmann, Rudolf, 'Die Literatur der Zaititen', *Der Islam* 1 (1910), pp. 354–68, and *Der Islam* 2 (1911), pp. 49–78.
Szombathy, Zoltán, 'Genealogy in Medieval Muslim Societies', *Studia Islamica* 95 (2002), pp. 5–35.
Szombathy, Zoltán, 'Motives and Techniques of Genealogical Forgery in Pre-Modern Muslim Societies', in Sarah Savant and Helena de Felipe (eds), *Genealogy and Knowledge in Muslim Societies: Understanding the Past* (Edinburgh, forthcoming).
Szombathy, Zoltán, 'The Nassāba: Anthropological Fieldwork in Medieval Islam', *Islamic Culture* 73 (1999), pp. 61–108.
Szombathy, Zoltán, 'Techniques of Genealogical Forgery and Procedures of Genealogical Verification in the Mediaeval Middle East' (unpublished manuscript).
Szombathy, Zoltán, *The Roots of Arabic Genealogy: A Study in Historical Anthropology* (Budapest, 2003).
Taheri, Amir, *The Spirit of Allah: Khomeini and the Islamic Revolution* (London, 1985).
Traini, Renato, 'La corrispondenza tra al-Manṣūr e Muḥammad an-Nafs al-Zakiyya', *Annali dell'Instituto Orientale di Napoli*, n.s., 14 (1964), pp. 1–26.
Treadwell, Luke, 'The Political History of the Sāmānid State' (DPhil thesis, Oxford University, 1991).

Tritton, A. S., 'Notes on the Muslim System of Pensions', *Bulletin of the School of Oriental and African Studies* 16 (1954), pp. 170–2.
Tyan, E., *Histoire de l'organisation judiciaire en pays d'Islam*, 2nd edn (Leiden, 1960).
Uhrig, Hans Ferdinand, *Das Kalifat von al-Maʾmūn* (Frankfurt, 1988).
Veccia Vaglieri, Laura, 'al-Ḥusayn b. ʿAlī, Ṣāḥib Fakhkh', *EI2*.
Veccia Vaglieri, Laura, 'Divagazioni su due Rivolte Alidi', in *A Francesco Gabrieli: Studi orientalistici offerti nel sessantesimo compleanno dai suoi colleghi e discepoli* (Rome, 1964), pp. 315–50.
Waines, David, 'The Third Century Internal Crisis of the Abbasids', *Journal of the Economic and Social History of the Orient* 20 (1977), pp. 282–306.
Weir, T. H. and Zysow, A., 'Ṣadaqa', *EI2*.
Winter, Michael, 'The *Ashrāf* and *Naqīb al-Ashrāf* in Ottoman Egypt and Syria: A Comparative Analysis', in Kazuo Morimoto (ed.), *Sayyids and Sharifs in Muslim Societies: The Living Links to the Prophet* (London and New York, 2012), pp. 139–57.
Winter, Michael, *Egyptian Society under Ottoman Rule, 1517–1798* (London, 1992).
Winter, Michael, 'The *Ashrāf* and *Niqābat al-Ashrāf* in Egypt in Ottoman and Modern Times', *Asian and African Studies* 19 (1985), pp. 17–41.
Young, M. J. L., 'Arabic Biographical Writing', in M. J. L. Young *et al.* (eds), *Religion, Learning and Science in the ʿAbbasid Period* (Cambridge, 1990).
Zaman, Muhammad Qasim, *Religion and Politics Under the Early ʿAbbāsids* (Leiden, 1997).
Zaman, Muhammad Qasim, 'The ʿAbbāsid Revolution: A Study of the Nature and Role of the Religious Dynamics', *Journal of Asian History* 21 (1987), pp. 119–49.
Ziadeh, Farhat, 'Equality (Kafāʾah) in the Muslim Law of Marriage', *American Journal of Comparative Law* 6 (1957), pp. 503–17.
Zomeño, Amalia, '*Kafāʾa* in the Maliki School: A *Fatwā* from Fifteenth Century Fez', in Robert Gleave and Eugenia Kermeli (eds), *Islamic Law: Theory and Practice* (London, 1997), pp. 87–106.
Zysow, A., and R. Gleave, 'Khums', *EI2*.
Zysow, A., and R. Gleave, 'Zakāt', *EI2*.

Index

ʿAbbās b. ʿAlī b. Abī Ṭālib, 3, 41n
ʿAbbāsid Revolution, 4
ʿAbbāsids
as *ahl al-bayt*, 3, 17, 29
black clothing of, 6n, 43, 56, 70, 88n
inter-marriage with ʿAlids by, 35, 40–3, 44, 49
niqāba of, 11, 53–4, 56n
relations with ʿAlids of, 4–6, 7–8, 35, 38, 68
ʿAbd al-ʿAẓīm b. ʿAbdallāh b. ʿAlī, 23
ʿAbd al-ʿAzīz b. al-Muṭṭalib b. ʿAbdallāh b. al-Muṭṭalib b. Ḥanṭab, 40n
ʿAbd al-Raḥmān al-Shajarī, 44
ʿAbdallāh b. ʿAbd al-Raḥmān b. al-Ḥārith b. ʿAbdallāh b. ʿAyyāsh, 40n
ʿAbdallāh b. ʿAlī b. ʿĪsā b. Yaḥyā b. Zayd al-Shahīd, 20
ʿAbdallāh b. al-Ḥasan b. al-Ḥasan b. ʿAlī, 5, 34–5, 39, 70
ʿAbdallāh b. Ismāʿīl b. Muḥammad b. ʿAbdallāh al-Bāhir, 25n
ʿAbdallāh b. Jaʿfar b. Abī Ṭālib, 24n
ʿAbdallāh b. Ṭāhir, 77, 79
ʿAbdallāh b. al-Zubayr b. ʿAwwām, 39n
Abū ʿAbdallāh al-Ḥusayn b. ʿAlī, 76
Abū ʿAbdallāh Muḥammad al-Aṣghar, *al-shāʿir* (*naqīb*), 61n
Abū ʿAbdallāh Muḥammad b. al-Dāʿī (*naqīb*), 55–6
Abū Aḥmad al-Ḥusayn b. Mūsā (*naqīb*), 55, 56
Abū Aḥmad Muḥammad b. Jaʿfar b. Muḥammad b. Jaʿfar b. al-Ḥasan b. Jaʿfar b. al-Ḥasan b. al-Ḥasan b. ʿAlī, 56n
Abū Aḥmad al-Mūsawī (*naqīb*), 56
Abū ʿAlī Aḥmad al-Kawkabī (*naqīb*), 55
Abū al-Bakhtarī Wahb b. Wahb (governor), 19
Abū Bakr Muḥammad b. ʿAbdallāh al-Shāfiʿī, 83–4
Abū al-Ghanāʾim ʿAbdallāh b. al-Ḥasan al-Dimashqī, 14, 21
Abū Ḥanīfa, 46; *see also* Ḥanafīs
Abū al-Ḥasan ʿAlī b. Yaḥyā b. ʿAlī b. Ibrāhīm b. al-Ḥasan b. ʿUbaydallāh b. al-ʿAbbās b. ʿAlī (deputy *naqīb*), 56n
Abū al-Ḥasan Muḥammad (*naqīb*), 60
Abū al-Ḥasan Muḥammad b. al-Ḥusayn b. ʿAlī Katīla b. Yaḥyā b. Yaḥyā b. al-Ḥusayn b. Zayd al-Shahīd (*naqīb*), 67n
Abū al-Ḥusayn ʿAlī, 57n
Abū al-Ḥusayn al-Mūsawī (*naqīb*), 56n
Abū al-Ḥusayn al-Ṭāhir, 58
Abū al-Ḥusayn b. ʿUbaydallāh (*naqīb*), 56n
Abū al-Ḥusayn Zayd b. ʿAlī b. ʿĪsā b. Yaḥyā b. Zayd al-Shahīd, 20
Abū Isḥāq b. Ibrāhīm b. al-Ḥusayn b. ʿAlī b. al-Muḥsin, 56–7
Abū Isḥāq Ibrāhīm al-Ṣābiʾ, 55
Abū Jaʿfar b. ʿAbdallāh b. al-Ḥasan b. al-Ḥasan b. al-Ḥasan b. ʿAlī, 35n
Abū Jaʿfar Muḥammad b. ʿAlī (*naqīb*), 61
Abū Jaʿfar Muḥammad b. ʿAlī b. Hārūn b. Muḥammad al-Mūsawī (genealogist), 27

Abū Jaʿfar b. Muḥammad b. Hārūn b. Mūsā b. Jaʿfar al-Ṣādiq, 76
Abū Jaʿfar Muḥammad b. al-Ḥasan b. Muḥammad al-Kābulī b. ʿAbdallāh al-Ashtar b. Muḥammad al-Nafs al-Zakiyya (*naqīb*), 65, 66, 67
Abū Muḥammad Ḥamza, 43
Abū Muḥammad Isḥāq al-Mūsawī (deputy *naqīb*), 61n
Abū Mūsā b. ʿAbdallāh b. Qays, 41n
Abū al-Qāsim ʿAbdallāh b. al-Ḥusayn b. Jaʿfar, 26
Abū al-Qāsim al-Ḥusayn b. al-ʿUd, 63n
Abū al-Qāsim al-Mūsawī (*naqīb*), 60
Abū al-Qāsim al-Zaydī (*naqīb*), 56n
Abū al-Sarāyā, 8
Abū Ṭālib al-Fawshaḥī, 29n
Abū Thawr, 84
Abū ʿUbaydallāh b. al-Ḥasan (*naqīb*), 60
ahl al-bayt, 3, 29, 30, 87; *see also* ʿAlids
Aḥmad b. al-Ḥusayn b. Jaʿfar, 26
Aḥmad b. Muḥammad b. Ismāʿīl b. ʿAbdallāh al-Arqaṭ, 61
Ahmed, Asad, 11, 35, 37
ʿAlī b. Abī Ṭālib, 1, 2–3
ʿAlī b. al-Ḥusayn b. Zayd al-Shahīd, 20
ʿAlī b. ʿĪsā b. Yaḥyā b. Zayd al-Shahīd, 20
ʿAlī b. Ismāʿīl b. Jaʿfar b. Muḥammad b. ʿAlī b. al-Ḥusayn (Ibn al-Makhzūmiyya), 39
ʿAlī b. Muḥammad, 69
ʿAlī al-Riḍā, 6, 41, 76, 77
ʿAlī b. ʿUbaydallāh (ʿAbdallāh) b. ʿAlī b. ʿUbaydallāh b. al-Aʿraj b. al-Ḥusayn b. ʿAlī b. al-Ḥusayn b. ʿAlī (*naqīb*), 67n
ʿAlī al-Uṭrūsh b. Ḥusayn, 29, 44
ʿAlidism, 1, 48
ʿAlids
  financial privileges of, 28–31, 62, 80
  genealogy of, 1, 2–4, 13, 17–18, 20–4
  geographical dispersal of, 26–7, 36
  green as colour of, 88
  numbers of, 87
  quietism among, 9, 34, 35, 41
  rebellions by, 5–6, 7–8, 28, 34, 64, 80
  relations with ʿAbbāsids of, 4–6, 34–5, 38, 42, 68
  as Shiʿite scholars, 9, 81, 83
  shrines for, 30, 87
  status of, 1–2, 72, 87
  trans-sectarian reverence for, 31, 87
ʿAqīl b. Abī Ṭālib, 3, 24
al-ʿAqīqī, Jaʿfar b. ʿUbaydallāh, 18
al-ʿAqīqī, ʿUbaydallāh b. al-Ḥusayn, 19
al-ʿAqīqī, Yaḥyā b. al-Ḥasan b. Jaʿfar, 14, 18–19, 26, 61, 69
al-Ashraf Shaʿbān (Mamlūk sultan), 88
Asmāʾ bt. Ibrāhīm b. Mūsā b. ʿAbd al-Raḥmān b. ʿAbdallāh b. Abī Rabīʿa b. al-Mughīra al-Makhzūmī, 39n
Asmāʾ bt. Isḥāq b. Ibrāhīm [b. Yaʿqūb] b. Salama al-Makhzūmī, 39n
ʿĀtika bt. ʿAbd al-Malik b. al-Ḥārith b. Khālid b. al-ʿĀṣī b. Hishām b. Mughīra, 39
al-ʿAṭṭās, ʿUmar, 32

Baḥr al-ʿUlūm family, 50
al-Bukhārī, Abū Naṣr, 2, 23–4, 26
Bulliet, Richard, 9, 43, 71, 73, 85
Burhān family, 71
al-Buṭḥānī, Abū ʿAbdallāh al-Ḥusayn b. Dāwūd al-Ṭabarī, 75, 76, 83
al-Buṭḥānī, Abū ʿAlī Muḥammad (*naqīb*), 60, 75
al-Buṭḥānī, Abū al-Ḥasan ʿAlī, 43
al-Buṭḥānī, Abū al-Ḥasan b. Zayd b. Muḥammad b. Aḥmad b. Muḥammad b. al-Ḥusayn b. ʿĪsā b. Muḥammad, 52n
al-Buṭḥānī, Abū Muḥammad al-Ḥasan (*naqīb*), 57n, 59, 75

al-Buṭḥānī, Abū al-Qāsim Zayd (*naqīb*), 60, 75
Buṭḥānī family, 9, 43–4, 59–60, 73, 75, 78, 86
as *nuqabā*ʾ, 59–60, 61, 82
al-Buṭḥānī, al-Ḥasan b. Dāwūd b. ʿĪsā, 83
al-Buṭḥānī, Muḥammad b. al-Qāsim b. al-Ḥasan, 43

Caskel, Werner, 16
Crone, Patricia, 86

Dāwūd b. Khalaf al-Iṣfahānī, 84
descent (*nasab*) as factor in marriage choices, 45–8; *see also kafāʾa* (suitability in marriage)
Donohue, John, 55

Elad, Amikam, 8

al-Faḍl b. Shādhān, 84–5
Fākhita bt. Abī Ṭālib, 39
false genealogical claims, 23–8, 31, 62
Fāṭima (daughter of the Prophet), 1, 2, 38
Fāṭima bt. ʿAbdallāh b. al-Ḥasan b. al-Ḥasan b. ʿAlī, 35
Fāṭima bt. ʿAmr, 38
Fāṭima bt. al-Ḥasan b. ʿAlī, 41n
Fāṭima bt. al-Ḥusayn b. Zayd b. ʿAlī b. al-Ḥusayn, 34n, 37n, 41, 49n
Fāṭimid, meaning of, 2
financial privileges of ʿAlids, 28–31, 62, 80
traditions promoting, 30
Franklin, Arnold, 89

genealogical registers (*jarāʾid*), 20–2, 61–2
genealogy, 13, 15–16, 36, 89; *see also* false genealogical claims; Ṭālibid genealogies

Ghaznavids, 53, 59–60
Gleave, Robert, 49

Ḥaḍramīs, 32
Haider, Najam, 8
Ḥakīm family, 50
Halm, Heinz, 83
Ḥamza b. al-Ḥasan b. ʿAlī, 41n
Ḥamūya b. ʿAlī (*ṣāḥib jaysh*), 80
Ḥanbalīs, 45–6, 83
Ḥanafīs, 43, 45–6, 83, 85
Hārūn b. Mūsā al-Kāẓim, 25n
Hārūn al-Rashīd (caliph), 41–2
al-Ḥasan b. Aḥmad b. al-Ḥusayn b. Jaʿfar, 26
al-Ḥasan b. ʿAlī, 41n
al-Ḥasan b. ʿAlī al-ʿArīḍī, 25n
al-Ḥasan b. ʿAlī b. ʿĪsā b. Yaḥyā b. Zayd al-Shahīd, 20
al-Ḥasan al-ʿAskarī, 36
al-Ḥasan b. al-Ḥasan b. ʿAlī, 37n
al-Ḥasan b. al-Qāsim al-Dāʿī al-Ṣaghīr, 55n
al-Ḥasan b. Zayd (*dāʿī*), 43, 77, 79
al-Ḥasan b. Zayd b. al-Ḥasan b. ʿAlī (governor of Medina), 5, 23, 43, 44
Ḥasanids
definition of, 2
political behaviour of, 34, 42
Hāshimites, 2–3, 4
al-Ḥaskānī, al-Ḥākim Abū al-Qāsim, 85
al-Ḥimmānī, ʿAlī b. Muḥammad b. Jaʿfar, *al-shāʿir*, 65, 66
Hinds, Martin, 40
historical chronicles, as sources on ʿAlids, 7–8
Hubayra b. Abī Wahb al-Makhzūmī, 39
Hunāda bt. Khalaf al-Makhzūmī, 40
al-Ḥurra bt. al-Imām al-Muwaffaq Hibat Allāh b. al-Qāḍī ʿUmar b. Muḥammad, 43, 59

al-Ḥusayn b. Aḥmad (*naqīb*), 61, 64–5, 66
al-Ḥusayn b. ʿAlī b. ʿĪsā b. Yaḥyā b. Zayd al-Shahīd, 20
al-Ḥusayn b. ʿAlī, Ṣāḥib Fakhkh, 8
al-Ḥusayn b. al-Ḥasan b. Muḥammad al-Kābulī b. ʿAbdallāh al-Ashtar b. Muḥammad al-Nafs al-Zakiyya (*naqīb*), 65, 66
al-Ḥusayn b. al-Ḥusayn b. Zayd al-Shahīd, 20
al-Ḥusayn b. Ibrāhīm b. ʿAlī, 77, 80n
al-Ḥusayn b. Zayd al-Shahīd, 20
al-Ḥusaynī, Sayyid Ṣadr al-Dīn, 76
Ḥusaynids
  definition of, 2
  inter-marriage with ʿAbbāsids by, 40–1
  quietism of, 34–5, 41

Ibn ʿAbbād, al-Ṣāḥib Ismāʿīl (vizier), 29–30, 44, 57, 81
Ibn Babūya, 47–8
Ibn Funduq al-Bayhaqī, 20–1, 22, 67, 76, 78
Ibn Khadāʿ (*naqīb*), 61n
Ibn Khuzayma, Abū Bakr Muḥammad b. Isḥāq, 83
Ibn Qutayba, ʿAlī (b. Muḥammad), 85
Ibn Taymiyya, 1
Ibrāhīm b. ʿAbdallāh b. al-Ḥasan b. al-Ḥasan b. ʿAlī, 5, 34, 39, 42n
Ibrāhīm b. ʿAlī b. Muḥammad b. Aḥmad b. Muḥammad b. al-Ḥusayn b. Ibrāhīm b. Ibrāhīm b. Mūsā al-Kāẓim, 27
Ibrāhīm b. Ismāʿīl al-Ṭabāṭabā, 39n
Ibrāhīm b. Muḥammad b. Mūsā b. Jaʿfar al-Ṣādiq, 77n
Ibrāhīm b. Mūsā al-Kāẓim, 24
Ibrāhīm b. al-Qāsim al-Shuhārī, 9
Idrīs b. ʿAbdallāh b. al-Ḥasan b. al-Ḥasan b. ʿAlī, 6, 34, 39
Imāmīs, *see* Shiʿism
imāms, 2, 34, 35, 48–9, 72
ʿĪsā b. ʿAlī b. ʿAbdallāh b. al-ʿAbbās, 42n
ʿĪsā b. Mūsā, 42
ʿĪsā b. al-Shaykh al-Shaybānī, 8
Isḥāq b. al-Ḥusayn b. Zayd al-Shahīd, 20
Isḥāq b. Ibrāhīm b. al-Ḥasan b. al-Ḥasan b. ʿAlī, 35n
Ismāʿīl b. Ibrāhīm b. Mūsā al-Kāẓim, 24
Ismāʿīl b. Jaʿfar b. Muḥammad b. ʿAlī b. al-Ḥusayn, 39
Ismāʿīlīs, 48–9

Jaʿda b. Hubayra b. Abī Wahb al-Makhzūmī, 39
Jaʿfar b. Abī Ṭālib, 3, 24n
Jaʿfar b. ʿAqīl, 39n
Jaʿfar b. al-Ḥasan b. ʿAlī, 41n
Jaʿfar b. Ibrāhīm b. Mūsā al-Kāẓim, 24
Jaʿfar al-Kadhdhāb, 36
Jaʿfar al-Ṣādiq, 9, 41, 47, 48, 49
Jaʿfarids, 3n
Jarrar, Maher, 8
Jews, concern for lineage among, 88–9

kafāʿa (suitability in marriage), 32, 44–9
Kennedy, Hugh, 8
Khadīja bt. Isḥāq b. ʿAbdallāh b. ʿAlī b. al-Ḥusayn b. ʿAlī, 41n, 49n
Khawla al-Fazāriyya, 34n
Khūʾī family, 50
khums tax, 28–9
Kohlberg, Etan, 84
al-Kulīnī, Muḥammad b. Yaʿqūb, 47

Leder, Stefan, 18
Linant de Bellefonds, Y., 46
local histories, as sources on ʿAlids, 9–10, 26, 72, 73, 76
Lubāba bt. ʿUbaydallāh b. ʿAbbās, 41n

Madelung, Wilferd, 40, 63
Makhzūm family, 35, 39–40
Mālik b. Anas, 45
Mālikīs, 45–6
Malikshāh, 60
al-Maʿmūn (caliph), 6, 41
al-Manṣūr (caliph), 38
marriage
  between cousins, 33–4, 50
  as indicator of relative status, 35, 40
  legal regulations on, 32, 44–9
  as means of building alliances, 34, 42, 43, 50
  preference for endogamy in, 33–6, 43–4, 88
matrilineal descent, 4, 11, 34n, 36–8
Mauriello, Raffaele, 50
al-Māwardī
  on *kafāʾa*, 45, 46
  on *niqāba*, 35–6, 52–5
Melchert, Christopher, 83
Mez, Adam, 11
Modarressi, Hossein, 9, 57, 67
Morimoto, Kazuo, 7, 11, 12, 19–20, 51, 68–9
Mottahedeh, Roy, 28, 71
Muḥammad b. ʿAbdallāh (son of al-Saffāḥ), 41–2, 49n
Muḥammad b. ʿAbdallāh b. al-Ḥasan b. al-Ḥasan b. ʿAlī (al-Nafs al-Zakiyya), 5, 34, 35, 37, 41–2, 69n
Muḥammad b. ʿAbdallāh b. Zayd b. ʿUbaydallāh b. Zayd b. ʿAbdallāh b. al-Ḥasan b. Zayd b. al-Ḥasan b. ʿAlī, 80n
Muḥammad b. Aḥmad b. ʿAbdallāh b. Mahmūd b. ʿUmar b. Muḥammad b. Mūsā b. Muḥammad b. ʿAlī al-Riḍā, 23
Muḥammad b. Aḥmad b. Ibrāhīm b. Aḥmad Ṭabāṭabā, 24n
Muḥammad b. ʿAlī b. Ḥamza b. Yaḥyā b. al-Ḥusayn b. Zayd al-Shahīd, 58
Muḥammad b. ʿAlī al-Murtaḍā, 27
Muḥammad b. ʿAlī al-Riḍā, 41
Muḥammad b. ʿAqīl b. Abī Ṭālib, 24
Muḥammad b. al-Ḥanafiyya, 3, 24n, 25n, 29
Muḥammad b. al-Ḥasan b. ʿAlī, 41n
Muḥammad b. al-Ḥasan b. al-Ḥasan b. ʿAlī, 42n
Muḥammad b. al-Ḥusayn b. Zayd al-Shahīd, 20
Muḥammad b. Jaʿfar b. al-Ḥasan b. ʿAlī b. ʿUmar b. ʿAlī b. al-Ḥusayn b. ʿAlī, 77
Muḥammad b. Jaʿfar b. al-Ḥasan b. ʿUmar b. ʿAlī b. al-Ḥusayn, 77
Muḥammad b. Mūsā al-Mubarqaʿa, 6n
Muḥammad b. al-Qāsim b. ʿAlī b. ʿUmar, 77
Muḥammad b. Ṭāhir, 28, 64, 77
Muḥammad b. ʿUbaydallāh b. ʿAlī (*naqīb*), 67n
Muḥammad b. Ward al-ʿAṭṭār, 68
Muḥammad b. Zayd b. ʿAbdallāh, 39n
Muḥammad b. Zayd b. ʿAlī b. al-Ḥusayn, 30, 40, 68
Muʿizz al-Dawla (*amīr*), 55
Murtaḍā Jamāl al-Dīn Abū al-Ḥasan al-ʿAlawī (*naqīb*), 57
Mūsā b. Ibrāhīm b. Mūsā al-Kāẓim, 24
al-Muʿtaḍid bi-llāh (caliph), 67–8
al-Mutawakkil (caliph), 6, 68

Nafīsa bt. Zayd b. al-Ḥasan b. ʿAlī, 41n
al-Nafs al-Zakiyya, 5, 34, 35, 37, 41–2, 69n
Nagel, Tilman, 8
naqīb al-nuqabāʾ, 56–7, 60
*naqīb*s
  appointment and succession of, 55–60
  deputy, 56–7
  duties of, 35, 52–5, 61–3, 88
  female, 60
  status of, 52, 53, 69n

Naṣr b. Aḥmad (Sāmānid ruler), 80
al-Nāṭiq bi-l-Haqq, as *naqīb*, 61n
niqāba
in Kufa, 65–7
origins of, 11, 51, 63–4, 67–70
Nūḥ b. Manṣūr (Sāmānid ruler), 81–2

Paul, Jürgen, 72–3
pensions, 29–30, 62, 80
Pomerantz, Maurice, 57

al-Qāsim b. ʿAbdallāh b. al-Ḥusayn, 70
al-Qāsim b. al-Ḥasan b. Zayd b. al-Ḥasan b. ʿAlī, 6n
al-Qāsim b. al-Ḥusayn b. Zayd al-Shahīd, 20
al-Qāsim b. al-Walīd b. ʿUtba b. Abī Sufyān, 41n
quietism among ʿAlids, 9, 34, 35, 41

Rabīḥa bt. Muḥammad b. ʿAbdallāh b. Abī Umayya b. Mughīra, 39
al-Rāzī, Fakhr al-Dīn, 23–4
Riḍā, Rashīd, 32
Robinson, Chase, 71
Rosenthal, Franz, 68
Rowson, Everett, 59, 82
Ruqayya bt. ʿAbdallāh b. al-Ḥasan b. al-Ḥasan b. ʿAlī, 35

ṣadaqa (charity), 28–9
al-Ṣadr family, 50
al-Ṣadr, Muḥammad, 50
al-Ṣadr, Reza, 50
al-Saffāḥ (caliph), 41–2
Ṣaffārids, 80
Saljūqs, 53, 60
Sāmānids, 80
*sayyid*s, 3–4, 86, 89
Scarcia Amoretti, Biancamaria, 9, 26, 33
Schacht, Joseph, 44
scholarship, as source of status, 71, 82–5
al-Shāfiʿī, Muḥammad b. Idrīs, 45, 84
Shāfiʿīs, 43, 44, 45–6, 59, 82, 83
and Shiʿism, 83, 84
al-Sharīf al-Murtaḍā (*naqīb*), 7, 47, 53, 55
al-Sharīf al-Raḍī (*naqīb*), 7, 53, 55, 56
*sharīf*s, 3–4, 86, 89
Shiʿism
vs ʿAlidism, 1, 33, 48
role of ʿAlids in, 9, 81, 83
Twelver, and Shāfiʿism, 84
views on ʿAlid marriages in, 47–50
Stewart, Devin, 84
Sulaymān b. Dāwūd b. al-Ḥasan, 39n
al-Suyūṭī, 3–4
Szombathy, Zoltán, 25

al-Ṭabarī, Muḥammad b. Jarīr, 67–8
al-Ṭabāṭabāʾī, Abū Ismāʿīl, 26
Taheri, Amir, 28
Ṭāhir b. Zayd b. al-Ḥasan, 23
Ṭāhirids, 28, 77
Ṭālibid genealogies, 10, 13–14, 17–23, 37–9
Ṭālibids, definition of, 2–3
al-Ṭūsī, Muḥammad b. al-Ḥasan, 46, 47, 48

ʿUbaydallāh b. ʿAbdallāh b. al-Ḥasan b. Jaʿfar b. al-Ḥasan b. al-Ḥasan b. ʿAlī, 78
Ukhayḍirids, 68
ʿUmar b. ʿAbd al-Azīz b. ʿAbdallāh al-ʿUmarī (governor), 6
ʿUmar b. ʿAlī b. Abī Ṭālib, 3, 29
ʿUmar b. al-Faraj al-Rukhkhajī, 64, 70
Umm al-Ḥasan bt. ʿAlī b. Abī Ṭālib, 39
Umm Ibrāhīm bt. Ibrāhīm b. Hishām b. Ismāʿīl b. Hishām b. al-Walīd b. al-Mughīra al-Makhzūmī, 39
Umm Kulthūm bt. al-Faḍl b. al-ʿAbbās, 41n

Umm Kulthūm bt. Muḥammad b. al-Ḥasan b. al-Ḥasan b. ʿAlī, 42n
Umm Salama bt. Muḥammad b. al-Ḥasan b. al-Ḥasan b. ʿAlī, 35n
*umm walad*s (slave women), 35, 75
Umm al-Zubayr bt. ʿAbdallāh al-Makhzūmī, 39n
ʿUthmānids, marriage patterns of, 34n

Veccia Vaglieri, Laura, 8

al-Walīd b. ʿAbd al-Malik b. Marwān, 41n
al-Walīd b. ʿUtba b. Abī Sufyān, 41n
women
  information in genealogies on, 36–9
  limits on marriage choices of, 35–6, 44–6, 54

Yaḥyā b. ʿAbdallāh b. al-Ḥasan b. al-Ḥasan b. ʿAlī, 6, 34, 69n
Yaḥyā b. al-Ḥusayn b. Zayd al-Shahīd b. ʿAlī b. al-Ḥusayn b. ʿAlī, 20, 65, 67
Yaḥyā b. ʿUmar, 28, 64–5, 82
Yaḥyā b. Zayd, 77
Yaʿqūb al-Layth, 80n

zakāt (alms), 28–9
Zanj revolt, 69–70
Zayd b. ʿAlī, 48
Zayd b. ʿAlī b. Jaʿfar b. Zayd b. Mūsā al-Kāẓim, 25n
Zayd b. al-Ḥasan b. ʿAlī, 34n, 41n
Zayd b. al-Ḥasan b. Zayd b. al-Ḥasan b. ʿAlī, 39n
Zaydīs, 18, 32, 48–9, 68, 77, 78–9
Zaynab bt. ʿAbdallāh b. al-Ḥasan b. al-Ḥasan b. ʿAlī, 35
Zaynab bt. ʿAbdallāh b. al-Ḥusayn b. ʿAlī b. al-Ḥusayn b. ʿAlī, 41–2
Zaynab bt. ʿAlī b. Abī Ṭālib, 4
Zaynab bt. Muḥammad al-Nafs al-Zakiyya, 41–2
Zaynabīs, 3n, 4
Zomeño, Amalia, 45
al-Zubāra, Abū ʿAbdallāh al-Ḥusayn Jawharak, 74, 82
al-Zubāra, Abū ʿAlī Aḥmad, 74, 78
al-Zubāra, Abū ʿAlī Muḥammad (last Zubāra *naqīb* in Nishapur), 74, 82
al-Zubāra, Abū ʿAlī Muḥammad b. Aḥmad (first *naqīb* in Nishapur), 74, 79, 80, 83, 85
al-Zubāra, Abū al-Ḥasan ʿAlī b. Ḥamza, 74, 78n
al-Zubāra, Abū al-Ḥasan Muḥammad b. Ẓafar b. Muḥammad b. Aḥmad b. Muḥammad, 74, 78
al-Zubāra, Abū al-Ḥusayn Muḥammad b. Aḥmad (*naqīb*, ‘caliph’), 57, 74, 79, 80–1, 83, 85
al-Zubāra, Abū al-Ḥusayn Muḥammad b. Yaḥyā b. Muḥammad b. Aḥmad (*naqīb*), 74, 79n, 81, 82
al-Zubāra, Abū Jaʿfar Aḥmad b. Muḥammad, 74, 77, 78–9
al-Zubāra, Abū Manṣūr Ẓafar b. Muḥammad, 74, 78, 83
al-Zubāra, Abū Muḥammad Yaḥyā (*naqīb*), 30–1, 57, 74, 79, 81–2, 83
al-Zubāra, ʿAlī b. Muḥammad, 74, 78–9
al-Zubāra, Abū Yaʿlā Zayd b. ʿAlī b. Muḥammad, 85
al-Zubāra, Muḥammad, 74, 78
Zubāra family, 43, 59, 73, 74, 78–82, 86
al-Zubayr b. Bakkār, 17, 18
Zubayrids, 17, 34n, 40